Copyright © 2025

All rights are reserved, and no part of this publication may be reproduced, distributed, or transmitted in any manner, whether through photocopying, recording, or any other electronic or mechanical methods, without the explicit prior written permission of the authors. This restriction applies to any form or means of reproduction or distribution.

Exceptions to this rule include brief quotations that may be incorporated into critical reviews, as well as certain other noncommercial uses that are allowed by copyright law. Any such usage must adhere to the specified conditions and permissions outlined by the copyright holder.

Book Design by HMDPublishing.com

LOOKING TO BECOME AN ENGINEER?

Join the FREE Problem Solvers Community!

As a token of our appreciation for buying the book, we invite you to our Problem Solvers Community!

If you are looking to be a part of the engineering discipline and want to learn the outside-the-classroom skills needed to succeed, all while connecting with fellow strivers with similar goals, join the (completely free!!) community!

Get Access and Connections to Information and Resources	Get Answers to Important Questions along your Journey
✓ Periodic "Ask an Engineer" Sessions	★ What do I have to do in order to level up and be prepared to become an engineer?
✓ Access to the Hidden Curriculum: The Sixteen Crucial Skills needed to be an Engineer	★ How do I get an internship?
	★ How do I get a mentor?
✓ Connect with others who are seeking to become an engineer	★ How do you deal with impostor syndrome?
✓ Connect with Current Engineers and hear their stories	★ How do you handle a job interview?
	★ How do I know if graduate school is right for me?
✓ Access to free development resources that will give you an edge in becoming an engineer	★ What are the best ways to network and meet others?

We Hope to See You There!
Meet and Learn from These Engineers and More!

Robert Hodge

Energy Providers Consultant

KiYett Brown

Traffic Engineer Jacobs

Jesse Milliken-Callan

Water Resource Control Engineer

Cory Payne

Sales Engineer Charlatte

Join the Community at

https://tinyurl.com/BeAProblemSolver

ACKNOWLEDGEMENTS

So many people were involved in the making of the book. First and foremost, thank you to the sixteen engineers who shared so many parts of their lives. There is obviously no book without you. They each had the goal of impacting those who seek to become engineers and anyone who is reading who wants to achieve a goal. If we do this right, numerous lives will be changed because of your decision to share your journeys. Thanks a million times over.

Thank you to our families and friends who supported us in numerous ways, whether it was listening to our ideas about this project when it was in its infancy or putting up with us not being available when we were very much in the throes of the book-making process. We appreciate you more than we can express.

Finally, we would like to thank the people at HMDPublishing for helping us put the final touches on this project. Their holistic approach is largely responsible for the book you are holding (or listening to) right now.

CONTENTS

Acknowledgements 5
Introduction 7
01 - Alex Luce 10
02 - Austin Sampson 32
03 - Cory Payne 56
04 - Nikeem Coleman 90
05 - Sibel Leblebici 111
06 - Jesse Milliken-Callan 131
07 - Katrien Herdewyn 159
08 - Cooper Whiteleather 183
09 - Anthony Hinojosa 205
10 - Ariel Leslie 222
11 - Seth Fortuna 246
12 - Krys Williams 269
13 - Joseph Harman 287
14 - KiYett Brown 304
15 - Robert Hodge 325
16 - Danny Murphy 345
Themes 363
Conclusion 370

INTRODUCTION

"A story is not like a road to follow ... It's more like a house. You go inside and stay there for a while, wandering back and forth and settling where you like and discovering how the room and corridors relate to each other, how the world outside is altered by being viewed from these windows. And you, the visitor, the reader, are altered as well by being in this enclosed space, whether it is ample and easy or full of crooked turns, or sparsely or opulently furnished. You can go back again and again, and the house, the story, always contains more than you saw the last time. It also has a sturdy sense of itself of being built out of its own necessity, not just to shelter or beguile you."
— **Alice Munro**

This book you are holding (or listening to) exists because we believe being an engineer is intrinsically a human endeavor. This book started out because of the observations of Kyle, the engineer among the two of us. He has watched new engineers develop over a decade in his career. He has seen promising engineers both grow and prosper while others fade and struggle. What was the difference? It wasn't content knowledge. It wasn't a lack of understanding of physics, chemistry, or mathematics.

What he noticed was a difference rooted in their relationships to themselves and to others. The ability to self-reflect, to communicate productively with others, to have a willingness and skill in asking questions, to be open to seeking out help, and to maintain the humility to say "I don't know" were all clear demarcations and predictors of success for young engineers.

Where are these characteristics discussed in our colleges and universities? Yes, content mastery is vitally important and necessary. Indeed, to paraphrase a common statement, we don't want someone building a bridge who failed physics.

But take a moment to consider the other side, hypothetically. Think about a student who has aced all of their classes, getting perfect scores in engineering and other STEM courses. What if we told you that this same student didn't work well on teams, was afraid to admit when they were wrong, struggled to collaborate with others, and hadn't sought out any mentors to help them along the journey?

Would you really want to cross the bridge that they built?

These human relational topics rarely get the attention they deserve, often getting a cursory glance in introductory courses. Our research of over two hundred institutions of higher learning indicates that very few had a dedicated class on addressing these topics as a precursor to being a good engineer, forgetting about showing a commitment to making sure that these topics were infused in *all* of their courses.

We think that the engineering community as an educational enterprise can do better than this.

This book aims to inspire all of us who find ourselves on a path toward a goal, particularly to motivate those who seek to be engineers. We hope readers move a little closer to understanding that they have what it takes to accomplish their goals. So what does it take?

In order to answer this question, we could have made a large (and expensive) textbook that would go through a set of topics in a rote and dry manner. This mythical gargantuan of paper would probably barely be more effective than a simple Google search or query from ChatGPT.

Why not just ask the engineers themselves? Why not have them talk about their journeys? Admittedly, this would be a lot messier, but such is life. We aren't going for order and structure as much as impact. After all, there is something profoundly different about learning the importance of networking through reading an abstract description versus reading the story of a successful engineer who details how they were afraid of it, how they overcame that fear, and discovered the tangible benefits of networking on their life and career. We decided on the latter option.

We went about asking sixteen engineers about their paths to their current positions, asking some fundamental questions. Here are a few:

1. What does it mean to be an engineer?
2. What do you wish you had been taught?
3. What have you had to sacrifice to be where you are?
4. What would you say to someone (who might be the reader) who is aspiring to be an engineer?

While these questions provide the basis of each of their stories, each interview has so much more, more than we could have imagined.

We shouldn't have been surprised. Being and becoming an engineer is a human endeavor, and thus, life shows up consistently. There are no easy paths in this book; each author has their own challenges to overcome. While each path in this book is uniquely its own, there is one major theme that we will spoil here, in the introduction:

Regardless of the extreme variety of backgrounds of the authors, ranging from extremely resourced to deeply impoverished, we are convinced that anyone with the drive to succeed, the support to push through, and access to opportunity can become an engineer. This might be a general life lesson, also. As you read these stories, be on the lookout for how (and when) each of these elements presents themselves.

That's it from us, for now. We will come back around at the end to think about some common themes that we noticed from the stories and to consider ways to engage aspiring engineers and the general public about what it means to navigate a path towards a goal.

We hope you enjoy the book and take something from your visits to the houses that the authors have built for themselves, and for you, hoping that you can come back again and again, finding more than what you saw before.

01 - Alex Luce

THE INTERDISCIPLINARY PATH

We are the sum of our experiences. What we do, how we do it, the people we work with, and the environments in which we work all play a role in who we become as professionals. Materials Engineer (and Venture Capitalist) Alex Luce epitomizes this. Studying overseas in Switzerland for an internship introduced him to a variety of people and professional experiences, confirming to him that positive exposure can be advantageous and rewarding for your life and career. Doubling down on this belief in graduate school, he found himself taking classes in business and law, making him, in his words, a better engineer. This undoubtedly contributed to him becoming a Partner at Creative Ventures, a deep-tech venture firm. This is the story of someone who decided to look over the fence, see that the grass is greener, and instead of jumping to the other side, tore down the fence and made a bigger yard. Read how he did just that.

Alex Luce, PhD

General Partner at Creative Ventures, San Francisco, California

PhD & MS in Materials Science & Engineering, University of California, Berkeley

BS in Engineering Physics, University of Arizona

Hometown: Los Alamos, New Mexico

Aris Winger: Alex, thank you for joining us. Are you an engineer?

Alex Luce: I am.

Aris Winger: What does it mean to be an engineer to you?

Alex Luce: Well, I'm sure there are multiple definitions. But, maybe one that I like would be… It's someone who's able to solve problems and all manner of problems. And be able to find tools and resources to use in solving those problems.

Aris Winger: And so your journey started in undergrad, where?

Alex Luce: I did my undergrad at the University of Arizona in Tucson, Arizona.

Aris Winger: Did you feel like you were prepared as an undergrad, as a 1st year coming in? What was the transition like?

Alex Luce: In terms of 1st year of college, it was a big transition. In some respects, I was prepared, and in other aspects. I definitely wasn't prepared. So my major in college was a major called engineering physics. Which the way I describe it is, it's like you're getting the full physics degree for your curriculum. But you're also getting a minor in engineering. So you take all the foundational engineering classes across different disciplines as well. So it really blends kind of the science with the practical aspects of engineering coming into college. I had a really hard 1st semester, actually. I think I was overwhelmed by how much freedom and agency you have.

Aris Winger: Overwhelmed by freedom?

Alex Luce: Well, yes, because essentially you can do whatever you want, and sometimes what you want to do might not be studying for the exam that you have at the end of the week. And my study habits really weren't great in my 1st semester. So I had difficulty in some of my classes. In particular, I was taking Calc 3, which is a pretty hard, pretty foundational, but also a difficult math class. So that's vector calc. And I had always liked math. I don't think I had ever, in high school, really studied that hard for math, and I think, coming into college classes where the coursework is just more rigorous, the pace is faster. I was unprepared for that. I didn't have great study habits. I wasn't good at time management. Previously, before an exam, maybe I could cram the night before, but I think that's less effective in a college coursework setting.

Alex Luce: So, despite loving math and having always done well in math, I got a D in that class, which was kind of a shock to the system, immediately.

Aris Winger: You didn't turn it around in the middle of the semester or anything?

Alex Luce: No. I remember going into the final exam feeling like I didn't really truly know the material. And so, finals week is here, and I'm staying up late and I'm trying to prepare. I think I had a lot of coffee, but I wasn't a coffee drinker then.

Alex Luce: It was just a lot of stress trying to do well on this exam. And I didn't do well on the exam. So, yeah, it was a shock to the system, and I would say there were some other classes in which I had had subpar performance, or I knew that I was capable of doing better in these classes. And again, I think a lot of it was due to not having great study habits. Doing everything at the last minute, instead of, say, pacing out the assignments or preparing for an exam. Things that I would say are just foundational, good study habits. I didn't have that in my 1st year. And there wasn't a whole lot of handholding or help along the way.

Aris Winger: Meaning what?

Alex Luce: It's a little bit up to you to sink or swim, which was my experience. So that was an eye-opening experience, and it was eye-opening because I knew I could do better. Upon having some reflection, I knew what I needed to do better. And I think it was a bit of a kick in the pants to do that the next semester. So the next semester of my freshman year, I really made an effort to turn things around, and I did. I retook that Calc 3 class, got an A. I got A's in most of my classes.

Aris Winger: You're skipping over the good stuff here. You mentioned a word that I'm not sure that we're emphasizing enough these days. You reflected. I want you to break down the reflection. Does that mean that you just sat in a room? How are you reflecting? Because you're not looking at your phone? You're not scrolling? What does reflection look like?

Alex Luce: Yeah, so. This was the end of the year. The end of a semester is a great time for this, because it naturally forces you to do this. So it's December 15th or whatever, and everyone goes home for the holidays. You get your grades over email essentially, and you have 2 or 3 weeks again before classes start. So you're home with your family and friends, and the holidays are happening. But at the same time, you also have that natural break, or that natural pause, to think about, Okay, here's what happened over the semester, because you're back with family, and for me, visiting and staying with my parents. There were just natural conversations around.

Well, how did the semester go? How do you think things went? A big part for me of my reflection is, I'm looking back and asking questions like, how do you think it went? Some good, some bad. Having space to not be immediately focused on the next thing because there's that 2-week break. You're not worried about what the assignment is that you have to turn in next Tuesday? You have a bit of a pause. You know, you mentioned phones. At the time, we didn't have smartphones. A phone was a flip phone, so you could play Snake, or maybe text people by typing out in a very convoluted way.

But you're right. There weren't any of these distractions. There was just more of, I would say, a natural time to think. At the time, I didn't journal or keep a diary. That's something I do more actively now. But at the time, had I been journaling or keeping a diary, that would have been a good opportunity to write down the questions and things I was thinking about. So, I think knowing that I had a very poor 1st semester academically, my 1st year at college forced me to ask some of these questions about, okay, what went wrong? What could have gone better? How much of this was …? So I didn't know it at the time. I really tried to think through and internalize. Were there steps I could have taken to change the outcome? And yeah, it turns out the answer was, yes, I sort of knew, though maybe I hadn't acknowledged or wanted to acknowledge, that my study habits were really bad. I was procrastinating on things like homework and prepping for exams. Whereas in high school, I felt like I could often do the bare minimum to get by, and that was definitely not the case in college.

Aris Winger: Great. I appreciate you going deeper on that. So you come back that next semester and are ready to go?

Alex Luce: Yeah, I was. I made some changes. There were a handful of things I did. I said, I'm going to actually spend a lot more time in the library. I'm not gonna stay out as late with friends if I have an exam due the next day. I'm gonna try and actually get my assignment done. But, with time to spare like before and not procrastinating, I instead do the homework. I think a lot of it was just knowing the 1st semester, I hadn't made a good faith effort. I hadn't been true to what I knew I was capable of. And now, upon that reflection, I knew I was kind of phoning it in or not trying my best. I said, Okay, I'm gonna go back, and I am gonna try my best. I am gonna try really hard. And I'm gonna see what happens.

Aris Winger: Something about it feels like, in some sense, you're saying to yourself, this is not me.

Alex Luce: Yeah, definitely. I knew that I was not giving it my all. I was not giving it a hundred percent. So that was, I think, fundamentally that was upsetting to me. It took a while to acknowledge that. So I did go back, and I said, You know what? It's a new semester. It's a New Year. It's January. Classes are starting again. It's a natural time to try something new. And so I went in and I really tried to make some of those changes and long story short, the changes were effective. I did much better academically. I was happier. I was less stressed, actually, because I wasn't trying to cram for an exam the night before. I actually had better relationships socially, because when I was with my friends I was able to be more present. And then, when I was studying, I was able to focus on that. So just overall, I would say I did a better job with time management, but I had to figure it out the hard way.

Aris Winger: So you mentioned socially. Who are we meeting? Are we in study groups?

Alex Luce: Yeah. So I was.

Aris Winger: Who are our peers in studying?

Alex Luce: Yeah. Study groups. I was much better about going to, or in some cases forming study groups, finding other classmates to study with, or to work on an exam together.

Aris Winger: And how does that happen? Pragmatically like, are you just asking people?

Alex Luce: Yeah, I was asking people, you know, hey, do you know we have this assignment due next Tuesday? Do you wanna meet at the library? 4 pm? And let's spend an hour or 2 working on this? Or let's meet at a coffee shop and go through this together. And I think I was a lot more collaborative in working with classmates and also going to office hours and asking for help. In my 1st semester I think I was still more of the mindset that I can do it on my own, and because I was doing things at the last minute, when I had questions, there wasn't time to go out and ask for help. So if I got stumped on a problem and the assignment is due tomorrow. I didn't have time to go to office hours. I didn't have time to email the Professor. I didn't have time to ask my classmates.

And so by being better at time management, by spacing out when I did the work, I would have time. There's a problem I'm stuck on, I could actually go to the office hours and get some help on it. Or I could ask one of my classmates in one of our study meetups like, Hey, let's work on this together.

Aris Winger: That's powerful. In the undergraduate time, do we have some mentors? People that we're connecting with Professor-wise or otherwise.

Alex Luce: Well, going back, one of my mentors, who I'm still in touch with to this day, is one of the people who set me on the path to a career in engineering. So this was actually, this was a sports coach I had had in high school. My high school water polo coach and he was an engineer. So he worked at the lab as an engineer. And he was one of the people who I had an internship with after finishing my senior year of high school, and he helped me get that internship and, really through him and being around him. He just conveyed so much excitement about science and engineering and in the field. I think he's a very passionate person, but really, his enthusiasm is palpable for solving problems. So when I think about the field of engineering, which is solving problems and coming up with practical solutions to problems. His way of problem solving got people really excited because he would draw other people in. So he's been a long-time mentor and, even though, when I was having this difficulty academically my 1st year of college, he's not someone I reached out to. I should have in hindsight. I probably was a little embarrassed.

Aris Winger: In hindsight, What would you have done? You would have reached out, and you would have said what?

Alex Luce: I would have talked through what I was going through with them. I think I ended up getting there on my own. But, in talking with him I probably would have gotten there faster. And when I say I've gotten there, I think, having the realization about study habits and time management and all of these things. So, I think a lot of people can figure things out on their own. But through having mentors, or peers. Sometimes family members or coaches, you get there faster.

Aris Winger: Powerful. So you're in undergrad. Anything else in undergrad that's impactful that you want to bring up mention as you're going through it. Are there other internships?

Alex Luce: Yeah, it was. It was really impactful for me to continue to do internships, and I started doing research as an undergrad. So, I connected with some different professors whose class I liked, or I was in the engineering library, and on the bulletin board, there was a job posting for an undergraduate research assistant in the aerospace engineering department. I thought the project sounded really interesting, or at least the one-page description. So I went and talked to the professor and ended up joining his lab. So I did, and I worked in a couple of different labs as an undergrad, and I think it was good to sample. I think it was good to work with professors on different research topics, some of which were in the physics department. One was in chemistry again, one in aerospace mechanical engineering. I think it was really good to have. Different perspectives on the different types of research. How different professors run their lab, the different work that you're going to do different tools you get to use. Some are more hands on, some are more computer oriented. I think being able to sample all of these things was very, very helpful, because it gave me a taste of different things, so I could start to develop a sense of what I wanted to do as I was thinking about when I finished college, and what I wanted to do next. So I think, having the multitude of experiences was incredibly impactful. And one of those experiences. Actually, I worked with a professor in the aerospace mechanical engineering department. He ended up having a grant from the National Science Foundation to send a student abroad. So he had a research collaboration with a university in Switzerland. I think the connection there was that he did his postdoc with the Professor, who's now in Switzerland. They had an academic working relationship. And he was able to get a grant from the NSF where he could essentially send over one student a semester, roughly, I think. and then their university would send over one to his lab. So it was an exchange program, funded by the NSF. So, I worked with him, and then this was my senior year. I spent the fall semester in Switzerland. The lab of this other professor, which was an incredible, incredible experience. The research led me there. and it showed me that science, engineering, that it's international. It's highly collaborative. People speak all sorts of different languages and come from all types of backgrounds. And working in this international setting, that's really got reinforced on me. And it was also fun.

Aris Winger: Right!

Alex Luce: Fun right? It's fun to be in a different country, a different lab. Working on, even though it was brought broadly. It was the same project overall. You're working on a different part of the project. So that was really fulfilling. That was really exciting. At the time I was pretty sure that I wanted to go to grad school after undergrad. Fall semester of your Senior year is when you're gonna start putting your applications together. It's when you take the GRE. And being out there at this other lab really reinforced. Okay, you know what I want to do as a next step is to go to grad school.

Aris Winger: Great. Let's unpack that. So what were the things they were telling you? They said grad school was the option. We might have some seniors reading this. What should they be thinking about?

Alex Luce: So I worked in this lab out there in Switzerland. I would say more of my focus was on doing research than it was in taking courses. I had enough credits that I knew I was gonna graduate. I only had to take, I think, 2 or 3 classes that semester. So it was a light load academically, as far as coursework. But really my project, my job was part of this research project. So I was spending a lot of hours in the lab. I was mentored and got to work with a couple of grad students there and some masters, some Phd students. They were great. Showed me a lot of things, answered a lot of questions, seeing what they did on a day to day basis.

Aris Winger: You were thrown into the Graduate school culture already of this space in lots of ways.

Alex Luce: Yeah. And I had had a taste of it before, because maybe during undergrad, maybe I was in the lab for 10-20 hr per week, or something for them, I think when I was out there I was in the lab 30-40 hr per week.

Aris Winger: Wow, okay. And then you're sold?

Alex Luce: And I'm sold. I'm like, I like this. I'm learning a ton. I felt like I was learning. I felt like I was surrounded by people who had all sorts of different expertise. You know, some of them were really good at it. Okay, we're making a circuit. This guy's a total whiz at circuit design. You know where I'm trying to program something in that lab. This guy's really good at coding. This other person is really good at analyzing data. So I was around these people who are just really good at what they were doing, and was able to learn things from them. And it was just a lot of fun.

Aris Winger: And so at some point, you pick a graduate school. Where do we end up going?

Alex Luce: Yeah, so I was a little torn, between which program which discipline actually to go.

Aris Winger: Interesting.

Alex Luce: All this undergrad research I had been doing, culminating in the time in Switzerland. What this professor had been in. He was in the aerospace mechanical engineering program. But really his research was on MEMS., micro electronic mechanical systems. micro fabrication, basically things you sort of cook up in a Fab that do all kinds of useful things. But I had some other research experience in material science, similar but different. And I mentioned my earlier mentor. He was also material science professionally, and that's what his degree had been in, and that's what he worked in.

I think that being in Switzerland and being in this lab reinforced how interdisciplinary science and engineering is and meaning, people who are working in this lab have different backgrounds. Some of them have math or physics backgrounds. Some have mechanical engineering or chemistry. There wasn't one single major or degree that people had. And I'd seen that across my different research experiences, so even say, working with a professor in mechanical engineering, not all of his or her graduate students were in mechanical engineering. But the coursework and research aspect, I really liked how interdisciplinary it seemed to be. And materials is a pretty central foundational engineering discipline. So when I was deciding what degree to go for, I was deciding, do I do Mechanical engineering? I didn't want to do physics and stay on what I would say is more on the science side. I really want to do engineering, and I would draw the distinction broadly between science versus engineering as engineering being the practical application of knowledge, whereas, science being the pursuit and understanding of that knowledge. and I felt I wanted to do something more practical. So again, they're very intertwined. So I decided on material science because it was interdisciplinary. I knew I liked interdisciplinary work. I'd had exposure to it as an undergrad. I felt that I wanted to continue doing that. In hindsight. I don't think that there was a bad choice, I think. Had I gone into mechanical engineering, for example, I think I would have been happy, and I would be doing something interesting now that's different. Maybe, from what I currently do. But I don't think there was a bad choice.

Aris Winger: Okay. And how was that time in grad school?

Alex Luce: Well, Kyle was there.

Kyle Clark: Let's start with. How is the transition from undergrad to grad school?

Alex Luce: It was less of a difficult transition for me than from going from high school to college for me. That was the pivotal, difficult transition. And so I am in grad school. I think some things are similar. So I would say for 1st year. Coursework is similar. It's certainly more difficult than what you have in your senior year as an undergraduate. But how do I study for it? How to do the courses is similar if you have good study habits, if you know that you need to find classmates, form peer groups, have study groups, go to office hours when you have questions. If you have good foundational study habits. I don't feel like the coursework itself is new or challenging. I mean, it is new and challenging, but not in a way that's unexpected. The research is, I feel like I was. I was decently prepared for that because I had done a lot of that throughout undergrad. So I knew what it was like to be in a lab and to work in a lab. And I don't think the research aspect got difficult until probably starting in the second or 3rd year. The reason is for 1st year. The emphasis is much more on coursework. as much more on getting ready, for at Berkeley they have what's called a preliminary exam. Where essentially demonstrate competency across, just like 5 or 6 different disciplines within the field of material science. And that's a big deal the format is gonna totally vary, probably depending on whatever school or department, but at least for Berkeley material science. Kyle, correct me if I'm wrong, but I think it was 6, 20 min oral exams.

Kyle Clark: That's how I remember it.

Alex Luce: Yeah. So you go and you have an oral exam, each with a different professor on a different topic. And they can ask you anything about that specific topic. So it might be electronic properties. It might be thermodynamics. so you have to study quite comprehensively. To be prepared for whatever it is that they're gonna throw at you. In some ways, I had had a little bit of a taste for that, because when I had done this semester abroad in Switzerland as a my senior year, some of the classes. Maybe just one of them was an oral exam at the end, which is generally not something we have in the US System. but as something that seemed at least was at the time more prevalent in that system out there. And so I had a taste of what it's like for the exam to be you and the professor one on one with any topic on the table.

Kyle Clark: In preparation for an exam like this at Berkeley, this oral exam. What was the value or importance of study groups or help from other graduate students? Was there help from other graduate students?

Alex Luce: I would say that maybe the most instrumental thing in preparing and preparing for this exam is forming study groups. Well, 1st of all, you also know that every generation of graduate students has had this exam. So 1st things first, It's so important to find the older senior graduate students who just took it the year before or 2 years before and learn from them what they were asked and what were the questions like. you're not going to get asked the exact same questions, but you get to understand what the format is. The types of questions, things that might be on the table. There's a long history of your types of questions that were asked in the past. So you get a sense of what's going to be offered and then form a study group, which we did, and basically practice with your peers. Because this exam format is a little bit different, we essentially took turns doing that and replicating what it would be like. And if you're not accustomed to it, being able to have this format where it might be, you are at the whiteboard, trying to solve this problem. So I think it goes back to something that I feel like. I learned that 1st semester in college, which is the value of preparation and the value in forming good study groups. And that ended up being helpful, not only for the exam, but they ended up being some of my best friends in the program.

Aris Winger: And it's fun to study together.

Alex Luce: We met up socially. It's a lot more fun than being by yourself, right, cause these other people are going through the same challenge you are. And it's a much more effective preparation. So I think. The field of engineering. And now, professionally. You are working with other people. So it's also preparing you for whatever job that you're gonna take. You need to work with others. To solve some of these problems. You have to do that collaboratively; everyone's gonna have different expertise. And being able to form groups. Figure out what's important and how to solve problems for me. I think that's a really foundational skill.

Aris Winger: Thank you for that. I'm thinking about it. The curve of a course, and then saying, Oh, I need to be working with 4 or 5 other people also, right? There might be someone reading this like, No, I'm competing against people. What is this balance of competition and collaboration when you're an undergrad?

Alex Luce: Good question. Perhaps this will sound self-serving. But in the courses that I had that were graded on a curve, I feel like, and I'm pretty sure, the people who work together and study together always did better, and we're generally in the upper quartile. And I knew that personally, I was going to do better. I knew that if I was studying with other people, I was going to do better. They're going to do better. I tried it on my own, that 1st semester, and did very poorly. So for me, it was clear night and day. There was no question. Collaboration versus competition. I knew if I was going to collaborate with other people, I was going to do better. I think, on a relative and an absolute basis, they would also probably do better. And the reality is not everyone did the same level of preparation for the exams, and I do think that people who were better prepared, who did things like study groups and come to office hours, clearly did better on the course overall. So there was a pretty clear relationship, I think, between, let's call it time, effort, and how smart you prepare, or basically what your study habits are. There was a pretty clear correlation between those aspects and how well you ended up doing in the course. So. Never, never for a second did I feel like I had to compete with others in order to do well.

Aris Winger: That's powerful. So talk to me a little about the collaboration being on the team. What makes for a good teammate? What are you looking to do? To be a good teammate, to be part of a team, and to be a good contributor to a team.

Alex Luce: Yeah. 1st of all, showing up.

Make a commitment or join a team, you know. First, Show up. If you say you're going to do something, it's very basic. But sometimes you're surprised when you do these group projects in a course, or we may get into this later. But I actually helped teach a course at Berkeley. Now, sometimes you're just. You're kind of surprised that some people just don't show up. It's so easy. Just show up. If you say you're gonna meet at this time, be there at this time. Honor your commitments. Respect again. Also very, very fundamental. But you know, everyone's coming from a different place. Everyone's got a different background.

Maybe in one course, someone already has it down. And someone has never been exposed to this material before. So there's gonna be a difference in the place that they're coming from. And you gotta respect wherever people are coming from. Asking questions. Also super important, not being afraid to ask questions. And speak up when you don't understand something. If you have a question, very likely someone else will as well. And there's a sigh of relief, whether it's in class or the study group, you ask a question, and it's like, Oh, it turns out 5 other people had that same question. But I didn't want to ask, so I think those are all pretty foundational to being part of a team. I think common or shared vision or goal. It is also pretty important. So, in the context of this graduate school anecdote about preparing for the prelim exam. We all had the same goal, which is, we all want to pass the exam. And it wasn't a case like only a certain number of people were gonna pass it; everyone who showed the level of competency needed was going to get there. So we had this shared goal and knew we all wanted to work towards that goal.

Aris Winger: Alright. So we're in the graduate school space at the moment. Anything else impactful that you want to mention during graduate school? I assume you passed the Prelims, and then.

Alex Luce: Sigh. Yeah, sigh of relief there! Maybe going back to a theme that's something that really resonated with me that I discovered about myself during my undergraduate work was continuing to work across disciplines. Continuing to seek out interdisciplinary collaborative opportunities. And in the context of grad school. I actually spent a fair amount of time in other departments so taking classes outside the field of engineering, which was not required.

Aris Winger: And why'd you do that? Did you have a need, a feeling to do it? Did you think it was going to be necessary for what you wanted to do?

Alex Luce: It's out of interest. It ended up being very necessary for what I ended up doing professionally, though I didn't know it at the time. But I sort of figured I'm here as a student. I might as well; I should try and take advantage of all of these opportunities. Rather than just try and rush through grad school. You're at your own pace. You determine the pace at which things go largely. And I wanted to take advantage of the fact that I was at this great, great university with a lot of other interesting programs. So I took classes at the business, law, and public policy schools. A big part of that was because my professional interest was renewable energy and climate change. And really, the topic of clean energy. And that's why I chose to go to Berkeley specifically as a graduate school versus other offerings. I felt like, if I wanted to work in the field of climate and energy. That would be the place to do it. And through joining one of the student clubs. So Berkeley has a very active, graduate student energy club that has membership from across the entire campus, engineering and sciences, business school, law, school policy, and humanities. And a big part of that is because the field of energy itself is so interdisciplinary. If you're trying to solve things in energy, you need engineering. But you also need things to happen on the policy side. You need things to happen on the business or finance side, and being in that club and meeting these other students and really developing, I think my passion for energy and wanting to solve problems within energy motivated me to pursue classes outside of just engineering as well. And then, the club did great things; they would bring in speakers who were doing cool things professionally. Would have a career fair and they would have an annual event. So you get to see or have snapshots of what different people are doing professionally in this field? And through seeing that, I knew. Okay, I'm here. I'm getting a Phd. In engineering, but I also want exposure to these other domains that I think are going to be helpful if I want to work in energy, which I did, and it ended up being really helpful in retrospect.

Aris Winger: There's something about what you just said, and there was another interview that brought this up, also about thinking about school as this vast opportunity to know more than just what you're supposedly majoring in. And then there's like so much value in that, right? So, I just wanted to mention that out loud for us to remember that. We often just think that we just need to be in our major, and that's it. But there's so much stuff over there that we might be interested in that might play a role in what we're gonna do. And to actually go over there, look, and take some other classes, and that could be fundamentally transformational.

Alex Luce: I think it is. Well said, I would a hundred percent agree with you. And I would say, this is true for school at any level. I didn't bring this up earlier, but I took a wide variety of classes in college, especially my 1st 2 years. I didn't quite know what I wanted my major to be, and I switched a couple of times. I think initially, I wanted to do chemistry, switched to physics, and ended up finding engineering physics, which I ended up doing. But along the way, I took a music class. I was in different clubs and different sports. I took a lot of foreign language classes, even though I wasn't required to, and I think the process of sampling different things was really helpful to reinforce what my path ended up being. But it was good. School is the best environment to try different things out, and what I think at 1st I was going to say you try things out without a consequence, but that's actually not the right framing. I think it's to try things out and expand your perspective. And you are in an environment where you know your job as a student is to learn. Learn as much as you can. You want to do well and understand. But you're in an environment where you can learn all of these other things as well. So why not do it, and that was certainly true for me, both in undergrad and graduate school.

Aris Winger: Right? So, okay, now we're roughly entering the workforce after graduation.

Alex Luce: I knew within the 1st 2 years that I wasn't going to be on the academic path. That I did not have aspirations to become a professor. It was good to have exposure to what that work is like through being part of a research group and writing papers and going after grants, and a lot of things that one does as a professor, you at least get exposure to as a graduate student. So you kinda understand? Maybe what it's like to walk in those shoes a little bit, and I knew I was less interested in that. So I focus my time more on what I would call some of these practical or interdisciplinary experiences. So for me. That was a lot of work with this energy club. I ended up being the club president for one year. I made an effort to do an internship going into my final year of grad school, which was at least for our program. Something that was not very common to do during your PhD research, say over a summer, and go work in industry or somewhere else. But my professor was pretty open to it, which was maybe a little bit of a surprise. But when I had the conversation with him, he was very open to it and supportive. So, as you know, another reminder to ask people and speak your mind. And so I did an internship. I actually went to Washington, DC, and I was able to secure a position working with part of the Department of Energy called ARPA-E. I was there for the summer. This is a part of the government that's focused on funding high-risk, high-reward research within energy, which is, you know, a topic I was very interested in. And that exposure to not only what it's like to work at the government in an agency, but also what it's like to fund that research. Again, going back to problem-solving is another aspect of how you solve this problem. It was really important. Even before then, I was also very interested in not only the application of science and engineering, but also the commercialization of it. Turning science and engineering into a business. Because I'd seen, you're doing this deep research in a lab. Your goal is to write a paper about it, even if it's an impactful discovery or invention.

I wanted to see if it gets to the next Bayes, which is outside of a lab. Okay, you know. Is it an impactful discovery? That means it needs to be used by people, outside of the lab. And it needs to be in the real world and being in in Berkeley, which is part of the Bay area ecosystem, which means there's a lot of startups of new business creation was exposed to this idea that one way to get from scientific discovery to making a big impact outside of the world is to start a company or Take that technology and license it out, or start a company around it. Just writing a paper about it was less fulfilling than wanting to do something practical with that work. So it was exposed to a lot of startups to this idea that science and engineering have to have a big impact.

One way to do that is to build a business around that, and so I also did that in grad school again, which is like just a great learning environment, you get to try a lot of things. So I tried to start a business around a lot of different things. Berkeley had a business plan. Competition. Held every year. Sort of go, and, you know, have an idea. Pitching in front of judges, prizes, and stuff. I entered that 3 different times.

We ended up meeting through one of our weekly seminar series. But connecting to another student. And we ended up forming a company together around a topic that he was working on. Got a little bit of funding for that. It's a real deal. We incorporated it. Working on those nights and weekends. Filing patents that would pitch that to investors. It was quite a formative experience. And I think there's no substitute for if you want to do something, actually trying to do it. And probably making a lot of mistakes along the way, but again, back to school as being a low, negative consequence, learning environment. It was great for that. So that experience, just really. Impressed upon me that that's something that I wanted to do professionally. So then, when I was going to finish and leave my Phd, leave graduate school. That's where my head was at. I want to do something to support the commercialization of science and engineering. I'm really passionate about startups. Whether it's starting, working at a startup, helping to fund or support them, I've had a flavor of this idea that you can go from impactful scientific discovery to making a broader societal impact. I knew I wanted to be part of that in some way, shape, or form.

Aris Winger: That is great. So I've gotten this feeling throughout your whole story here about you having interests that were gonna go beyond the traditional path. And there might be people who are just like, Oh, I'm an engineer. I can't think about this, or I have to do this. It has to be that it feels like you. Be very open to looking elsewhere, wherever your passions decide to have you look, and to embrace those things. And that turned into you being able to ask your Phd Advisor. Yo, I want to go do this other thing and be gone at the end of my Phd, right where typically you don't do that. And typically, you don't do A, but you did it. And typically you don't do B, and you did it right, and so talk to someone who's reading this, that who might feel like. No, I'm an engineer, or maybe they're stuck in a box. It feels like they're not stuck in the box. They don't have to be.

Alex Luce: Yeah, I think my mindset, maybe, has always been: You can always try something. And what's the worst that can happen in the context of taking courses? I took courses at Berkeley Law, at the Law School. Guess how many other engineers were in those classes? I don't think more than a handful. It was hard. But what's the worst that's going to happen? You do bad in a course that's not essential for your degree, and learn something along the way.

Aris Winger: But what did you get from doing that?

Alex Luce: Well, I met my wife as well.

Aris Winger: Okay.

Alex Luce: So totally worth it.

Aris Winger: Yeah.

Alex Luce: Going back to what it means to solve problems. You need lots of different disciplines to come together and solve problems. And whether it's in the domain that I'm interested in, which is energy and climate. Or any other field in aerospace. Health and medicine. Artificial intelligence. Engineering is a very important component of that. But so are these other disciplines, like law, policy, business, or finance. Even things like communications and how that narrative is portrayed across society. So I think, having this interdisciplinary mindset. I wanted to see how these other disciplines or other fields approached solving these problems, and I figured I might as well try. What's the worst that can happen if I take a class that's outside of my major, even if I'm totally failing, I don't need to be taking it, anyway. So I could audit. It didn't at all matter for my transcript if I was there. I didn't need the credit.

Aris Winger: These are all free shots for you.

Alex Luce: Yeah. You know, I figured, okay. I could take a couple of classes at the business school. What's the worst that can happen? So my mindset has always been, you know. Try something once. Maybe you'll like it. Maybe you won't. But you've probably learned something about yourself along the way.

Aris Winger: Yeah, so tell us what you do today.

Alex Luce: So today, I do a couple of things. Primarily, I work in venture capital. So now I'm on the funding side of helping to start and support those businesses. Those who are spinning or coming up with new technologies. Oftentimes, out of a lab or university, and trying to build a product around that, and trying to turn that into a viable commercial enterprise. So I'm part of, let's say, part of an ecosystem that goes from New sciences discovered in a lab. It gets supported generally by maybe a grant from one of the agencies. NSF, DOE, it's worked on by grad students and postdocs. Maybe one of them decides that they want to start a business around that. So we'll generally come in at the earliest stages and provide money to help start that business. I think having a scientific mindset is really important because no one knows if these businesses, if these efforts are gonna work or not. And maybe going back to what I said earlier, you have to try and see what happens. And I have an opportunity in this case to, if one of these things works, it can have a big impact. Often positive, meaningful impact on society.

Aris Winger: That's 1 thing.

Alex Luce: Then the other thing I started doing is I help teach a class at UC Berkeley now. So this is actually a class that I took when I was in graduate school called CleanTech to Market, and for me was a pretty foundational class as a graduate student. It's taught out of the business school that has students across the campus, engineering MBA, law, policy, and so an applied practical course where students over the course of the semester work with an actual startup company and help them develop a strategy for how to bring their technology into a new market. So the students get a very hands-on experience. How do you introduce a new technology into the market, develop a strategy around that, and generate testable hypotheses? And do all of this market research to try and make informed decisions. So I help out in a part-time capacity in teaching that class.

Aris Winger: Excellent, now that you're in the professional space. If you could look back to undergrad and dream about what you wish they had taught you, giving you a class about giving you information on that would have helped you much quicker. You may have found yourself saying, Oh, why didn't someone teach me that? What would those things be that you wish you had gotten more guidance on earlier?

Alex Luce: Study, habits.

Aris Winger: Okay.

Alex Luce: I, for whatever reason, didn't need to or failed to develop them in high school. So I feel like I have good foundational study habits. You know, actually, one fairly prolific author whom I've read a number of his books. Cal Newport coined the term "deep work", but I know he's also written books about study habits and how to succeed in college. I wish I would have had a book like that at the time. So, just really the 101 of how to study and how to be successful as a student would have been a lot easier than figuring it out the hard way.

Aris Winger: Excellent. Regret anything that you wish you had done differently on your voyage that you just described.

Alex Luce: Not really, I think, because I did try a lot of different things. In the context of picking different classes, having exposure to different fields and careers. Stuff outside school sports, music, and meeting people socially. I think that today prevents me from having big regrets because. A lot of regret is like, what would it be like if I had done this other thing? But in school. I got to try all of these different things. So I feel like I got a sense of basically what these, almost what these different life paths are like. And I feel like I chose a good one, that I'm happy with.

Aris Winger: That's powerful.

Aris Winger: to be where you are at this moment? What did you have to sacrifice?

Alex Luce: I had to figure out a balance that worked for me. So I had to sacrifice some aspects of my social life, go to all the parties, and do all these things with my friends. I still did some of that, but had to find the balance. That let me focus on school. Focus on my career. Still making some time for friends, but being balanced with that. And I definitely feel like it was totally worth it.

Aris Winger: Excellent. All right. Last question. You know, we're going to have some undergrads reading this, some seniors, lots of people. What would you say to them? You're talking directly to them. What would you say to them if they're going through some problems right now, struggling with how to get through this degree and become a professional in the world? Say whatever you want to say to them.

Alex Luce: Ask for help. Don't be afraid to ask for help. There are so many people around you: classmates, friends, family, teaching assistants, professors, mentors, and advisors. You know it's never too late to ask for help, so don't feel shy about that. If you don't have a mentor, find one, make one, find someone out there whose work or wisdom inspires you, and try to reach out to them and build a connection. If there's no study group, start one and take the initiative to ask for help and build. If those support systems aren't there, take the initiative to build and put them there.

02 - Austin Sampson

CHANGING PATHS IS NOT FAILURE

Choosing a new direction isn't always easy. Software Engineer Austin Sampson was on his way to being a doctor, but a voice in his head kept telling him, "are you sure you want to do this?" Persistent and convinced that he had to do what he said he was going to do, he continued on that path, even when others echoed that voice in his head. Revelation struck as he realized that the thoughts questioning his own path weren't negative thoughts, but ones that could liberate him. A new path soon opened, and he set out diligently, night and day, working to make a career in software engineering a reality. Dive into the story of a young man who came to understand that the path you are on doesn't have to be permanent, and that oftentimes changing paths comes down to dealing with the biggest obstacle: yourself.

Austin Sampson

Software Engineer at Capital One, Richmond, Virginia

BS in Biology, Howard University

Hometown: Fayetteville, Georgia

Aris Winger: Let's just jump into it. Austin, are you an engineer?

Austin Sampson: I am.

Aris Winger: And what does that mean to you?

Austin Sampson: So, engineering to me means seeing a problem and creating some, coming up with some creative solutions to solve those problems, and software engineering is using software to create those solutions.

Engineering used to mean something very bad to me. I used to think it was putting something together and taking it apart. And I mean, is that right? It's just putting a problem together, right? It's taking the problems and taking the bits and pieces of problems and then making it into one cohesive solution or something even better than where it started.

So that's what I'm learning. And the idea for definition changes for me every day as I grow.

Aris Winger: Thank you very much. So let's go back to the summer before your first year at Howard.

Austin Sampson: Okay.

Aris Winger: Going in, how are you feeling about university? Are you feeling prepared? And how was the first semester and first few years? And how was college in general?

Austin Sampson: So summer before freshman year, I was ecstatic. I couldn't wait. I was going to Howard University. This is my dream school. I had my plan and everything mapped out. I was going to go to college for four years, study bio, and be pre-med. And then, after that, my fourth year, I would go ahead and take the MCAT. Then I would go to Med school.

This is what I knew. This is what I wanted to do. I came up with the plan probably like 2 years before this. This is what I'm going to do.

And then I got to college. I had an amazing time in college. My freshman year was awesome. I had the time of my life, and with that time of life comes, you know, some things... If you don't manage the time of your life and your schoolwork, you're going to start to get some of your first F's...

And so my freshman year, I received my first failing grade. It was in genetics. This was in part because I was in a kind of accelerator program. So, you know, I was doing a lot freshman year, anyway, and then, like..

Aris Winger: Genetics in your first year, is that usual?

Austin Sampson: So usually it's BIO 101 and then 102, and then you go to genetics. And it was kind of an accelerated program, the Honors program, and I had credits that allowed me from dual enrollment, from high school, that allowed me to jump right into genetics.

You look around and you're like, "Oh, y'all are used to this, you know what's going on. Okay, cool. Maybe I do, too." And then the class. It was one of the tougher courses in genetics, too. It varies by Professor. If you go to "rate my professor," you see. Oh, gosh! Everybody feels this way. But that's when I received my first failing grade, and I'm like, "Wow, my GPA is down the drain. How am I going to become a doctor?"

But honestly, that really didn't deter me from pursuing premed.

Aris Winger: What would you tell old Austin now about taking genetics? What would you have needed to have done differently in genetics?

Austin Sampson: What I would have told Austin back then is to actually study. I think at that time, like I thought, I was doing the studying that I knew how to do. From high school, I didn't really have to. Everything was kind of just... I can grasp it. I could maybe go through a few flashcards. It kind of clicked like that. And that was high school. And then when I got to college, I used those same study habits, and I knew, and I felt like they weren't practical and working. But you can tell, "Okay, this is not sticking." I knew it wasn't sticking.

But I was like, "Okay, I read this chapter. I did the homework. I got it." Now I'm about to go, you know, have fun. Or now I'm about to focus on anything else, or just live college life.

Aris Winger: So what does real studying look like?

Austin Sampson: Right. So real studying for me at least… It's different for everybody. But real studying for me is actually looking, taking notes… rewriting the notes if you have to, in your own words. It's actually going through the problems, the homework, understanding why you are being assigned this homework, and looking through those questions… It's thinking through the work, not just reading, because studying for me used to be just reading and remembering, which is a form of studying. But it looks like thinking through it and wondering, "How does this actually apply?"

And because genetics is trying to figure out…you know, we're doing fly genetics. I don't care about flies, Drosophila melanogaster. I don't care.

Aris Winger: Let me just get through it.

Austin Sampson: Yeah, so I just got through. Just remember everything. Remember, remember. And I mean, I was remembering. So, for me, if I want to study well, I need to find a way to make it click. I need to actually figure out the purpose of this. Sometimes it doesn't have a purpose to me at that moment.

Aris Winger: But this didn't deter you?

Austin Sampson: Yeah, so it didn't deter me, because I was stuck on the path, right? And so I stuck to the path. At this point, I'm like, "Alright. You know what, you don't have to have a 4.0 to get to Med school. You don't need to have a 3.8 to get into Med school."

So those stories are true. And there are so many people… I had a great community of people who had the scores that got in, who didn't have the GPA. I just stuck to that path, and so began looking into summer programs, doing more internships, and just staying on the path and getting the grades back up that summer. I ended up taking the class again. Got almost a 100.

I don't know if it was because I had seen the course before, or maybe this professor was just a little more lenient, but…

Austin Sampson: So I went on and kept the pre-med track going all the way until I graduated. In my brain, until I graduated, I did not think about anything else.

So I graduated in 2020, and I was supposed to graduate in 2021, but because I had so many credits built up from before Howard, I would take higher-level credit courses while I was at Howard. I was told that was enough and that I didn't have to come back for last year. The world is ending. No one knows what's going on. I'm like, "Okay, wow."

Remember, I had this four-year plan. I was going to study in my senior year. This is where I'm studying for the MCAT. I'm getting ready. This is like my chill year. So that was kind of like thrown off. Now, I graduated early, and so after I graduated, I'm kind of like, "Okay, Whoa." And then the world is the same way because it's 2020. But I'm still on my Med school route and still determined. This is what I'm going to do.

And…I think one thing that I wish I'd known sooner, or that I wish I could accept, is that there were times, a lot of times, where I was like, "I don't know if this is for me. I don't really know if I really want to do this."

But I didn't listen to those voices because I already do this. This is my path, you know. And so I didn't really listen to those.

Aris Winger: So this is a little voice in your head saying, "Are you sure you want to do this?" the whole time.

Austin Sampson: The whole time, the whole time. It was small, but it came back. It wasn't making me stay up all night.

But it was also like, "Well, you know what? You didn't really care about that class. You don't care about this class. Okay, you are doing a lot of this biology work, but I want to get to anatomy. Okay, that's your interest. But you don't like a lot of this.

So it's just those small things.

But the thing is, I had this idea to see it through. You said you were gonna do it, do it.

Why?

I don't know why. I mean, everybody told me: "Hey, if you want to change your mind… My parents and my counselor from high school… They told me it was okay for me to change my mind. And I think they also know that this is kind of just something I may have...

I don't know. They just know me. They're like, "It's okay. If you want to change your mind, if you want to do something else, if you want to pursue another career. That's what college is for, exploration."

But in my head I'm like. "I told you I was going to do this. I'm going to do this. So I'm making y'all proud. I'm going to do this. And then I was like, "Oh, is that it?" I want to make them proud because I said I was gonna do it. So I want this because I said I was gonna do it.

I don't care about anything else except doing it. I don't care if it makes me kind of unhappy. I don't care if it's not really what I want to do. I said I was going to do it. So I just, I'm just gonna stick to it. And so that was what I realized that I was doing by the time I was a 1-year post-grad. I'm studying for the MCAT. I don't care about this MCAT, I really. And I'm studying hard. Then I realized: I'm studying. And then when I got the passing grade to get into Med School, at least 500, I got to go into med school. Now, I have to do this all over again, which wasn't exciting me anymore. That whole process wasn't exciting me anymore.

And if it hadn't been for a friend who took me to the side one day and just said, "Do you want to do this? Do you actually want to do med school?"

I think that was the 1st time somebody ever actually asked me that amongst my friends, my family, counselors, and professors.

I replied with "No, I don't."

I mean, I just… I want to be successful, right? I want to help people. I want to make money. I want to make people, my family, proud. And my friend responded with "Yes, that's a hard way to do all those."

That's when the seed of "Wow, I can actually do whatever I want." I can say, "I don't like this." I was okay. That was the first time I ever said, "I don't want to do this." And that seed sprouted. Then I said to myself, "Okay, well, what do you want to do?"

And so I just started talking to more people. I was teaching high school at the time that this was all happening. So, one year post-grad, right after I graduated, I started teaching high school sciences. I knew I didn't want to do that. No matter what. I've got to get away from these kids. I loved them, and they were great. But it's the loud minority. They really do it sometimes.

So I didn't want to teach anymore. I'm kinda like, Wow, I don't want to be a doctor anymore. I can't believe that. Okay, let me tell my mom.

She said, "Okay, great." I said, "Okay, well, let me tell my counselor." She said, "Oh, yeah. Well, I was waiting for you to say it because you kept complaining. All you were doing was complaining, complaining, complaining. She was telling me there were signs.

So then I had a friend who was almost taking the same route.

She didn't care. She was gonna try everything. She started with English. Then she went to Dental, then to business, and then she ended up in cyber security. She told me to look into it. She went the bootcamp route, and that kind of introduced me to bootcamps.

Here's the funny part. What actually made me even consider trying the boot camps was my students. The first time I actually tried computer science was while I was teaching. I had students who were taking AP computer science.

They were doing a free Codecademy. They would come into my homeroom and say, "Mr. Sampson, I bet you can't figure this out." I'm getting competitive and seeing if I can go faster than them, not realizing that I just did their homework for them. So they got me. Then I'm like, But I found it kind of cool. This is interesting.

That's when I started to look at software engineering. After that year, I stopped teaching. I moved back home and did a boot camp.

Aris Winger: I have two questions for you. I'm thinking about an undergrad who's reading your story right now, and they might have these little voices in their head. Would you have listened to that inner voice now if you had the chance?

Austin Sampson: I would say yes.

Aris Winger: How do we get someone to say... What is your message to someone who may have this voice that's consistent? It may not be loud, but it's always there.

Austin Sampson: My message would be: It isn't a negative thought. The problem is that that's not a negative thought. It's maybe a true thought. Just because it doesn't align with your idea of what you want to do or what you thought you would do, it doesn't mean it's negative or bad.

Aris Winger: That allows you not to ignore it, because when it's something that's getting in the way, then you try to push it away.

Austin Sampson: Exactly. Maybe it's not getting in the way. Maybe it's something that's guiding you, that's pushing you. It's trying to lead you in a different direction. Right? It may be telling you, "Hey, let's look around. Let's look at other avenues."

And so I think that's what it is, because it felt negative, even though it wasn't loud. It always felt negative and felt bad. It felt wrong. It feels like you're giving up.

But the only time that you give up is when you decide that you don't want to do anything with your life. That's the only time you really give up. But just because you change your major or mind doesn't mean you gave up. You're just now going on a different path, and I think that is one thing that I wish I also knew: is that changing a path doesn't mean giving up. It's not giving up. It's just pivoting.

Then I think when you get into the field, you realize that it's always about the pivot. Everything is pivoting. When you get into working or come up with an idea that doesn't work, pivot to something else. It's not that you're giving up on the problem. You just realized this wasn't the solution to your problem.

Aris Winger: Yeah.

Austin Sampson: Look at startups, you always hear how people have this big idea that they put everything into, and then it didn't work. So then they pivot, and then they just go right to the next thing. It can be almost seamless. They had an idea, and they saw something that could be better.

Aris Winger: It sounds like you already have a big support network. Did you always have that?

Austin Sampson: I've always had a big support network. So I've always had it. So I've had my family, mom, dad, and sister.

My sister went to college. My mom went to college. My dad didn't. So I wasn't 1st generation. But then I had my high school counselor, who was always there every step of the way.

Everybody at Howard was super supportive. I would say I had a huge, huge, huge network. But the crazy thing is… I didn't use it. I didn't tell people. I didn't like to talk about my feelings. I didn't really say the things I felt.. My family doesn't know that I failed or got an F.

Aris Winger: Why don't they know that? Why not?

Austin Sampson: Because it felt like a failure. I felt like it was just wrong. It was bad.

And…My scholarship was in jeopardy. So I just couldn't tell that.

Aris Winger: So when they read this, they'll know for the first time?

Austin Sampson: Oh, yeah, when they read this, they'll know, and then they'll also realize that I ended up losing the scholarship. So I'm glad if they do read it, we'll put it here, so this could be the easiest way to tell them.

Aris Winger: I'm glad we're doing you a favor.

Austin Sampson: And I told them about everything else. But I didn't really tell them about those things. I would often tell them that everything's good.

Aris Winger: So what did you need them for? If the support network wasn't for academics, then what was it for?

Austin Sampson: They were good for reaffirming that the path I'm on is the right path for me.

They were constantly saying that they were proud of me. They were giving me that reassurance that I was doing a great job.

And maybe that was negative since I wasn't giving them the truth. But they were always letting me know I had people in my corner who were there for me, no matter what.

And so I always have this thought, too, that even in the worst-case scenarios, if I just flunked out, or didn't do well on a test, or can't afford college next year, I would always have them to fall back on. I think having them in that way also helped.

So I think that is definitely a lesson I wish I had learned: just talk to your community about

everything. That's what they're there for: your network, your community, and your village.

They don't want to always just hear that everything's good. They love it, but it's not what they're there for.

You don't have to be a yes man in your own life. You can tell them the truth. You can tell them. Talk to them more about how you're feeling.

Aris Winger: I appreciate that. That helps me as a mentor myself to just be more explicit in saying that I'm here for more than just the good times. I'm also here to listen when things aren't going fine, and I'm very open to hearing that.

Here's another question. Tell me about the switch to software engineering. Is there no doubt? Any worry about not knowing enough? No impostor syndrome?

Editor's note: He is shaking his head and shrugging in response.

So where did that come from? We've been talking with so many people about making these pivots, as you talk about. But behind software engineering is a bunch of stuff that you may not know. That's not an issue for you?

Austin Sampson: I really have a belief that you can learn anything. You can become good at anything that you really want to. Am I good at a million things? No, because I don't really want to be good at a million things. I say I want to, but I don't really want to put in the work or learn it. So I didn't go in with a scared mindset.

And then another thing is, I had literally just seen my friends go this route. My friend Aaliyah went the cybersecurity route, and her boyfriend went the software engineering route. They were enjoying it, the problem-solving that was showing up every day. It made me think that this was doable.

This was around 2020, and everyone was really talking about getting into technology big time. That also made it more welcoming because it felt like it was the next big thing that everyone was getting into. All of the research that I did about getting into the area was welcoming. It didn't give me the full story of what software engineering would entail, but it helped me not be worried about being prepared.

So I decided to do a boot camp. If I hate it, I hate it. It's only 3 months. Luckily, I have a support system where I can go home, live at home, and not have to pay rent. I don't have a job. Well, I ended up working overnight at a hotel and then doing the boot camp at the same time. My focus was on the boot camp for 3 months, and then I can figure out what I want to do after that.

Aris Winger: What did the boot camp entail?

Austin Sampson: Yeah. So the boot camp was Per Scholas, which you know, if I can ever give a plug, Per Scholas is such an amazing program. It's a nonprofit boot camp for people who just don't have the funds to pay for a boot camp or maybe go to school right now. It's amazing and one hundred percent free. And it's a real boot camp. It was a 3-month boot camp, 9 to 5, and it was essentially web development.

I believe we go through front-end development, HTML, and CSS for the first two weeks, I believe, and then we go into JavaScript and manipulating the DOM, and then we go into making a full-stack application. So at the end of the boot camp, you are able to build a full-stack application.

You learn a lot very fast. Some people did well, and some people didn't. But I enjoyed it. I was blown away because I began to realize that I can be creative with the work.

I feel like I'm creative. But I can't draw. I don't sing, I can't paint. But I realized I could be a creative tech.

I have ideas and I could put them on paper. So I was making projects that were fun. For my new godson, I imagined him having a website where his mom can upload pictures of him, giving him a time capsule forever. People can go and send messages to him as he grows up.

Aris Winger: This clicked really intimately with other parts of your life.

Austin Sampson: You realize, and I guess this is the engineering part, there are problems that you want solutions to. You have ideas that you think could make life better. So it started to play into my interests.

I started to ask, "What do my interests miss?" I started to see how that can be fixed through the tech side. So I started enjoying it. It's funny because at the end of the boot camp, you have your capstone to create the full-stack project, and I am still pursuing my full-stack project.

I want to actually get this out and released like to this day, and that was like 2 years ago. This is something I really enjoy, a problem I see in my passion. I want to work on it and make a community around it.

Aris Winger: I want to go back to the boot camp. So you're sitting at home for 3 months, 9 to 5. There are no distractions? I guess Covid? I guess the context of Covid is helpful?

Austin Sampson: Well, so this is 2022. This is 2 years post-Covid. So I taught high school for 2 years, and then went home.

So yeah, we were back in school. So Covid is a thing of the past. It's like Covid didn't even happen.

Aris Winger: So are you going in person at this point?

Austin Sampson: No, this boot camp was still virtual. But…

Aris Winger: How are you staying focused?

Austin Sampson: How am I staying focused? Really? I mean, I'm just locked in from 9 to 5. I'm here on my computer, in my room. I bought a desk and I made my little zen den. This is my little locked-in corner, and from 9 to 5, I was locked in.

But it wasn't hard because I was interested. I really enjoyed it. I think that's another thing. I'm learning this new skill. And I had the carrot at the end of the stick. I might get a job. That's the whole reason why you're doing this is…

I had these plans that I…Like I said, I had my 4-year plan. I made a new 6-month plan. I'm gonna do this boot camp for 3 months, then give myself 3 months to find a job. And then I'm gonna leave this house.

That may have been unrealistic. But I just kept it, and I was okay with that. At this point, I had realized that plans don't always go the way that you want. So I was more ready to part with that plan. But that was my plan. So I had a plan and I'm enjoying it. So I'm locked in. I'm enjoying it, and my schedule was crazy.

So I'd do the boot camp from 9 to 5, and then I would take a nap, and then from 11 to 7, I work at the hotel, and then…

Aris Winger: Sorry. 11 PM. To 7 AM?

Austin Sampson: Yeah. I would go and work the overnight shift at the hotel and then go home, take a 30-minute nap, and then get back on at 9.

It was a fun schedule, but I mean… I was just determined. Right? When it becomes your schedule, it becomes your schedule, right? Like, once you get into a routine, it becomes routine, so…

Aris Winger: I did want to hit up a word that you've said twice so far, and it's the word "plan." We might have some people reading this who may not have a plan. So tell me when you first started to realize that plans were super important. You started making plans. You had a 4-year plan. You had a 4-year plan 2 years before graduating from high school. Why are plans important? Where do plans come up for you?

Austin Sampson: So it's interesting. So I hate plans, actually. My mom is a big planner. So that's where it comes from. But my mom was always wondering what the plan was.

Not that I hate plans, but I'm a very spontaneous person. Let's say that I don't hate plans. I'm just very spontaneous. I don't live in a plan, but when I have a big goal, I think having that plan and steps and actionable steps, it actually works.

When I make plans now, I always imagine the end. I have this vision of the end. How am I gonna feel at the end? How am I gonna feel? What am I going to achieve at the end of this plan that I want?

The 4 Year Plan was obviously: I'm going to be a doctor. I'm gonna make everybody proud. The achievement was not being a doctor. It was going to be the gratification of making people proud. I am going to make myself proud, for once.. I'm going to make some money. I'm going to have that title in front of my name. So that was driving me then.

Going back to my new 6-month plan, I knew after those 6 months that I wanted to be out of my mom and dad's home.

I had this idea. I wanted to buy this couch, which is so weird. I wanted this leather couch, and I knew that if I got a job, I could afford this couch and this one lamp that I wanted. So I was going to give myself a gift with that. So I don't know. I always had external goals at the end.

It was always the vision of where I would be at the end of those 6 months or the end of the 4 years that really kept me going, rather than the actual thing that I'm trying to do. When I think of my plans, I think of those external effects that I am rooting for.

I was talking to my student one day, and he said the same thing you just asked. He mentioned that I always had a plan and how do I stick to it. I replied that I may not know if the plan works out for sure, but if it does work out, I know I will get the things that were the reason for me trying in the first place.

Aris Winger: So then you finish the boot camp. That's 3 months. So you're halfway there, and then start applying for jobs?

Actually, before that, I want to ask something else. Is there anything after going through the boot camp and doing all this stuff?

Austin Sampson: So the boot camp has this thing where you can't apply for jobs until like 10 weeks into the boot camp.

Me, I don't listen. I started applying for jobs way sooner. And so I saw this one job that I actually applied for before and got rejected. And it was a Capital One CODA program. And so Capital. One has a program for non-traditional software engineers who come from anyone who wants to become a software engineer and doesn't have a computer science degree.

So this is probably around a 3-month mark or probably around like 10 weeks. I remembered that I did apply for this, and they rejected me. I decided to apply again. And then, if I do happen to get an interview, since I'm probably not going to get this job. It'll be good interview prep.

I ended up getting a call back. I did the phone interview with Capital One and got another interview with a startup. I can't remember what it was called, but I got another one with them, too, but that one didn't go anywhere. They were definitely looking for a very experienced developer. But it was fun. It was good practice just to hear what they were looking for.

Capital One moved me onto the next step. And so they have their next interview process and coding process. A few weeks later, I found out I got the job. I was in the boot camp. So that was really amazing. I had to tell my team. They were happy for me.

The job wouldn't start until after the boot camp, around the 6-month mark of my plan, which I found interesting.

Aris Winger: But now you have even more motivation in the boot camp to get all of this information, because you're going right into a job.

Austin Sampson: And so to retain it. Right, because that's another thing about boot camps…

I was very lucky. I was very fortunate to actually find a job directly during, or even anytime near after. The market is difficult for entry-level workers. I mean, I had the grit. I wanted to do it. But it was also a blessing.

And so I think what I've noticed with a lot of my colleagues is that if you don't have anything lined up afterwards, then it starts to stick less and less, you start to stick less with it. If you're applying and not hearing back, and if you don't stick with it, you'll lose it. You have to sharpen your skills after the boot camp.

Austin Sampson: So the job coming up helped me stick with it.

I kept coding. I kept working on my personal projects. I kept preparing for this next phase of my life, which… was another boot camp. So the CODA program for Capital One is a 6-month boot camp. Then you go into their rotational program, which is their true software engineer rotational program for recent college grads.

Aris Winger: So you go through another boot camp with Capital One. When do you feel like you are getting into the everyday experience of being a software engineer there?

Austin Sampson: So that doesn't happen until after six months. You join their Technology Development Program. That's when I got hit with the software engineer label and everything that comes with that. I started my rotational program and officially joined my 1st team at Capital One.

We work on the Capital One app that everybody uses, and it's in Java. I'm like "Whoa! I never learned Java. I don't know anything about Java." It's because it's a legacy system app. And so it's Java. And my team is focused on migrating all of the services to serverless. So we want to go serverless. We want to go to the Fargate containers.

I'm like, "Whoa!" We didn't talk about any of this in my boot camp. We didn't talk about this in the first boot camp. We didn't talk about this at Capital One at CODA. In those boot camps, you're focused on web development.

Austin Sampson: So that's when that imposter kick syndrome started to kick in.

Okay, I'm here. I don't know what I'm doing. I really don't know Java. One thing that helped me. The mission of CODA was to teach you how to learn, grasp technologies, where to look, and where to find answers you need when you're at work. And so that definitely was something that it did teach me. So that helped me get up to speed. It didn't deter me, I guess.

The program is two rotations, and they're both a year. At the six-month mark, I'm not feeling great. I still…I don't understand. I can deliver my stories, although not as fast as everybody else on my team, because everybody else is a senior engineer. Okay, not thinking about that, right? But I'm not delivering as fast. I don't like the work. I don't understand the work the way that I understood it before. Then I realized this is software engineering. It's more than web development. That was my first taste of that.

Around the eight-month mark, something clicks. I realize what we're doing now. I get it. I don't know what it was. I noticed myself getting better at the stories. But it took 8 months. Oh, my. I just felt terrible.

Aris Winger: Terrible about what? You felt terrible about how long it took?

Austin Sampson: Yeah, it felt terrible that it took so long. And the other thing about this is that:

I'm not talking to anybody. I'm not telling anybody how I feel. I'm not really expressing my confusion with my team. I'm not really expressing anything.

I'm telling myself, "I'm on a team doing their work. Let me just do it."

Aris Winger: Would you go back and do that differently?

Austin Sampson: Oh, yeah. Oh, yeah. Oh, yeah, yeah.

Aris Winger: Ok, now go back, and what would you do differently?

Austin Sampson: So if I go back, I would embrace the newness. I would literally embrace where I am. I am six months into software engineering. I don't need to know everything about Java. I don't need to know what Spring Boot is. I don't. I'm not expected to know this. So this expectation that I had to just come in and know everything in the 1st week or 2 months, I would take that expectation off me. I would really go in there and embrace the newness of it. I'm new to this. I'm gonna ask you questions. These questions are going to be dumb, and they're going to be repetitive in the beginning, because I might forget what you said or I might not understand how you said it. But I'm gonna ask these questions. I would have done that instantly. But I didn't do that.

Aris Winger: But to whom? Who would you have done that to? Who would you have picked?

Austin Sampson: My team. So my team was great. I love my team. We were awesome. We always talked every day we had. But I wasn't really me. You know me. I told you I don't really express negative thoughts.

I just say everything's good, right? So I don't express that. So this is something that I was learning, even to this day.

Back then, I would ask a question and then they would give me the answer, and I wouldn't understand the answer. And I'd say to myself, "Okay, well, I'm not gonna ask another question because I already asked my question." But what I do differently is I'd ask that question again. I'd say "that didn't make sense to me. I really don't understand it. Can you please explain it again?"

I realized they were open to it, they were willing to. That's what you're supposed to do. When you're essentially a junior software engineer. You are supposed to ask questions. You're supposed to make these little mistakes. And I was so afraid of making any mistakes. So

Therefore, I wouldn't actually try to do anything like push to production, because that's where you would make a mistake. But if you are going to make a mistake, make it here, because obviously, you won't do anything huge yet.

So the eight-month mark is the first time I made a mistake, and that's where I learned so much. I finally got comfortable, and then I made a mistake, and then we learned how to fix the mistake. And then we learned. Then we talked through the mistake, right? And then my manager realized that I didn't know some things. At one point, I expressed that I just didn't feel super comfortable with the team. So then she paired me with a mentor.

This is where I learned how to talk. She was adamant. "Oh, you need to talk. You need to say more. If you have a question, ask it." The biggest thing she taught me is that pull it up when you have a question and can't explain it in words.

Pull up your screen (we were on Zoom), share your screen, and get the answer that way. Share, explain it that way. So I'm just learning new ways to explain my thoughts and my questions as a software engineer.

So with this rotation approach, on my second team. So I went to my second team. I took those principles that I said to the next team. So to the reader:

Ask the questions right away. Ask them again and again, and again and again. If you need to ask for clarification, don't be afraid to speak up. Don't be afraid to say you're lost.

If they don't make sense to you, but they make sense to everybody else. It's okay for you to ask for more clarification. Right? You're new to the team.

Aris Winger: This is what I'm learning from you. I'm learning that the title Junior gives you permission...

Austin Sampson: Yes.

Aris Winger: To ask, to go deeper, and to say when you don't know something.

Austin Sampson: 100%. And Junior, anything that's not senior right? Well, if you have somebody above you, that means that you can ask them questions. It gives you permission to ask them questions. But the Junior level, especially for us. That is the time to be new, right?

So I recently got a promotion. Initially, I thought, "Now I'm not a junior anymore." I thought this meant my question-asking was going to change. But no, I'm not going to stop asking questions just because I have a promotion.

I'm going to keep asking questions, and they'll be different and they'll be better. Now I'm understanding the long term and the long game. It's still a million questions.

If anything, I think my journey is teaching me: Speak. Share how you feel. Ask the questions, reach out to your community.

I'm a very sociable person, but I don't really get to the root of who I am. I love listening. I love talking. I love chatting. But I won't share. I won't open up about myself too much. That's only been doing me a disservice.

Austin Sampson: As soon as I open up, people around me will respond, "Oh, I have a solution for this," or "I can help you with that."

Aris Winger: Almost immediately, right?

Austin Sampson: Immediately. There have been times when I have had a great community. I needed to move my apartment. I didn't tell him anything. After I moved, they said, "Why didn't you hit me up. Why did you say anything?" I didn't want to bug them.

When you have a community, the community is for you to commune. You could talk to them about this. You can ask for help.

You don't get a prize for not asking for help. You're not better than anybody because you didn't ask for help.

Ask for help. Be open. Be vulnerable in this journey. It's not easy. That's the biggest thing that I'm learning, and it applies to my personal life and my professional life.

Find somebody to talk to, to ask the question. To say that a small negative thought, you had to see what it sounds like outside your mouth and your head.

Aris Winger: Powerful

Austin Sampson: Yeah, that's been huge.

Aris Winger: Okay, good. We got a few more questions. So now you're, you know, on the team and a software engineer. When you look back to your undergrad, what class or curriculum do you wish they had told you? What information do you wish they had told you about being a professional that they didn't teach you? What did you have to learn on your own outside of the software engineering discipline? Because at the time, you're in a different major, but you wish they had told you about being in the workforce.

Austin Sampson: Being in a corporate world, I realized there's like a corporate strategy and hierarchy.

The other thing…I wish I had taken more classes outside of biology and electives.

Aris Winger: Why?

Austin Sampson: That's what college is for. College is for experimental and exploration, and learning. You literally go there to learn. If you want to learn something new, take that course right. Take that elective that doesn't really apply to you. If you have an extra credit course, do something that interests you instead of doing something random. I just never knew I had the ability to take an intro to computer science class.

Aris Winger: So you would have taken that if you could go back.

Austin Sampson: Even if I didn't major in software engineering, I would have taken some classes just because knowledge is great. That's just who I am. I like to ask questions. I would have taken a lot more courses.

I would have taken a political science course, also. I love philosophy, thinking about something else other than science. I love this.

Aris Winger: And so, how are you feeling today about your status as a software engineer?

Austin Sampson: Yeah. So today I'm feeling great. I'm feeling just as new as I felt when I started. I realize I have permission to ask more questions and to explore more.

Also, I'm working with the biggest tech nerds in the world, and while I'm not a tech nerd yet, I'm slowly becoming one.

So it's like my newness is allowing me to really ask questions and try things. So I'm feeling good and exploratory.

Aris Winger: You sound free.

Austin Sampson: Yeah, free. I have the freedom to figure out whatever path I want to go into within software engineering. If I want to say web development, I could do that. If I want to go into cloud development, let's do it. So that's what I'm feeling right now. I'm still charting my path. But I'm excited about where I'm gonna end up as a software developer and a software engineer.

Aris Winger: Two more questions. First: to be where you are right now, what have you had to sacrifice?

Austin Sampson: I had to sacrifice time. But there are a lot of social things that I wanted to do that I chose not to do. Living in Richmond and being close to DC, I sacrificed not visiting my friends there. All of my friends are in DC. So I had to sacrifice, like a lot of times, where it's like I would just go back and forth. I couldn't do this as much as I wanted. So it's just time and social. I had to sacrifice that.

I had to sacrifice my comfort zone, allow myself to be uncomfortable, and be okay with that. And like, lean into the uncomfortable.

I was always comfortable with knowing what I was doing, with what my path was. So I had to sacrifice that comfort, and knowing what I was doing and what I wanted to do, with not knowing and learning something new, and being terrible at something.

Aris Winger: Last question. We might have some undergraduates reading this, some people who are majoring in engineering. Some people listening are majoring in biology and are thinking about engineering.

This is your time, as we end. Talk directly to them about your process, how you got here, and any remaining lessons.

Austin Sampson: I think my biggest, my biggest thing is typical. But do not, do not, do not, do not give up. That doesn't mean stay in something that makes you completely uncomfortable, and you completely hate. But it means don't lose hope. Don't lose sight of the end goal at the end of the day.

You're in school to be successful, and your idea of success is right, and only you truly know what your idea of success is, so continue striving towards that. Your idea of success may change. And that's okay as long as you always strive towards that goal.

You're doing all this for yourself: the person that you're going to be. If you know you want to be the best engineer that you can be, then you need to lock in. You have to make those sacrifices you need to. Make those choices to study harder, study longer, and study smarter.

Actually, that's the biggest thing: studying smarter, not harder or longer. Learn your studying skills, do it. Take that time to do it.

You're doing this for you. You have you, and you know what you want. Just lean into your idea of success.

Don't be afraid. And don't say, "Okay, I'm not gonna do it," because of fear.

03 - Cory Payne

THE NONLINEAR PATH

Life can be a winding road, seemingly turning back on itself, at times. Sales Engineer Cory Payne was once a mechanic for boats in South Carolina, also helped track and maintain the grazing land of cattle in New Mexico, and ran a distillery in his neighborhood, all with a biology major background, as he wanted to initially become a doctor. His realization finally came to him. What he wanted to be in terms of a doctor was really being a problem solver. He left the field, returned to college, and pursued engineering. In what comes next, you will find the details of someone who was using his talents with his hands and his unyielding curiosity to build a career of which his father and grandfather would surely be proud.

Cory Payne

Sales Engineer at Charlatte America, Abingdon, Virginia

MS & BS in Mechanical Engineering, New Mexico State University

BS in Biology & Minor in Chemistry, Emory & Henry University

Hometown: Nashville, Tennessee

Aris Winger: Cory Payne, thank you for taking the time with us. Would you call yourself an engineer?

Cory Payne: I do now, yeah, yeah.

Aris Winger: What does an engineer mean to you?

Cory Payne: I would just say, just a problem solver. I mean, that's maybe the main thing I learned in engineering school was how to break down large problems and start tackling them piece by piece, instead of getting crippled with the fear of something large and looming. I think the difference between what an engineer does and what maybe a different profession trying to tackle the same project would be, is like this panic of not knowing where to start, and not realizing that it takes time to produce some valuable insights and solutions. So that is kind of what engineering school did for me, beyond my other academic endeavors, was just. It was kind of like a framework or a methodology of thinking through problems and making it so that you have a way to start something, a way to track something progressing through stages. And then, of course, everybody knows the adage about engineers. What do they say? A great engineer knows when to stop. So then there's also defining what the end product should look like, getting as close to it as possible, and knowing when it's time to move to something else.

Aris Winger: I want to stay there for just a second. What do you mean by this quote about a great engineer?

Cory Payne: Yeah, I think a lot of, I mean, let me also preface this by saying I had the opportunity at a large Fortune 500 company, where I helped manage our Co-OP program. So I was hiring 18 to 20-year-old aspiring engineers.

Aris Winger: So that could be some of the people who are reading this right now.

Cory Payne: Absolutely. Yeah. I would imagine so. I would imagine.

Aris Winger: And what did you notice?

Cory Payne: Our pool was all local college students from what I would consider prestigious Universities s for engineering, and what I noticed was they would get a project, 90% done within the timeframe, and then they would sit on it for months, because they couldn't get this last little touch, or the perfect fixture in place. They couldn't find the fitting they were happy with, or their inclination was to always try to build something like a spaceship. That or they would respond, "I emailed so and so a month ago and I'm still waiting on their response". We worked in an industrial environment where things were going to be abused, so you often had to really do that fine line of design work, where it was, make it robust, make it industrial. Make it good, but don't keep overthinking it... This is not a nuclear facility.

A lot of what gets studied in engineering school is control systems for space exploration, satellite launches, you know, nuclear facilities, and their reliability and robustness. And I think that was a huge thing that I noticed was, you know, young engineers that were coming out of school and interning and trying to just cut their teeth. They would just beat these like really small problems, like not realizing that they're focused on this little teeny, tiny thing when they still had done so much, and they could have just said, "Okay, like, this is where it ends." Let's put it out there and see what happens with it. They would just kind of beat it to the ground.

Aris Winger: Was that tied to perfectionism? Or what they thought a good job looked like?

Cory Payne: So I think it was partial perfectionism. I think it was also really engineering students. They really hold their heads high. They're really proud of what they're accomplishing. That was not so much the case for me, but especially when you're 18 or 19 years old and going through one of the more rigorous undergraduate fields of study. So I think there was also an intense desire to prove their intelligence at times.

At work, it seemed like they really wanted to have things super polished, spending 90% of the time on a 5% increase in whatever they were trying to accomplish. In some engineering disciplines, that is necessary, but in ours, speed outdid perfection.

Aris Winger: You started off with biology. How do we go from biology to now as an engineer?

Cory Payne: In undergrad, I wanted to be a doctor. I thought for sure that was the path I was going to go down when I was in high school every summer, or even early college. During my summers, I would rotate through. I was really close with the orthopedic medicine doctor who helped me overcome some big injuries in basketball, and they really took me on. I was able to sit in on surgeries and help with the clinic. So yeah, so go to undergrad, I thought, "For sure, I know what I want to do. I want to be a doctor."

And then, just kind of slowly over time, I got really, really bored with, you know, hindsight is 20-20. I didn't realize there was bureaucracy in whatever profession you go through. But I got really frustrated. I don't know if I've shared this story with you, Dr. Winger, but I can remember the day I decided medicine wasn't for me. I was in the orthopedic office. So I was in the clinic one day, and there was a lady who came in every 4 months to get a greater trochanter steroid injection in her hip.

It's a steroid shot to calm down inflammation, but she was morbidly obese. I was like, Why don't we provide some lifestyle suggestions instead of just continually bringing her in here and shooting her full of drugs? Why don't we make an impact in the long term? The Doctor said that it would be illegal for me to do so, that what I should be focused on is a medical intervention or medical treatment for the problem that she had, and then she can seek that advice elsewhere. So instead of really trying to solve for the root cause of her problem, it just seemed like we were throwing medicine at it - I'm sure there was more to it, but that is how I interpreted it.

That didn't feel like problem-solving to me. And then there were other things, you know, in terms of pharmaceutical sales practices. And so I just kind of did some reflection and said, "You know what? I don't think that this is the profession I want to pursue anymore."

My grandfather had been a mechanic my entire life. He was a Diesel mechanic in the coal mines in West Virginia. My dad was a really handy guy who ended up getting into sales, but they both told me forever.

You can't be a mechanic. You can't be a mechanic, can't be a mechanic. So naturally, what did I do? After undergrad, I went to Yamaha school and became a mechanic on marine vessels out on the coast of South Carolina.

So I did that for 3 years in Hilton Head Island. I worked for a 100-ton master Captain, who was maybe the most talented mechanic I've ever been around and ever interacted with aside from grandpa. And it was funny. I really fell in love with it because it felt like the same thing as being a doctor to me in my head.

You had a problem that you didn't know the solution to. You had to take all the information and feedback that the system was giving you. You had to understand the system to truly diagnose anything, and then you could start to maybe make suggestions or theories as to what was wrong, and then you would go about fixing them.

I say it all the time. It makes my wife, who is a physician, crazy: I'd say mechanics and doctors are the exact same. There's just a higher consequence of failure for a doctor.

The mentality and the thought process really feel very similar. In mechanics, you have to understand systems. As an example, I would realize "Oh, I know this sound means that the spark plugs are bad, and I started to understand what the spark plug does in the engine. Then, all of a sudden, I could start to diagnose it in a totally different way. It wasn't just from experience, but it was like, I understand the system. I understand there's a flaw in this system. Now I'm going to go fix that.

So I did that for 3 years on the coast. I got to go on amazing fishing trips. It was an incredible but challenging experience. I worked in flip-flops and shorts all day, came home greasy, loved it, loved every minute of it, came to the Southeast, back to. I was the head mechanic at Laurel Marina and Yacht Club on South Holston Lake, working under one of the finest small engine repairmen and a heck of a bluegrass guitar player.

So I did that for 2 years. And after the 1st year, you know. I just realized that it's kind of a young man's game: you're crawling in and out of bilges of boats, you're busting knuckles every day, you know. And then there was also the family component. I didn't want to... I don't know if "disappoint" is the right word. Still, I knew that I had an education beyond what anybody in my family had ever had. So, on a whim, I applied to a chemical manufacturing company to be a tech, and after my second year at Laurel, I got an offer letter from that company that was triple the money. So I said, "Hey, let's give it a go."

And that's where all my introduction to engineering came. I was a technician, so it was my job to come up with different tests. For example, I worked in the medical polymer business. When a doctor goes into surgery there's often like, if you go to cardiac surgery, there's a kit that the doctor has all the tools they need to perform the surgery. It's usually a polymer-based tray with a thin sheet of plastic on the top, and it gets sterilized and then sealed in different methods of sealing that sheet, that thin film, to the top of the tray.

We noticed that we had a 20% failure rate on those seals popping open, which de-sterilizes the instruments, meaning the doctor has to literally throw that kit away and grab another one. And the same thing with blood bags. They undergo a rapid phase change. So those seals were popping upon, freezing and thawing rapidly. And so it was my job to develop different protocols for testing the strength of the seal. So the PhD scientists would kind of have different theories about changing the formulation of the polymer. Then I would be the one to physically build fixtures, set up strain gauges, pull those things apart, and measure the efficiency of the seal.

And shoot, man, I just kind of found out I didn't know what a Young's modulus was at the time, and it was like I was learning on the job…

Aris Winger: From what you just described, there is a lot of expertise that's tied to it. They didn't talk about any of that in biology in undergrad. So, how much of the time did you have to spend learning this whole new process of what it means to do this engineering stuff?

Cory Payne: Oh, for sure, for sure. I mean if when I look back and reflect, I thought they hired me because I had some chemistry knowledge (as a minor). But I think that they saw the potential…I guess I would say I'm strong at taking tools and like making whatever I need happen, if that makes sense.

I was really handy. For instance, when I was on the coast of South Carolina, we were a two-man shop with very limited tools, and, like the guy I worked for used to always say, it would drive me nuts. Still, he would be like, "Every job is possible. The right tools just make it easier." (as I was complaining about needing the perfect sized screwdriver).

I just kind of absorbed that mentality of like, okay, like there's got to be… I know I can fix this, or I can build this. I may not have that beautiful router bit that I need, but I can still find a way to make that shape close enough, and I think that's really why they brought me on board.

At this company, there was a piece of equipment that they were unfamiliar with, called the tribometer, and they were like, We need you to build fixtures to make these two things stick together so we can test the coefficient of friction. I generated the graphs. I wasn't really smart enough to interpret them at that time, probably still not now. But I was really, really probably the best in the entire building at building those things that were necessary for the scientists to get the data that they needed. Plus, I was stubborn enough not to stop until I figured it out.

Aris Winger: I wonder, how is it that you're presenting yourself on your resume in such a way that the company comes to understand that you are this type of person with these qualities? Is this a special line item on your resume?

Cory Payne: No, it's not. I mean, I thru-hiked the Appalachian Trail in 2012. It gets brought up in every interview, I put it on every CV, every resume, and unequivocally, it is brought up in 80% of every interview I go through. I will talk about that. And so I always put something like "demonstrated ability to critically think and problem solve via this accomplishment." And so maybe they just were willing to roll the dice on me, I don't know. Maybe that, plus my mechanical aptitude.

Yeah, you know, I've always known the significance of education. It was beaten into me by my non-collegially educated parents.

So even when I was a mechanic, I was one of the few guys who would go take the Yamaha and Mercury tests to become a certified technician. And so I also carried a lot of those credentials. It's a little bit different than saying "I know what I'm doing." It's like here. Here's a certificate that says I should know what I'm doing, and I'm likely capable of figuring it out. I think that's why they rolled the dice on me.

Aris Winger: Okay. So it's at this company that you gain a lot of these, what you call engineering skills. Okay, keep going.

Cory Payne: So, I'm in year two. I have an engineer who I worked with who pulled me aside. Bachelor's level mechanical engineer, and he's like "Dude". I think you can get an engineering degree in 2 years," and he's like, "your salary will double here." And he was like, "I think you're crazy not to do it." I said to myself, "Well, shoot, man like I would like more money. I like the work you do a little bit more."

I'm still kind of having to come in early. I'm getting my hands dirty every day. It's like, I'm pretty interested in this CAD software we're working on. So the next thing I know, my wife gets into medical school in New Mexico, and I submit my resignation.

We go to New Mexico, and I have a hell of a time finding a job with my biology degree and chemistry minor. I ended up landing a job with the Bureau of Land Management, and I was in charge of inventorying the cattle grazing lands that are owned by the Federal Government.

It was one of the coolest jobs I've ever had. I show up in this new state, in a place I don't know. I was given a government truck and a government gas card, and I was to go out and inspect water troughs for cattle on the range. And they're operated, so what they typically do is they'll take a train tank car and install a solar pump to fill it at the top of a hill, and that gravity feeds like five different cattle troughs out on the range.

Cattle, free-grazing cattle, follow their water source. So if you want to move them and prevent overgrazing of certain areas, you drain certain troughs and fill up others, but they're all operated by float valves, and those float valves would break. So I would go out in the middle of the desert to perform repairs as necessary. But mostly I was geotracking where they were located, because these were huge swaths of land in the Badlands of New Mexico, I mean middle of nowhere. Again, most likely landed this job due to my proven ability as a competent outdoorsman and in-field troubleshooter.

So I did that. This was 2016. The Bureau of Interior Budget was cut, and they came and fired the last three people who were hired at our field office. So I found myself without a job, was kind of wondering what I was going to do, and found out that New Mexico State was one of the cheapest state schools in the country to attend as an in-state citizen. They had a pretty good ABET-accredited engineering program. So next thing I know, I'm going back to undergrad, riding my bicycle to school.

Aris Winger: You decided that engineering was tied to what your co-worker had told you?

Cory Payne: Yes, oh, absolutely. I knew at that point, because I also had the engine aptitude. It just seemed like the only way I could go back to doing what I really like to do, which was fixing mechanical pieces of equipment, but still make the money that I was kind of interested in making. While not for everyone, the technician work was amazing for me, and it's like what probably helps me the most today in my professional life. But I also wanted to solve bigger and different kinds of problems. So I knew that I was going to go back for engineering if I went back to school.

And let's be honest and feel free to use any of this you want. I was a doofus at Emory and Henry. I mean, I was just… I didn't take my academics very seriously, and so I felt like I had a little something to prove, which is what was a big driver to send me back to school as well. I felt like I got through Emory and Henry because I'm a hard worker, but I never really absorbed the information I was getting. I can remember working on some things where I would call you [Editor's Note: Aris] for what I now would say were simple formulas that I needed help with. I felt like I should know how to do these things. So anyways, that was a huge reason.

Aris Winger: Let's break this down a bit. So what does a doofus look like? That means what?

Cory Payne: Oh, I mean, that just means doing the bare minimum to meet the standard that you set for yourself. If I could not learn a certain topic and still get a B+ in the class, I was the kid who was going to do that every time.

Aris Winger: And instead, you're suggesting you would do it differently.

Cory Payne: Yeah, yeah. I mean, it's so funny to go back to undergrad as a 30-year-old, right? Like, your professors really don't ask that much of you. It's like, show up. If you follow their guidance most of the time… I mean, this is not always true. There are some stank professors out there for sure, but for the most part, I found that, you know… I guess what I would say is, I was good at school. I knew how to talk to my professors.

I knew how to show that I was putting in a bit of effort, but I was certainly not to the point where I was putting in the consistency required to absorb and understand the knowledge. You know, I was like the classic kid who could talk to you all semester about a topic. And then it was like when that semester ended, I wiped the hard drive, and got ready for the next one. I wasn't really carrying things with me, and I certainly was not able to apply them in the real world like I would like to.

Aris Winger: And if so, if you could go back, how would you be a different student? What would you be doing differently day to day in your mind?

Cory Payne: Yeah, I mean, maybe just more attentive, and then constantly striving to see how what you're learning in the classroom, especially in the math classroom, can be applicable to your life, right?

We use these formulas for so many things, but to me, it was like, I only needed to pass this exam. And then, as I got further along and became more interested in more sophisticated technologies, it was like, No, math is the rule governing how these things work. So I would have just tried maybe to have been…You know, I kind of knew I was never going to be a super great academic. I'm a hands-on fellow.

That's the world I come from. It's what I know better. But I do wish I would have taken more time to see where my class studies could be applied to my real life and the things that I'm interested in, and I think there was a lot of that overlap. I know there was, but I didn't see it when I was an undergrad, for a host of reasons.

So consistency, really, I think, is a huge part of school. And in life in general, right? Showing up every day. Yeah, yeah.

Aris Winger: Dig into the consistency piece.

Cory Payne: Like, truly understanding what you're doing right?

I was like a cheat sheet fanatic. I could understand and apply a lot of the principles we learn in school, but in the classroom. I would be trying to solve the problem so I could learn something in your classroom. Then I could be doing something with my group of friends, trying to, let's say, make some cider, and I could have learned the formula needed to solve the thing I was covering in your classroom, and I would have never used that in real life. I would go back to Google.

I wasn't consistent enough. It wasn't applicable in my everyday life.

Aris Winger: So you head to grad school in New Mexico.

Cory Payne: Yeah. So I initially (before going back to undergrad) applied to grad school, and they said they would not let me in until I had my basic mechanical engineering undergrad classes taken. So I actually had to get another undergraduate degree. So I had to take statics, dynamics, vibrations, you know, just the core fluid mechanics. So then, I went back to my undergraduate studies. I'm…

Aris Winger: Okay. And now this time, are you more serious about it?

Cory Payne: So I also love rock climbing. So I guess the important thing to note here was that I still probably could have been a lot more serious. I was a little jaded that I had to go back to undergrad, but honestly, the Administration, New Mexico State… I sing their praises; they didn't make me take, you know, from Emory and Henry, we have the Liberal Arts degree. So I had to take zero humanities classes. It was purely math and physics that were needed to succeed in graduate school. I think I would have…I think I would have floundered had I not been forced to go back and solidify some of those topics.

So like going to Cal 2. Super frustrating. But going to differential equations. Something I didn't study as a biologist. Immensely helpful. That's where you really get into engineering math. And so I needed those courses.

But yeah, so, anyway… Yes, I was a much better student at New Mexico State. I still had a lot of hobbies outside of the classroom, but I was just much more mature, and they were much healthier hobbies that went to better brain function the next day. So you know, it's like, you go rock climbing all day. You still can get up at 7 o'clock and do what you need to do in the classroom. So I think I was much, a much better student nearing 30 than I was at 19.

And it's really funny. So one of the reasons I agreed to move to southern New Mexico was for rock climbing. About 45 minutes from Las Cruces, New Mexico, is a place called Waco Tanks. If you're a rock climber, you certainly know of it. It's one of the best boulder fields in the country, and it climbs year-round. It's beautiful. You have to have a guide to climb at the majority of Waco Tanks. This all kind of ties together…

I go. I had met a guide two years before I moved there, when my wife and I were considering it. We went to climb at Waco to see if we thought we would like it there, and met this guy, and called him up a couple of years later. I said, Hey, will you take me on a trip.

We're cruising down to Waco Tanks, and he says, "Cory, I'm thinking about starting a distillery. You know, you're from Tennessee. You know anything about making whiskey?" And honestly, lying through my teeth, just to be excited about the opportunity. I was like, "I know everything about making whiskey."

I had run a still twice in my life in college. My friend and I manufactured a bit for a few years, so I didn't know much, but he said, Well, you know, I want to bring you in from the very beginning and get this thing started. So I immediately bought every book I could, and just became "Mr. Distiller." I mean, it was like the sole focus of my entire life outside of the classroom and crag.

So I'm going through undergrad again. And I am charged at this distillery to build a glycol manifold, to keep all the condensers cooled, as you know, as the hot vapor of the alcohol is coming to the condenser. I kept having a problem where I was lacking the pressure needed to keep the lines chilled. Well, I was in fluids at the time, and so I pulled my professor aside, and I said, "Hey, like I'm designing this Glycol manifold. I drew it up. I brought him out there. He explained to me "we're learning this right now," you know, he pulled Bernoulli's equation out. He's like, "here's what you need to do to fix this pressure issue. You have to make this elbow not as sharp because you're generating turbulent flow…" I mean, all these things that I just had not thought of. And so he and I developed a pretty good relationship.

Fast forward 6 months. I'm about to be done with undergrad round 2, and I don't know what I'm going to do. He is a PhD Fluid mechanicist. So he's a DOD employee for the Army Research Lab, and he says, "Hey, man, I've got an intern spot open. You should come work for me this summer…" and I mean, that's like that's how it happened. So I applied. I got hired as an intern.

I go to the Army base every day, and I'm telling you it's one of the best summers of my entire life. I mean, I just took to it like I love it. I got it. It became fascinating. We were doing fundamental weather research. So you know, it was cool to see fluid mechanics being used not for fluid, but for studying the atmosphere, which is governed by the same mathematical equations.

I got to work on some amazing projects, which we can get into if you guys want. But anyway, I discovered something in some data that we didn't quite understand at the end of my internship. So, a lot of my work was in charge of doing field repairs on weather instruments. So in the desert again, I think I got hired because they needed somebody to run a sonar and keep a generator filled for 5 days off the grid, and nobody was willing to do it except me. I was ecstatic.

Going out to go see aliens or something (Roswell is only a couple of hours away. Many stories of aliens in the desert). So I took the internship and found this weird anomaly in the data. He goes, "Cory, I think there's something there. I'd be happy if you could be my graduate student at New Mexico State if you think that is something you would want to do?"

It was insane. I missed all the deadlines for applying to grad school, you know. I kind of had hoped that I would get into graduate school, but I was also kind of over school. The distillery was doing great, and yeah, long story short, he sponsored me. We went to the Administration, said, Hey, like, here's all my application forms. It was one of those programs where I didn't require the GRE because it was the same institution. I had a 3.9 coming out of my undergrad, you know, as a 30-year-old. It's a little bit easier. So crush through that.

So then I started my graduate studies. And oh, my gosh, I don't know how you guys did it as PhDs.

Aris Winger: Would you have gotten this internship if you hadn't brought him in to talk and look at that stuff?

Cory Payne: Absolutely Not.

Aris Winger: There's something about you going...And I'm saying this for some of our people who are reading this, who are one of 250 in their classroom. What compels you to actually go to your professor and say something?

Cory Payne: Sure. Yeah, I mean, that's a great question. I mean, I'll give him some credit. He was a very cool professor as a younger guy, PhD from Notre Dame. That fluids class is probably 40-50 students.

And so it was really funny, like, I asked him the initial question, and he was kind of like, What are you doing this for? Like I think you could tell it was something that, had I not had a business, I probably should not have been doing. And then, as we just kind of developed a relationship, I also thought it was awesome because he was super excited. Right? Like I think he was. It ended up being the least scary thing I've ever done.

He was so happy that he had the knowledge to help me. After that kind of initial discussion, we started talking about all kinds of weird problems after class. Had I not had the courage to go up and ask him that question, or just the stubbornness to say, "I can't figure this out. I'm gonna find somebody who can." Here's this great resource that I'm kind of already paying for, someone who I would consider one of the great fluid mechanics experts in the country. Let's just see if he knows what's going on.

Aris Winger: How was grad school?

Cory Payne: It's brutal, you know. I mean, I'm in trouble all the time because I'm getting the opportunity to go out on these big, extravagant adventures like elk hunts, climbing at some of the most recognizable areas in the country, racing in 12-hour bike races, etc.

Graduate school is just... It's a wild leap. It's like going from high school to college in sports, right? I don't even know... even though I was older and more mature. I don't know that I was quite ready for the demand that's placed on you through graduate school - especially with what I had going on in life, and of course, I was trying to do it in a year, which didn't pan out. My research was not done. So it took me 3 semesters instead of 2, but the coursework, I mean. Other than taking more outside learning, the coursework was kind of the same.

At that point, I was like settled back into a routine of studying, and so I had to put in some hours. I had to ask for help from other engineering mentors in order to get through some of the classes. But again, it seemed like most of the folks who were in Academia were more than willing to kind of give me the help that I needed to get through some of my classes.

I should also say something about the work I ended up doing in graduate school. I really loved the way my professor presented fluid mechanics in undergrad 2.0. And then my graduate fluids course was taught by a guy who was all about hyper-speed travel. It was shockwave theory, and it was tough for me to grasp. You know I've done plumbing work in many houses in my life, so I understand head pressure, right? But when you're bending gravity by how fast you're going and there's extra friction because you're breaking through invisible barriers…it was just really a challenging course for me. That, plus we had to do all of our coding in FORTRAN. So it's funny, and it was hard.

I like to say I do fluid mechanics, but it's such a broad field that you know I do this little teeny, tiny part of it, or I have to contribute to a very small part of it.

Aris Winger: With all that you have said so far about what you have done in school and your number of interests outside school, how were you finding balance?

Cory Payne: That's a great question. I mean, that's like the bane of my life. It's funny, because I tell people all the time, like "I don't know that you would want to hire me for your business," because I do have hobbies and passions outside of work. And so as much as I'm willing to give my 50-60 hour work weeks of full focus to the company I work for, I still really cherish the time I get to go out and pick tomatoes in my garden, ride my mountain bike, and rock climb. So yeah, I could tell that even back in academia, especially in graduate school, where the classes are small, I could tell people were frustrated that I had things going on outside of the class.

And so it was tough to explain at times how significant an opportunity it felt like for me when they're like, I don't care if you're going to get through my graduate level. I'll give you an example. I got the opportunity to go on an elk hunt in the backcountry of New Mexico after winning a lottery in a hard-to-win zone in the Gila Wilderness (one of Teddy Roosevelt's favorite wildernesses). I knew people that have tried to draw an elk tag for a hunt in this wilderness for 18 to 20 years of their lives. Here I am in my 3rd year in New Mexico. I got this amazing opportunity. So I go to my professor, and I say, "Hey! Like I've got this amazing opportunity. I will make up the time. I was going to miss 2 class sessions.."

He responded, "I'm docking you a letter grade on your grade for this course." And that was his response. There was never a "tell me more about this opportunity. I may not be interested, but if it means that much to you…" I never got any of that.

And so, anyways, long story short, I had to get my advisor involved and the department head, and that professor still kind of massacred me. I passed the class, but it was the worst grade I got in graduate school.

Aris Winger: Was it worth it?

Cory Payne: I would say, Yeah, yeah. I got to see part of the country most people never have the opportunity to see. I got to live this visceral lifestyle that I love. I mean, just like those little things for me... Which is probably why I'm not a "great" student. Those things recharge me. The Cory *not* doing that is worse in that class than Cory doing that and coming back with this like vigor for life. It's just like I'm back excited, and I don't feel like there's this monotony or this drollness on, just getting through the motions. You know, those things like waking my spirit up, you know, and in turn make me far more productive as a human being and as a contributor to whatever I'm doing.

Aris Winger: So then we're almost at the end of graduate school. And where do we move on from there?

Cory Payne: Yeah. I think I mentioned it, but my wife is a physician. So that's what got me to New Mexico. So that got me all these awesome opportunities. I didn't know how Residency worked. You get an envelope in the mail. Every doctor who graduates from medical school does. On the same day they open it, and half the students cry, and half the students are excited about where they're going. So that's the match process. And then my wife matched at Emory in Atlanta.

So I have my last semester of graduate school about to start...well, and then before that, COVID hit. So as a matter of fact, I'm like, I'm 65% of the way through my research. And one day I go to my office at the Army Base, hand them my cat card, and they say you can't come in.

I say, well, why not? And they're like, there's this virus that's getting serious, and we're not allowing anyone in under a certain credential level. And so it's pretty crazy. That was the last time I got to go to my office. So all of my printed research, you know, we were studying levels of the atmosphere. So up on the wall I had taped different pressure plots as the atmosphere moved up so that I could kind of see what was going on in a 3-dimensional space. I lost all that, like I never saw it again... till this day, my boss said it's still hanging on the wall in our old office.

So then, all school classroom research, everything goes remote. So I'm working in New Mexico. Then that summer we moved. So summer of 2020, we picked back up and moved to Atlanta. And so I actually defended my thesis, you know, via Zoom from Atlanta to finish my graduate degree.

Once I got done with school, I actually continued to work for the Army Research Laboratory remotely for about 6 to 7 months, and then the research money just kind of dried up. I don't know if it was just time for me to go, but you know all the money was coming from … some sort of fund that they provide to the Army Research Lab, and I don't know what the circumstances were, but we thought it was going to be a much longer term solution, and it just didn't happen to be that way. So about 2 months before my time at the army was done, they told me, "Hey, the money's not going to be there. We're not going to be able to pay you. So, you know, get ready for that."

So that's when, an Emory and Henry connection, who happens to be managing director at a large company based in Atlanta, I reached out to her, and just said, "hey? You know I'm in Atlanta. I'm not gonna be here for super long, but I would love to see if there's any work that needs to be done at your company," and she said, sure enough, 'we got a department that's looking for a guy right now.' and so I did one interview via Zoom, and the next thing I knew I was hired as their quality and production engineer for the ground support equipment (GSE). That was the title that I accepted.

Aris Winger: Yeah. And while we're here… I'm a mathematician. So I'm always fascinated by the names. I see so many different names for engineers.

Cory Payne: They're ridiculous, and I'm sure Kyle would agree with that. I mean a common friend of ours, who has a chemistry degree, but has never attended an Engineering institution, has the exact same title as me for a chemical company as a sales engineer. My personal opinion is that I think the market's a little saturated right now, like it just seems like a lot of companies are just after that title. And then people who are doing any sort of technical work are being given that title. So you know it. It fascinates me, too. I don't have a clue. We had tons of people who were called engineers who had no engineering degree.

Kyle Clark: Yeah, that's certainly something Winger and I have talked a lot about, because I've got a materials engineering degree. But I've never carried any professional certificates, or…I can't design anything with CAD. I can look at it, but I don't design any of it. But I've been a process development engineer for my whole career. So you know, where does that come from? And you know, there are a lot of degrees like quality engineer, which probably lands in this category. But you can't get a degree in process development.

Cory Payne: Nope! It doesn't exist.

Cory Payne: It doesn't. There's not a degree, yes, exactly.

Aris Winger: Yeah, yeah, this. So it sounds like that. There are so many titles that aren't tied to degrees. Right?

The other thing that's coming up is these people that keep showing up, that step in and say, "Oh, I got a place for you! Oh, you should go here! You've named a number of them, but it seems like they have played a role in your direction. Lots of them feel like accidents or happenstance.

For the reader, it might feel like "Wow, it sounds like you ran into the right people at the right time." How do we make that more actionable? What are they supposed to do?

Cory Payne: Yeah, I mean, that's a great question. I'd like to sit here and give some really insightful and enlightening answers, but I was just nice to everybody, but you know…

I do think, I mean, I think I listen to folks. I think when I build a connection with somebody, I'm okay to let it fester and mellow as a peripheral connection, and not necessarily like we don't have to be best friends, and you know, but I also like to talk to people and hear stories. So you know.

I think, just keep an open mind, and like talking to all walks of life. You know, I never got into the little cobbles of social groups. I would never not talk to someone because of who or what they were affiliated with. I don't know. I think there's just, you know, I'm 6 foot 6, maybe people just remember me.

Aris Winger: Be nice to everybody is a good one.

Cory Payne: Listen to people.

Aris Winger: Yeah.

Cory Payne: You know, I can identify with these stories. I mean, when I was at the chemical company, I would tell you what made me successful was my ability to bridge the gap between the PhD chemical engineers and the guys that were running the equipment, because those two groups of people cannot talk to each other. I mean, even if the Phd guy or the doctor is trying to convey something that's not necessarily meant to sound degrading. These people just could not... It was just like, "You're the doctor. I know you're coming down on my intelligence level."

But that was a huge part of my success. Hell, my whole career has been... I've carried that as something that I'm really proud of: being able to work the interpersonal relationships between the academic side of the business and the operation side of the business.

Aris Winger: And so, but those require skills, where are you getting these skills from?

Cory Payne: I mean, different experiences, learning basic human psychology, you know, like understanding when somebody is frustrated, and you know, but sharing stories and listening to folks and meeting people where they are. I mean, honestly, what I would say. One of the main reasons that I have been successful at this is that I'm willing to do the dirty work with both parties.

You know, if you were to ask me to build a spreadsheet that I didn't know how to do, I would try my best, and if somebody in the operations was having an issue, you know, I would go put the Tyvek suit on, and go and get hot and sweaty, and wrench on whatever I needed to. You know I'm not afraid to kind of try to meet whoever, wherever they are.

Yeah, I certainly don't think any work is beneath me, you know, when I started at the distillery, it was like my 1st 2 weeks. I was sweeping, staining the floors, and squeezing lemon juice for hours, you know. I am willing to kind of go there on any part of a project. You know. I think that's huge. I think that's where I build a lot of rapport with these individuals.

This is especially true on the operation side, you know. I mean, I do my best on the academic side, and I think I do understand a lot of what's being discussed or why it's being discussed. I can have intelligent conversations, even if I don't know the fundamental science behind why you guys are making the decisions you're making. I can still understand how to translate that down to the operations team, which is going to be like performing most of the work that's getting done.

Aris Winger: It's powerful.

Kyle Clark: That definitely resonates with the experience I've had working for the last decade or so. There's been a lot of disconnect sometimes between your operators and technicians and the guys in the office.

Cory Payne: Yes. Yes, absolutely.

Kyle Clark: I've also worked extensively with international or cross-country offices. And so when you add that distance, disconnect, I've seen it build a lot of resentment between different groups to the point where it makes it very difficult to continue. So. That's an excellent skill to have and carry with you.

Aris Winger: How do you end up in the middle? What happened?

Cory Payne: My wife likes fine French dining, and I like big trucks and dirt. Maybe it's that I can find joy in almost any situation. Oh, it's a delicate balance, I mean… and especially when you get into the corporate world where we have middle management... I mean, it comes with a lot of frustrations. The chemical company was better than my later employer because it was set up in such a way that I was encouraged to have those conversations and do those things.

But a big, big corporate beast like the company I worked for, I mean, they're all they care about is efficiency, right? They want me to be able to track how much money I'm saving. So if I'm down there helping install a sensor for a project I need done, you know, my boss, who doesn't have any engineering background whatsoever, is like, "I don't know why you don't just pass that off?" and it's like that's why everybody downstairs hates you, dude.

You know, like that's why you, when you go down there, you are public enemy number one, because your mentality is "just pass it off", make them do the legwork of figuring things out. That's just not my style of working at all.

But it is really tough. I mean, it's really tough, and it always causes animosity, you know. If you go out to lunch with this group and then the other group the next week, then people are frustrated. I mean, that's just working politics…

Aris Winger: That sounds like high school.

Cory Payne: It's very much like high school. Yeah.

It's horrible. Listen. It's one of the reasons I left that company. I took a pay cut to have my current job. Now, there were other circumstances which we can talk about if you want to help me make the decision. But most certainly, the best career decision I have made was leaving a company of 100,000 employees for a company of 90 employees in terms of impact. The impact of your work. You know, taking a little bit of a higher risk tolerance to actually do some developmental and innovative things. Those kinds of things were almost impossible at previous companies unless you were hand-selected, and that comes to more politics.

I have found I can enjoy that because I know how to play the game, you know. Oftentimes, I could work on side projects at big corporations, because again.

I took the job at my previous company and spent 2 and a half to 3 years of my life working on numerical data sets, right? I love to tell a story. I got started with true data analysis in the army. You know. I had to get a top secret security clearance, which for me felt like, "Oh, man, I've made it kind of." So I go through all the rigamarole they call my old roommates. I'm worried as heck about people saying something ridiculous.

I got the security clearance, I'll never forget my 1st confidential government email. I was like, "Man, I'm about to know about nuclear codes and other government secrets." And it was a 4 GB Excel spreadsheet of numbers. No headers, no nothing. I mean, it was literally just sensor data, and I was just like this is ridiculous, you know.

This doesn't seem like a top-secret government email. And I would come to learn that it was really, really powerful.

Aris Winger: So, while you are out of Atlanta, is that company content to have you remote?

Cory Payne: No, no! I was for a year of my life… We bought a house in Abingdon, and I never spent a five-day week there. I think in my 1st year, I lived here for something like less than 80 days.

I worked for an airline, so I had flight benefits, which meant I could fly for free on the standby list. Monday or Tuesday morning (I usually was awarded one to 2 days a week from home), and I would hop a flight from my new home airport to Atlanta, and I rented a room from a colleague, a really cool couple.

 So I would go to Atlanta, and I would work in Atlanta for the week, and then on Thursday or Friday, I would hop a flight back as long as there was a seat, and come back and live at home for the weekends, and they were fine with that. I mean, if there were a couple of days, I would have to take personal time or something, because there was just no seat on a plane. So, it was frustrating. It was taxing, I mean, you know, to fly out at 6 am. You gotta leave the house at 3: 30. So yeah. I made the decision to leave. Oh, I was telling you about the spreadsheet of numbers, right?

Cory Payne: So that was the experience I had coming out of graduate school into my previous role. And so they hired me as their quality person. But what they really wanted was a reliability person, right? They wanted to see which of the fleet types of the vast number of types of equipment we were buying were performing the best. Who should we be purchasing in the future to save money in the long run? And I quickly found out that they were not collecting any of this information.. I mean to run a 12,000-unit fleet; the company has, like, the 5th biggest ground support fleet in the entire world.

Cory Payne: And it was when I started. There were 14 people and a software package that looked like it was made by my friends at Emory. I mean, it was just... It was pitiful. You could not extrapolate any information. Everything was custom, text input fields. So you couldn't really run queries to understand what was going on. And you know… so I can't tell you the number of conversations I had with my supervisor about… we cannot do anything with this.

For me to perform the job you're asking me to perform, we have to take a step back and start gathering, you know, high-quality information, right? I can't make numbers say something if we are not collecting this information.

I eventually convinced them it's what we needed to do, and we were able to build some good systems at that company. But again, Nothing like we could have had if we had the right systems in place and the desire to gather.

A lot of my supervisors, you know… they were business school graduates, and so it didn't make sense to them. Right? They were reading these articles about what was happening out west in Silicon Valley. And they're like, "We know, this is possible." And it's like, Yeah, man. But those guys *set it up* to be possible.

Lots of conversations like that. So yeah, and I'm sorry to both you guys... what I did at my previous company.. I worked on the ground support side. So if you're sitting on an aircraft and looking out the window, all those tractors are moving bags... Jet fuel is about 4 times more expensive than Diesel, so like when you are on an airplane, it's a Diesel tractor that pushes your airplane out into the runway. They're not firing up the jets until the last minute that they need to, just for cost savings measures.

So all those, all those pieces of ground support equipment, including the baggage systems. I was one of the 3 engineers who oversaw that entire fleet. So we were responsible for maintenance, purchasing, moving, innovating, and developing. If something was going wrong, how could we engineer that problem out? I mean...

Aris Winger: Biggest airport in the world.

Cory Payne: Yeah.

Aris Winger: And where are you now? And now you are at.

Cory Payne: So now I work for one of the ground support equipment manufacturers that I worked for back in Atlanta.

Aris Winger: How did that come about?

Cory Payne: I was getting ready to leave the airline. I had met one of their salesmen, and it was really funny. I was telling a colleague of mine where I was moving to. And of course, everybody in Atlanta asked, "Why in the world would you move to the Appalachian mountains?" and I was like, "Why in the world wouldn't you move to the Appalachian mountains?"

Cory Payne: One of the guys who had been there for a long time said, Well, the Charlatte factory, which is the company I work for now, is in Bluefield.

And so I struck up... I just emailed the Vice President of Sales out of nowhere. He's the only one I've met, and just said, "Hey, here's my situation. I'm looking to kind of make a career change. I've already got some good industry insight, and I think I can help your team grow, but there's no way I'm gonna drive for 1.5 hours every day. So if we can't work on some sort of remote work, then this conversation can die here." They were super excited to have me so…

Aris Winger: So you humbly say, "Oh, I contacted the Vice President. Oh, I went to talk to my professor. Oh, I reached out to this person. I want to make sure the reader understands these big moves, like sending this email.

Cory Payne: It just comes from experience. I'll add that one thing to keep in mind when having these conversations is to know your goal. Do not droll on or bore these individuals. Ask your question and let the conversation grow organically from there. And yeah, this has been great, and you know the flip side is, I was telling you guys at the beginning of our discussion. I was in charge of hiring engineering co-ops at my previous company. And Kyle, to your point. I quickly learned that I will never be a super successful engineer if I want to do design work on CAD because this new generation…I was hiring kids who had been playing on SolidWorks since they were 7 years old.

I mean, they could… I would give them something to mock up that would take me a week, and they would have it done in 4 hours. It was insane. I quickly realized that, like, that's not the skill that's going to make me successful. And so, as much as I like doing that work, and I do it for fun and 3D printing projects, I wiped that off as even a potential career course for me. I was never going to be that guy, you know. No one's calling you to become the next designer when you have 2 years of CAD experience. And again, like some of these kids, they could do this with their eyes closed. So… My best friend at that company had done design work for some of the largest defense contractors in the world. He also solidified that I was very far behind if I wanted to be a full-time designer. My interests were more along the business side anyway.

I also have been pretty strategic in that way. You know, I never really got so set on. "Here's what I want to do as an engineer." I was just kind of always willing to jump in and take, you know, oftentimes the crappy projects, I mean, at a big company. Nobody wants to do quality or reliability. I mean, that's like the job that most people kind of scoff at, you know. But I was like, "Heck, I know I can do the data work. Let's go for it." Right? So...

Well, now, I feel really fortunate because this is probably the happiest I've been as a professional, because, finally, or I guess, I've just had to do some reflecting, and I think I'm particularly good at understanding the technical side. But still, having a social part of my job, I got a little frustrated at my previous company... like I just... I'm not that... I wish I were more intelligent, a little more academically inclined. But I'm just not.

But I can have conversations with people. So now I kind of have this 2 pronged approach to my job, where you know it's on me. So my company is owned by a parent company in France. I'm the only engineer who sits in the United States. So any development stuff I have to understand. But then I'm going and having conversations with leaders of major companies that are purchasing this equipment, and I find that I really like that balance a lot, you know.

Is that all they said in France? So if I have an American customer who needs something changed to your point, it's been a really crazy experience trying to learn how to communicate with people from another country, you know. I mean, that's been a huge part of what I've done. I've only been at this company for a month and a half. I have been tasked with bridging the animosity between the stateside guys and the French guys. And that is totally new... That's a problem like I've never experienced before, you know.

But I really enjoy it. I love the ability to socialize and do some of the things that are involved in the whole process of understanding equipment from a technical side, but also a marketable side. But still, being the technical lead, you know, my job is sales engineer, but none of my compensation is based on commission or sales quotas. I just support the entire sales team from a technical perspective.

Kyle Clark: And another title that you don't get a degree in.

Cory Payne: Exactly. Yeah, there's no learning how to do this. Right? Yeah.

Aris Winger: So now, suppose you get to go back. What are some crucial skills that you wish you had gotten in undergrad that would have helped you along the way, that you may have had to pick up, or you were just like, "Wow! I never knew I needed to know this. I wish I had been taught this 4 years ago." What are some of those things?

Cory Payne: You know, like, especially when I went back to school, I wish I had taken the opportunity to practice some soft skills more.

I think you realize once you get out of like just the CAD jockey work and you're starting to run projects in engineering. You have to learn how to tell stories with information. You have to have great presentation skills and understand how your contribution fits into the business.

The number of times I've seen somebody have this immaculate idea in corporate America, and it just gets completely ignored because they couldn't translate that into the benefits to the other functions of the business, or couldn't convince the finance guy was important, or they just left all that out when they had this beautiful technical solution. But they didn't worry about budgeting. They didn't worry about the timeline like they focused on their own little piece of it. I kind of wish I had spent more time massaging those skills when I was an undergrad.

Kyle Clark: Oh, yeah, because at the end of the day, you have to be able to explain it to other people. One of the stories, I don't remember if I've told you this Winger, but you know we had our defense for the Phd. And having gone through the materials engineering program, I actually worked in a lab for an electrochemist. So I just learned how to talk, think, and talk about the subject. I was researching electrochemical terms, not material science terms. And so we spent half an hour not understanding each other because we were discussing the same thing with different terms.

Cory Payne: Yeah, and you know, you're fortunate enough to have the aptitude to work in this theoretical, technical world. But in corporate America, it's like at the end of the day, you're trying to save or make money, and so you have to be able to present this to someone with an MBA that has never taken calculus. Right? Like you're not... You're not trying... You cannot get into the weeds of this super detailed technical understanding, like they don't care. You know, like hell, I wish somebody had taught me how to make a 1-pager in undergrad.

Kyle Clark: That's a good one.

Cory Payne: Huge. That is a huge part of my monthly life...

Aris Winger: Why?

Cory Payne: Because it demonstrates, or it presents your understanding of your topic, the same way you've always heard of, like an elevator pitch in business school. It's like you're handing it to someone who has infinitely more responsibilities on their plate. They don't have much time to digest anything. They need to know who, what, when, where, why, how much it's going to cost me, and what I'm going to get out of it. And that's what they need to know.

You know, it's funny that we practice in school writing 5 to 10-page papers when the.

The majority of my successes have come from 3 quarters of a page, one diagram. Here it is distilled down to the most basic thing it could be for you to understand.

Aris Winger: Anything else?

Cory Payne: I wish that I would have taken more initiative myself to apply things I was learning into my everyday life. Ultimately, that's what drove me to go back to school. I wanted to stop having to call Dr. Winger to understand how much volume I needed to dilute this liquid down to where I needed it. You know. I mean.

But that might be very unique to me. I want to know. I want to have as much knowledge as I can, so that no matter what I go to do, I can hopefully have some sort of understanding of what I'm doing.

Aris Winger: Now you're saying you're tied to sales now. So this whole money-making piece is showing up. How does this impact curiosity? How much does curiosity still show up in terms of wanting to learn more?

Cory Payne: Yeah, that's a great question. I'm the only engineer in the States for my company. The team of engineers does the design work on these tractors. They all sit in France, and so a big part of my job, like what I've done for the last month, is understanding where our customers are going and preparing my team to be on the cutting edge of innovation. And also knowing what not to waste our time on, right?

So I still have a pretty intense curiosity. I mean, it's just that I'm no longer really doing a lot of the work itself. I'm not changing the brackets. I'm not designing the high voltage system. Now, I'm listening to what the Vice President of FedEx wants to see in his fleet moving forward. And I go to my engineering team. And I say, "Okay, we've got to move into high voltage like everyone's ditching low voltage stuff."

Aris Winger: Happy with that? You're out of the trenches, and you're okay with that?

Cory Payne: Yeah, I am, because next week, for instance, we're installing a telemetry system that we're gonna start doing off the production line, and no one knows how to do it. So, like my job will be figuring out the problem and writing instructions for my production team to follow. So I'll be in a mechanic's outfit all week. Next week, running wires, running tests. I still get to scratch that itch.

But I also am like, maybe what I would say is like a more significant part of the business. Now, like, I'm making large financial decisions and participating in high-level discussions, which I also find a lot of, I find interest in that. Now, as I get older, I'm getting more interested in being involved in my community. I live in the southeast. This place is undergoing a rapid transition right now.

I feel like I almost practice these conversations at work to bring them to my community, which has been really kind of a little hobby for me. It's like trying to find how I can work in and where, so my skills can be appreciated. And then I just view work as this opportunity to practice it like crazy.

I'm also trying to start a little business. So it's like trying to understand from cradle to grave how something works to get produced and sold.

I get to go through all that now, and as much as I love technical work like I told you, I have to be honest with myself, like I'm not. I'm not a top-tier

Fellow, like I'm not gonna be able to mock something up on CAD. I'd be better off hiring a 3rd party contractor to do it. It would cost me less money to pay someone for it than to do it myself. You know I can solve the problems. But I know that's just not my strong suit. I think putting pieces together and motivating a team to action is probably more my thing.

Aris Winger: Well, this leads to a couple of questions. So about ego. It feels like you are operating without ego, without being better than somebody else, without competition, without being better than your fellow employees. I didn't hear any of that.

Cory Payne: Yeah, that's not. I don't. That's not the environment I wanna work in every day, like.

I don't know if it was… I got it out in sports as a young in. You know, took a bunch of lumps in the process, or I mean, I certainly I don't want to sound like I'm Mother Teresa here… like I certainly there's certain people that I don't get along with as well as others and I'm still a competitive person, and you know there's some friction points. But yeah, as far as trying to outprove myself, I don't feel like that's really what I'm after in terms of my professional life, you know. If I could equate it to rock climbing, I would say I'm more of a big wall climber than a sport climber. Sport climbing is about who can do the hardest moves. Big wall climbing is about conquering a common objective with your partner, the latter being more in line with who I am.

Like I said I would say, most people, if they were hearing this story, they would call me crazy. I left a Fortune 100 company, which has amazing profit sharing and other benefits… I mean, the compensation is better at my previous company.. The work for me was not as engaging. I find that I make a much bigger impact on this small company, and I find a lot more reward and sleep a lot easier after weeks at what I do now than I did at a major globally recognized Brand.

Aris Winger: A couple of more questions. What if you had to sacrifice to be here where you are now?

Cory Payne: Wow! Golly! I feel really fortunate. I mean, I've just told you guys stories about how I went through graduate school and went on multi-day elk hunts, and I've climbed in Moab and got to help start a successful business. I feel really fortunate in terms of what I've had to sacrifice. I mean, the hard work is the hard work, you know.

So for me, it's like, I've always worked hard, and there's a part of me that really appreciates my parents beating academia into me. Because a little bit of a sacrifice for a couple of months of going through school to get a credential that's gonna carry you forever is this... I mean, I would have been doing it by dragging my knuckles over concrete, changing impellers, you know.

So I don't know. I just have always been a hard worker. I'm not a very lazy fella, like I wake up early because I wake up early, you know, I mean…of course, there are sacrifices, right? There are many things I would have rather done than studying differential equations on a Wednesday. But I think I've been able to strike a really good balance of, you know, keeping myself personally fulfilled while still making those sacrifices. I mean…Maybe I have a unique perspective, too, because I watched a partner go through Medical school and a great friend become a Navy SEAL, where those people literally give themselves up. And so…It's almost selfish for me to be like "I sacrificed so much." I had to make a couple of extra egg sandwiches to get my wife through Med School, you know. I still had way more fun as a graduate student in engineering than she did as a medical student, was able to socialize a lot more, and I was able to build connections in town. I was able to start a business.

The largest sacrifice I had to make was time away from my immediate family. My mom and sister had to sacrifice a lot for me to pursue all these endeavours. We are a tight-knit family, and I have been going full steam ahead, wherever it takes me for a long time, and I think if anyone suffered from my persistence, it is them.

Aris Winger: All right. So now again, this is directly to the reader. There's someone in this nation who is just at the end of reading about your story. They're in the middle of their undergrad for engineering, or maybe not for engineering. What do you want to tell them about being successful about the journey and lessons learned? Anything you want to tell them?

Cory Payne: I would say it's worth it. It's worth it, you know. I think the people that I find to be extremely miserable in this world are the people that can't see things through, and you know as much as my ego is not a big factor of how I work in my day to day life like there's a part of me that's a little sad that I didn't push through and go become a doctor.

You know. It's like when you set down a path, I think that there's a lot of validity and a lot of insightful things that you can gain by going through the hard stuff, and you really don't gain that much by stopping it. If you know it's not for you, don't do it, but you know almost nothing I've accomplished all the way through, do I look at it in a negative light? Even if it wasn't the right thing, right? I didn't need a biology degree to be an engineer, but I'm still grateful that I went through it and completed it.

I think once you commit to something, seeing it through, you're never going to do yourself wrong. You can always change it later, you know. Well, unless you go to Med school, take on a ton of debt, and don't want to be a doctor anymore. There's not a lot to change there. But yeah, just finish it out. I mean, I started the Appalachian Trail in 2012 in Georgia, you know, of the 10 people I met on my 1st day, only 2 of us finished, and all those others email us every year talking about how much they wish they had seen it through.

Yes, and you know they didn't go through the sore feet, fungus, and sicknesses, and I mean the hard days and being wet for days in a row, and they all still wish they could have finished. You don't think about that. You think about the accomplishment, you know.

As much as I didn't like grad school, I mean... I knew, like at first, when I went to New Mexico to be an engineer, I wanted to get my

PhD, that's what I wanted to do. And then I realized it wasn't for me. I chose mechanical engineering because I wanted to be a generalist, able to work on anything. When I realized that getting a PhD set me down more of a specialist route, I decided to stop at my master's. To clarify, though, I started my graduate journey in a master's program. I was never admitted into a PhD track.. Want a graduate degree? Go see it through, get it done, and then, if it's not for you, then you can make changes from there, right? But it's just worth it. It's worth seeing it through and pushing through the hard times. If you want to hike the Appalachian Trail, you'd better commit to the point you will finish, unless both legs are broken. If you want to pursue higher education, you'd better commit to the time required to reach that success, all while finding the balance in life that keeps you happy.

04 - Nikeem Coleman

DON'T QUIT, LIFE IS JUST TESTING YOU

No two people have the same life experience. Everyone's path is necessarily different. It's what makes us each unique from anyone else who has ever lived. This military veteran from an impoverished background details the challenges that he overcame in becoming one of the world's problem solvers. From the moment his high school math teacher told him to leave the classroom to adjusting to the demands of the US Air Force to grappling with his daughter's lessons about love, Cybersecurity Engineer Nikeem Coleman provides a testimony reaped with perseverance and fueled by relentless optimism.

Nikeem Coleman

Senior Software Security Engineer at Gates Foundation, Seattle, Washington

AA in Information Systems, Community College of the Air Force

Hometown: Atlanta, GA

Aris Winger: Thank you for your time. Nikeem. Are you an engineer?

Nikeem Coleman: I am.

Aris Winger: And what does that mean to you? What does it mean to be an engineer?

Nikeem Coleman: It means being able to find a solution amongst all of your issues or endeavors, even if that means coming up with some kind of solution out of nowhere, with or without resources, and utilizing that to come up with whatever solution you need. It can be something as simple as something in your personal life, or it could be for your professional career. But to me, engineering is just designing a solution for a problem.

Aris Winger: And what subdiscipline of engineering are you in?

Nikeem Coleman: Security. Information security.

Aris Winger: And what does that mean? What do you do day to day?

Nikeem Coleman: Basically defending the company from outside adversaries, but also internal adversaries as well.

Aris Winger: So, okay, so take us on the journey. So you've been in lots and lots of places. So you start wherever you want to start. We usually start people right before getting into college. So imagine yourself right before your college experience. Where did you end up going, and did you feel prepared and ready to go?

Nikeem Coleman: Before my college experience… and everybody's story is unique, and they have their own paths that they've taken. But before college. I was living in a poverty area of Atlanta, Georgia, on the east side of Decatur, Georgia, specifically, and obviously, before college, I was in High School.

I went to Southwest DeKalb High School, and my experience with that was my last year of high school…I was working at UPS, night shift or graveyard shift, and I came into school one day in math class, after working until 3 AM. So I was at school at 7 AM. I was very tired, and my math teacher couldn't understand why I kept falling asleep.

I tried to tell her that this was due to me supporting my family, my mother was a single mom with 5 kids, and was struggling. I told her I was just tired from working, and she said, "Well, if you're gonna keep falling asleep, you can get out of my class."

I was very upset and disgruntled at how our system, especially in the Black community… How in certain areas, certain poor areas… I know some teachers, since they're underpaid, can get overwhelmed, and especially if the students aren't really trying to learn, but to take it out in a negative way towards one student, actually trying to do the best that they can in all aspects, made me decide to just get up… I went to the administrative office and withdrew from high school. I went and got my GED the next week, then applied for college and got in the next 2 weeks.

Aris Winger: Wow! So there are a couple of things here. So were you the oldest?

Nikeem Coleman: No.

Aris Winger: I'm wondering about the graveyard shift. So is this something that you decided that you were going to do or that you needed to do?

Nikeem Coleman: Yes, something I need to do, because nobody else was stepping up to help my mom take care of things, because she was already working 3 jobs, taking care of 5 kids, and I figured I'd try to contribute somehow, some way.

Aris Winger: And at this point, you're how old?

Nikeem Coleman: I'd say around 17.

Aris Winger: And so how was the GED? You just took all 4 parts?

Nikeem Coleman: Yes, I did, as I was already educated enough for all the high school curriculum, or all the classes in themselves. I was doing pretty good as a student. So I figured, well, what's the point? If I'm gonna be treated this way and nobody… the students aren't taking school seriously enough, and the teachers are exhausted and tired of, you know, the students' lack of attention and trying to actually get the education they need. Then there's no point for me to be there.

Aris Winger: Did you always have college in mind?

NC: Not really.

Aris Winger: But you applied pretty quickly.

Nikeem Coleman: I did, because I thought if… once I got into college, I could make something out of my newfound interest, desire, love, and passion with computers. I first fell in love with that and music.

Aris Winger: And so you apply. Where did you apply to?

Nikeem Coleman: Westwood College, and it was at the time, it was out there in Tucker, Georgia.

Aris Winger: Really? I'm looking around now. I'm Tucker. Where?

Nikeem Coleman: No, it's no longer there, and I can't remember the exact street. I remember I used to always take two buses and two trains to get there… so I think the last stop was on Tucker Road.

Nikeem Coleman: It was tucked out in a back corner somewhere in a business district.

Aris Winger: And so how was that experience?

Nikeem Coleman: Oh, that was amazing. I loved it because I got to meet so many different people, especially my professor. And my degree was in computer network management. I was learning material on top of knowing what I knew, going into it, and then learning new things, such as all the types of distributions for Linux, and how networking works. I started to meet individuals through my professors. He takes us to conferences, and then I started networking with more and more people. So going through that portion of college, I ended up making the Dean's list and a whole bunch of other accolades. But I had another roadblock. I wasn't making enough money.

At the time, I had dreadlocks, and I lived on the Southside with my grandmother at the time, and there's a Publix down the street. So I tried to apply for the job, and the manager said, "Hey, you know.. Individuals with your type of hair are looked at as deviants or individuals who have malice intent to harm and hurt people, you know."

And he said, If you cut your hair off, and my dreadlocks were probably almost past my shoulders, and he said, If you cut them off, come back the next day, early in the morning. I'll give you the job.

I went to my barber and had him cut it all off. Right before they opened, I came back the next day and went in there, and he told me, "I'm sorry the job has already been filled."

So I couldn't keep trying to pay for college and commute to college with no money. I then withdrew from that college and joined the Air Force.

Aris Winger: What was that decision like? How long was that decision? How long did you think about that?

Nikeem Coleman: That was probably only, I'd say, about a month at the most.

Aris Winger: Okay. And did you find an office somewhere or...

Nikeem Coleman: Yes. So where I lived on the south side, with my grandmother at that time, there was an Air Force office off Mount Zion Boulevard, right off the highway... So I think it's 75 South.

Aris Winger: So you go in. So are you telling anybody this, or are you just doing it? Are you alone in this process?

Nikeem Coleman: Yes.

Aris Winger: Okay. And how is that?

Nikeem Coleman: I've always been alone because everybody else in my family all had their own aloneness or solitude. We're all bred to just be our own individual person, and to be strong.

Watching my mom try to support all 5 of us. I looked at her as a superhero: To be able to take care of that, 3 jobs, and the rest of the world, since she was a Black woman.

Aris Winger: So is this something you just announced to them, "Yeah, I'm going to the Air Force."

Nikeem Coleman: Yeah, at the time. I only announced it to my grandmother, aunt, and sister at the time, because they were also living at my grandmother's house with us. It was a bunch of us at my grandmother's house.

Aris Winger: Got it. And how was the Air Force?

Nikeem Coleman: Eh…There are good things about it, and I would say the benefits were good… The base… Well, I didn't really care for the first base I went to, but the politics led to my decision not to go as far as retiring from the Air Force.

You learn a lot, and you meet a lot of good people, but then you also meet the other side, and being exposed to certain things and certain information due to my clearance…It made me realize that this isn't something that I want to stand behind. I'm still proud of what I did.

My job in the Air Force was basically a systems administrator. And I was met with a lot of backlash from certain people as… About the color of my skin at my first base in Texas.

And then it just wasn't working for me anymore after almost five years of service.

Aris Winger: Five years is a long time.

Nikeem Coleman: It is. Though you know, at my second base in Germany, I was lucky to have met my current wife of 11 years. She also was serving in Germany as well alongside.

So whenever anybody asked me, "How was the Air Force?" I'll say it's just like any place that you go to. For the most part, there's gonna be ups and downs. There's gonna be people who are there who have intentions at heart, and you have the negative side, where people are trying to tear you down and not see you succeed, or even try to help you, you know, guide you through that path.

Aris Winger: So you know, we might have a few people who are reading this, who are encountering some of the similar challenges that you just described, particularly in terms of race. What would you say to those people about how to navigate this? How did you do stuff like this for 5 years?

Nikeem Coleman: This is a tough one. I'd have to tell them to always stay positive and understand those types of individuals…You know whether they like you or not. You know we'll have to learn how you respond with your actions towards them based on who you are as a person. Don't let the words hurt you. Take the right avenues and path to reach out to the right people. When you encounter those kinds of situations, those types of situations… never have any hatred and anger in your heart towards those individuals, because some could just be ignorant. Some could just be affected by the product of their environment, some could just have pure malice intent. But don't let that destroy your character. Don't let that destroy your mental state. Just take the right path. Talk to certain people in confidence about what's going on. Keep your integrity about yourself and your morals, and your values. You're always gonna be challenged every single day. You will always be challenged.

Aris Winger: And so, tell me some of the positive things that you got out of the Air Force?

Nikeem Coleman: Well, the first thing, which is one of the major things for me, was, you know, growing up in Atlanta, Georgia, 99% of people that I encountered were African American..So when I first got into the Air Force, I was exposed to more diversity of individuals. I hadn't ever really been around that many different types of ethnicities and different types of minds, points of view, and opinions. It provoked my curiosity because I'm a very curious individual. And so that made me just want to speak to everybody and gain their life experiences and everything. And because it just intrigued me. And so that's one major positive, at least for me.

The other, being like I mentioned before, the benefits, especially the education benefits.

Knowing that you have this job, and more than likely, as long as you do what you're supposed to do, it's gonna always be there for you, you know?

So the security and comfort of knowing that you have something that pays the bills but also gives you an opportunity to further your career by college and other kinds of vocational programs that you can go through and healthcare, especially if you have a family. You have that security in your mind of knowing that your kids are going to be helped being taken care of. They can also get paid, you know, through college and everything else. So the benefits, the diversity,

the exposure to different tools and technologies. And I love aircraft and engineering in itself. So, being a part of the Air Force. I got to see a lot of different types of aircraft that you guys can't see, but I have a whole display of different aircraft on my shelf, so I got to see that. I got to speak to pilots since I had to work in an office with all the C. 130 J. Model pilots, and they allowed me to go into the Air Force's 1 million dollar flight simulator, and I got to fly in this beautifully engineered simulator. So those are some of the other benefits that I got out of it. And then traveling, depending on your job and the need for your job. And wherever the base is, some people get to travel to some of the best bases in the world. Some people get shafted with the less desirable bases.

I had the opportunity to be able to go to Germany and get more exposed to so much more culture and different accents, and just different mindsets. It's just a beautiful thing to me. So I was in Germany for almost 3 years.

When it came time to leave, that's when I was... I had already been thinking about that in the second year. I was thinking, is this something that I really want to do? Because, even though being in Germany was an amazing experience, the base was the largest Air Force base outside of the United States and the largest one in Europe. And so they had about 10 generals at the time, fourteen-star generals.

When you have that many generals, or if you have that many high-profile individuals on one base, the base is really political, and it was just a lot of pushback and blockage on certain things. Whenever you know people want to achieve certain things or they want…How do I word this?

It's not a lot of opportunity for dedicated growth when you have that many people trying to compete for the limelight of those higher-profile individuals. So everybody's trying to fight to look their best. They're trying to get all these awards, trying to get promoted, and it's so difficult. And then the politics kick in when those individuals are either tied in somehow with that higher-level individual. So they kind of block you from being seen.

As you know, when you're doing the best that you can or going above and beyond, and somebody else is being mediocre… So it's just all of that. And then the long hours that I worked at that time, I was working sixteen-hour days, six days a week.

I didn't have any time to even take care of my mental state, or even do the things that I love, you know, on the side, or I've never had time to travel around Europe when I was in the military. All the time I was there, I only had a chance to go to two other countries, and that was because I was working too much. So on top of working so much alongside politics, everybody else is trying to, you know, stop you from growing as a person.

It just became too much and too overwhelming. I told myself, "I don't want to deal with this anymore. I have to have a plan."

And so I decided. Once everything was said and done, I moved back to Georgia with my aunt, since I didn't have a place to stay. I went straight from leaving college right into the recruiter, basically from my grandmother's house straight to the Air Force. I didn't have a real place to come back to, of my own.

Aris Winger: And so how is that coming back to the aunt's house?

Nikeem Coleman: To be honest, it made me happy. It made me happy to stay with my aunt, who is still one of my best friends today. So, being with her was amazing.

I'm the type of individual who does not want to stay stagnant. So I applied for, I say, a little over a 4-month period, I applied for at least four hundred jobs between LinkedIn, Monster, usajobs.gov.. I mean, I was on a rampage, and I sat there with my aunt's computer every day, and I took care of everything in the house. She worked during the day. I'd make sure I clean the whole house. I did everything that I could, since she would allow me to stay with her with no job at the time. But also make sure I put in that effort so that I can get the job as quickly as possible, and she was gracious enough to tell me, "You don't have to leave as soon as possible. You can take your time." I thought, "This is your house. I'm not trying to intrude on your space." Plus. I'm an adult. I don't know… I don't think you want an adult just living with you the entire time.

So after about four months, I got a couple of phone calls and interviews, and the one offer I got was from Rockwell Collins. Now they are called Collins Tech, I think it's Collins Technologies now, an Aerospace and Defense Company based out of Cedar Rapids, I think. I moved to Carrollton, Texas, because they had an office out there. And that was my first official cybersecurity engineering role.

And my job would normally be to configure and manage customer SIEM systems, the system information, and the event monitoring system. I would get the equipment, configure everything, the policies, and everything needed to secure and monitor for anomalous or negative behavior within the network.

I would create those systems, firewalls, and all the network, make everything communicate with each other, and build them out on servers, and also manage servers as well. Once I had everything configured, we'd have it shipped to the customer, who at the time were nuclear sites.

Then we go out there and have everything configured like it's supposed to be. Make sure everything is polished. Teach them how to use the system, what to look for, and if they have any problems or have questions, we come back out and work with them. So that was my job for

about a year and 8 months, almost 2 years.

Aris Winger: Where are you getting the skills to do any of this? Not just in terms of the content, but also interacting with people and being on teams? Is that from the Air Force?

Nikeem Coleman: Self-taught. I literally taught myself. All the certifications I got. I did that on my own. I didn't go to any classes for them. I got the books when I had money for them. I get the books, and I'd read through them. I'd go online. I tried to keep studying and studying, and then once I felt confident enough, I'd go take the exam.

And so I did that for my Network+ certification, Security+ certification, and Ethical Hacking. I did that for all of them, all of my certifications. And so, as I was growing in the career field, there were other individuals whom I would ask questions about to learn, especially at Rockwell. I was probably one of the youngest there. Everybody else was well seasoned, should I say…

And so I figured that they have a lot more insight into how a certain thing works. And I just asked. Be inquisitive. Just ask questions and start taking notes.

And then, yeah, apply that to myself.

Aris Winger: So then you're there for some time, and then?

Nikeem Coleman: Once. Let's see… I got a LinkedIn message from a specific woman who was a recruiter at Microsoft.

I still appreciate her to this day. Yeah, she was phenomenal. I never thought… I still have her message saved. I archived it for moments to remind me how far I have come, and it's a very emotional part for me.

She messaged me, saying, "Hey, we're at Microsoft having a recruiting party at the House of Blues in Dallas," and she would like me to come. At that time, my wife was still serving in Germany, and I said, "Well, my wife does the same thing I do. She'll be here to visit me around that time. Can she come as well?"

And she said, "Yeah, sure. Bring her along." So we got all dressed up and went down there.

Aris Winger: This LinkedIn message was just out of the blue?

Nikeem Coleman: This was out of the blue. There were a lot of recruiters there, but most of them were just for customer service positions for Richland, Texas, because that's where Microsoft has a lot of its customer service agents.

So my wife and I were having some free drinks, and we were deciding, since there's no security recruiters here, we should just leave. So as she's finishing her drink, she puts the cup down about to walk away. The bartender fills her cup back up. I look at her and say, "Looks like you gotta finish that one, too."

Had that not happened, we wouldn't have seen the only two security recruiters finally walk in, and we had been there for about an hour already.

They asked if we were security engineers, and we confirmed that we were. They said they hadn't found anybody here who was looking to be recruited as a security engineer. They had only seen customer service. They had computers set up to go ahead and apply. We applied and got the calls in the next 2 weeks to come in for an eight-hour interview with eight different individuals from different teams at Microsoft, and after I'd say another week or so, we both got a phone call and both got offers.

Aris Winger: Tell me about this 8-hour interview.

Nikeem Coleman: Yeah. So you get an hour. It's eight different individuals... At least in my interview, I can't speak for my wife. I don't know if she had eight people or not, but I know I did. And so you get somebody from the networking team, the security team, the project manager, the actual hiring manager, and some people from some quality assurance. You get all of these individuals from different teams.

Aris Winger: And is this a conversation with them? Or are they asking questions?

Nikeem Coleman: Yep, answer these questions, and it's very tense. Very, very tense, especially when they have you get up on the whiteboard doing scenarios and mapping out different things, especially the coding portion.

Aris Winger: So this sets you up to be in Washington for some time?

Nikeem Coleman: That's why I tell you it's really emotional for me. When I think back to the recruiter from Microsoft, had she never mentioned me, I wouldn't have gotten the opportunity. I'm fortunately happy that she reached out. My wife still currently works at Microsoft today.

Aris Winger: Do you see Le Bond often?

Nikeem Coleman: Yeah, I've reached out to her before on LinkedIn and have kept ongoing communications with her. She no longer works at Microsoft. But I've thanked her profusely, multiple times, for reaching out.

Aris Winger: There's something for the reader here about that LinkedIn profile.

Nikeem Coleman: I have a friend who lives down the street, and he recently separated from his last job. But he's not that technologically inclined, and he's also not really savvy when it comes to how to get your name out there and how to be able to get a job. He's used to temp agencies and going on Indeed, and calls it a day.

I tried to show him the importance of LinkedIn and gave him my story. I told him that while not a lot of people use LinkedIn, there are a lot of people who don't. I helped set it up for him and helped structure it the right way.

So if I can stress that, enough for any of the readers…To me, that platform is amazing when it comes to looking for the jobs you want and connecting to the right people. They'll see how a prospect may be connected to their friend. It makes them want to dig deeper into who you are, and that might possibly lead to a job offer.

Aris Winger: I did want to talk about being on a team. Are you often on teams with other people?

Nikeem Coleman: Yeah, I've pretty much been on the team at every one of those jobs.

Aris Winger: Do the certifications give you skills to be on the team? Where are you getting the team skills of being a good teammate? Where's that coming from?

Nikeem Coleman: I'm just so… How do I say this…

I'm a strong introvert. I like to be alone. I am working on trying to be more available emotionally and socially. But I can be very social when need be.

As odd as it is, I find human behavior fascinating. So whenever I am around people, like how you and I met on the airplane, with a conversation about technology, it ends up being this deep conversation. I got to understand who you are and got to know you.

I'm very passionate about understanding how people work and their interests. I don't know why it fascinates me, even though I want to be alone. But it does. So I end up being one of those people where everybody kind of feels comfortable being around me, even though sometimes I don't really want to be around so many people.

I found myself in a lot of social situations, and people have told me I'm kind and all of that. I criticize myself a lot in my head. I'm thinking, "I don't know who they're talking about, but it is definitely not me."

Aris Winger: So I just want to make sure. At this point, you do not hold a bachelor's degree.

Nikeem Coleman: No.

Aris Winger: How are you feeling about that? Is there impostor syndrome? Do you feel like you need to get one? Do you need validation? Any of that?

Nikeem Coleman: No. That's another thing to tell the readers. A lot of people get stuck on, "I need to do this, I have to do that, I have to go here, have to go there, I have to get this, I have to get that." You don't. It depends on what you're trying to do.

What organization are you trying to work for?

If you want to be a doctor, of course, that's societally known, where you need a degree. I don't think that there's any doctor out there without a degree.

But for me in my field, you don't. At first, I was a little nervous when I only had two certifications when I was applying, but when Rockwell called me. I knew it said that the bachelor's degree was one of their requirements, not desired, but one of their requirements. So I was a little hesitant about getting hired because I didn't have one.

But the manager who hired me at the time, who turned out to be a really awesome manager, probably in my top 3 favorite managers, made me feel better about it. He loved my passion. He told me that I reminded him of himself. He said he was willing to give me a chance. He said I answered all of his questions above expectations, and I had the certification. He was willing to waive the degree requirement.

He told me that as long as I was willing to learn, as long as I was willing to go above and beyond, we should be good, and I'm glad for Greg. I hope he reads this one day.

But don't think that you have to have a degree just to get to where you want to be. A lot of people will stress themselves over and over and over again, trying to work themselves into debt and the ground just to get a piece of paper. They think that piece of paper is the only way in. It's not. I'm living proof that it's not.

Aris Winger: So I'm thinking about you applying for this job. You see, something is required. And you apply anyway. Why?

Nikeem Coleman: There is a saying, "You miss 100% of the shots you don't take."

At the end of the day, if I don't try, I'm gonna be in the same exact place I was before I even initiated anything. It's like when people wonder why I would call to see where my application is. If they tell you "No," you're still in the same place you were before. But what if they say yes?

Just show them. Just prove to them, and you might get that opportunity. You might be surprised.

Aris Winger: So tell me about your time in Washington.

Nikeem Coleman: I've been here for about nine years, almost in April, and I've been living in this house for 8 years as of last month. Yeah. So I've been here for about 8 years in this house, 9 years overall, and I love it. I absolutely love it. It's because I'm a person who loves natural beauty, and Washington state has just about everything you can think of. It's such a biodiverse state, whether you want deserts, rainforest, flatlands, rolling hills, mountains, lakes, glacier lakes, lakes, rivers, or ocean. It has it all. And it's in a really nice location in the world. I love being in the Pacific Northwest and the people. The culture is such a melting pot here with so many people from all walks of life. And obviously the tech industry, because Washington State is…Microsoft is headquartered here, Costco, and Expedia. A whole bunch of big companies are here, including Amazon. So I feel like they contributed to bringing in so many different people from different walks of life.

Work-wise, it's been… It's so many different types of companies out there, at least from my field that I work in. There are so many different companies I can work for, and I'm not limited like I might be when I was in Texas. There were the DOD, DOE, and contractor places like Raytheon and Lockheed. And there are a lot of those kinds of companies. But at that time, there weren't a lot of major tech companies per se. I mean, Microsoft did have an office out there. And Google has an office somewhere down there. But it wasn't… I felt like there weren't as many opportunities. So when I came out here, I was surprised. I literally go down the street and find the next company right there. I can go to the Facebook office or the SpaceX office. I can go to all these different companies, all relatively within the same city, whether it be Redmond, Seattle, or Bellevue. They're right here. So that has been phenomenal.

Aris Winger: So you've mentioned some people along the journey. I'm wondering whether you are gonna call some of them mentors? Did you have mentors?

Nikeem Coleman: Yes, I would, I would definitely say, well, I just appreciate Lee Bon. I would not necessarily say she's my mentor. I would say my 1st manager at Rockwell was a mentor for me and stayed in contact with him for a long time. My Professor when I tried college. He's still my mentor. I still talk to him once a week, and my other manager, from my previous role, Thomas Clark. I met him at Microsoft, but then also met him at his second company, which I ended up joining. He ended up recommending I go, and I got hired there through him, so we've been close friends ever since. He's a good mentor as well.

Before, in my life, I didn't have mentors. So it was kind of weird for me to have my first one being, you know, my first manager. I just thought it was weird because it was…

Aris Winger: What was weird about it?

Nikeem Coleman: It was just uncharted territory for me. Having to go to somebody and talk about yourself, and then hear how they feel about what they just had to digest, and then give their opinion about it. I never had that kind of back and forth with just about anybody.

Aris Winger: That's powerful. What is next for you? What are you thinking about these days in terms of goals and what you're trying to achieve?

Nikeem Coleman: To be honest with you, I am really trying to retire as soon as I can because the work that my wife and I do, which is similar work but at different places, is very taxing. We are each at the front lines defending our companies, which can be one of the negatives of the career.

There have been times when my wife and I both had incidents simultaneously, and we had to determine which incident was more severe and who would watch the kids. My oldest daughter, when she was eleven, even commented on this. She said we are always working. So I am getting to a place where I can retire as soon as possible. I just want to spend more time with my kids.

But what I have right now going on is my notary business, and I partnered with one of my close friends I met at one of the companies I was working with. We have started our own security consulting business, and we've been working to get that off the ground. For now, not too much has happened. I've talked to a bunch of different potential clients. Hopefully, that business does well, and it starts to do gymnastics on its own, and I could just step away and benefit from the fruits of the labor and be able to just spend more time going outside with my kids and traveling, and just be stress-free.

Aris Winger: Yeah. Got a couple more questions for you. Maybe three. Are there any skills that you wish someone had taught you back in the day that you had to learn on your own? What would you want if you could build a curriculum early on for high school or college?

Nikeem Coleman: This might seem like an odd one. And this is less technical. It would be how to navigate people in the industry, how to read people.

Trying to learn new things would be one of them. It's just. I wish somebody had given me the tools that I felt like I needed, whether it be on a particular type of tool, whether it's a whole other type of cloud. Let's just say a cloud provider like Azure. I did all the homework, learned how to study, and built my knowledge on Azure, whereas we had a dedicated Azure team, but nobody else had the time or wanted to give me the time. That stuff is normal.

But I wish somebody had sat me down and showed me how taxing it is, how some of the people will be, and where some of the struggles you'll face. But I didn't really have that too many times along the way.

My first manager told me a bit that I met certain people, especially the one that I want you to meet, Victor. I met him at Microsoft, and he and another guy were basically my two mentors. They were giving me the rundown, especially being a Black man in the industry. They gave me the rundown on how certain things operate, and had they not, I would have just ended up probably in the worst situation because I probably would have gotten too frustrated in trying to figure it out. I would have questioned what I was doing wrong and why I wasn't being looked at fairly.

Aris Winger: I appreciate that. All right. A couple more. What have you had to sacrifice to get to where you are?

Nikeem Coleman: Time is definitely one of them. Nobody can escape that. But I'd sacrifice more time than probably a lot of other people had to also.

Sometimes it seems, since I was always a loner, I'd say… Sometimes I feel like I'm sacrificing, not my… I wouldn't say my dignity, but my pride. I'm sacrificing my pride. Sometimes, when I had to go and ask the questions, I felt I might be looked at as ignorant or stupid.

So that was one of the hardest by itself. Because a lot of times, since I was self-teaching myself along the way, I did build myself up strongly. So why did I have to ask them? I just go find the information myself and retain it. But sometimes it's not as easy as that.

And the blockades of being told "No." Like I said, those 400 applications that I put in for jobs. I told myself, "somebody's got to say yes." But sitting there stressed me out the most.

"What am I really doing wrong? Am I pushing this the wrong way? Am I using the right words? Am I going to the right app, platform, and avenue? What do I need to do? Because it's my name? My name is not average. It's not Jacob. So like, what is it that's causing me not to get traction?"

That really put a damper on my mental state.

Aris Winger: Why did you keep going? Why didn't you give up and try something else?

Nikeem Coleman: Because I told myself…I had a very, very hard, traumatic childhood, and I did not work so hard to get out of it to just quit. I convinced myself that there's gotta be light on the other end of that tunnel, so I'm just gonna keep pushing until I find it.

And there've been many points, many other points along the way. I've even had points when I'm here over the years where things are getting rough and I've wanted to quit, but my mind was like, "Nope. We're already in the thick of it. We came way too far for you to quit now."

And then my kids are looking at my kids… They are…

I mean, everybody's gonna say their kids are their inspiration. But no…

The kind of love that my kids give me is love that I had never experienced before with anybody, and so trying to show love to your kids with love you've never been given… It's hard, but also learning from their love is beautiful, but sad a little bit sometimes for me. So my kids are definitely my inspiration, too.

Aris Winger: Why is it sad?

Nikeem Coleman: Because I wish I could… I wish I knew the love they're giving me because they expect a certain level. I mean, they're obviously kids, and they'll be what they are. But they, you know, they've always wondered, "Daddy, why don't you show the same love as mommy does it, or how auntie does it? " So I'm always being compared to these other individuals.

I'm like, "Well, look, one day as you get older and mature, I'll give you a rundown on my background of why I am the way I am today. But until then, I want to learn from you. You know Daddy wants to learn from you. You are one of my biggest inspirations, you and your siblings. Y'all show me how I can be a better father, friend, better person, show you the right type of love, the love you deserve and want."

Aris Winger: This is the last question. As you know, we have some people reading this who are going to be thinking about engineering.

This is your time to talk directly to them. Some of them might be struggling. Some of them might not know where they're going or what this is about. You can say whatever you want to them directly at this moment..

Nikeem Coleman: What I would say is, like I mentioned a couple of moments ago. When faced with adversity or when faced with these blockades, don't quit. That's just life testing you; if you can prevail, you can accomplish just about anything you set your mind to. So don't allow those kinds of blockades to hold you back.

Also, don't be afraid to reach out and ask questions. At times I have my pride, and also I was taught by my mother that part of being a man meant not having to ask for help..

But I realized that it's not demeaning to my sexuality as a male or my gender to feel safe enough to ask questions. So put pride aside, ask questions.

When it comes to you trying to improve technical skills, there are a lot of free solutions out there, a lot of free information. And now we have, in today's age, data is all out there on the Internet. And there are so many ways to get it. If you don't know how to get a certain type of information, there are always communities on forums on certain Discord servers. There are certain communities out there, like Reddit, that have subreddits.

Just join some of those groups, ask those, ask those questions. Get the information you need and keep pushing until you get the result that you're looking for. If the angle you're going at constantly gives you the same result, get a different angle.

Like I said, if you can't figure it out on your own, ask, because somebody's probably been through the same situation and probably knows how to get out or navigate that particular type of situation. So never feel like you're alone. Never give up. Always ask questions and keep striving to keep that fire alive inside you.

05 - Sibel Leblebici

RISE TO THE CHALLENGE

You've heard the cliche before: It's not about getting knocked down, but how you get up. Facing an extremely rigorous undergraduate experience and threatening to quit multiple times, Process Integration Manager Sibel Leblebici found ways to keep going and eventually succeed at the University of Illinois, Champaign-Urbana. She would go on to get her Doctorate Degree in Materials Science. She persevered by tapping into her support network and intentionally branching out to find those outside of engineering whom she could rely on. In reading her story, you will engage with the journey of someone who was clear and articulate about her struggles, and how that clarity and humility ultimately led to her getting back up and prevailing.

Sibel Leblebici, PhD

Process Integration Manager, Meta, Ireland

PhD in Materials Science & Engineering, University of California, Berkeley

BS in Materials Science & Engineering, University of Illinois, Urbana-Champaign

Hometown: Champaign, Illinois

Aris Winger: Sibel, thank you for joining us. Are you an engineer?

Sibel Leblebici: I am an engineer.

Aris Winger: What does that mean to you?

Sibel Leblebici: That I make new things. Things that didn't exist before. Or I make things better than they were before.

Aris Winger: What subset of engineering are you in?

Sibel Leblebici: I am a materials engineer, electronic materials specifically, and I have been my whole education and career.

Aris Winger: And what does that mean you do day to day?

Sibel Leblebici: I make microelectronic devices. In undergrad, that meant I studied materials, how they're formed, how they behave, but then, because of my specialty in electronic materials, it meant that I also had to understand the devices that they were put into, and how those behave. Also quite a bit of physics on top of the standard material science, and then some electrical engineering as well. And I specialize in optoelectronic devices, to get even more into the weeds there.

Aris Winger: Take us back to the summer before undergrad. As you're going into your undergraduate institution, are you feeling prepared? How are you feeling? And how is this 1st semester in undergrad?

Sibel Leblebici: I did my last year of high school in France. I was part of the Rotary Youth Exchange program, which was an amazing program. And then I came back. I was going through reverse culture shock, getting ready to go to college. And one thing that made it quite a bit easier is that I went to the University of Illinois, and I'm from Champaign-Urbana; I was born and raised there. So at least the location wasn't new. And I was really excited.

Aris Winger: Did you stay on campus, or did you stay at home?

Sibel Leblebici: I stayed on campus. Staying in the dorms. And I specifically chose to stay to move into a dorm that was not really an engineering dorm. It was mostly art students.

Aris Winger: But you had the option to stay in an engineering dorm. Why didn't you do that?

Sibel Leblebici: I felt I didn't want everything to be too much the same. I didn't want the people that I was living in the dorms with to be the same people that I was going to class with. I felt it was gonna be too much of the same thing all the time. And I wanted some more variety. And I already knew I was gonna study material science, that's the program I had applied to.

Aris Winger: Where did your interest in material science come from?

Sibel Leblebici: With my mom's help, getting ready to apply for college, I was lucky. Because we were in Champaign, my mom was like, 'You want to be an engineer, you probably want to do something related to electronics or computers. But you don't really know. I'm gonna set up appointments for you with professors who can explain to you what their field is.'

Aris Winger: And when was this?

Sibel Leblebici: I had these appointments before I studied abroad.

Aris Winger: And that was back in?

Sibel Leblebici: 2005.

Aris Winger: Before your senior year of high school.

Sibel Leblebici: Yes, because I left for France, I had to do everything beforehand. I even applied; I submitted all my applications before I left for France to have it out of the way.

But my mom set up these appointments for me. I met with a professor in electrical engineering and met with a professor in materials. I feel I met someone in mechanical engineering. Also, because we were living in Champaign, my parents had connections to different departments. And understood how the university works. It wasn't a scary thing. There was a lot of knowledge about the system, and it was fine to reach out to email these professors and see if they'll meet with you.

So I met with Professor Paul Braun at the University of Illinois. He has a polymer focus. He taught the intro to material science class. He had all these perfect examples in his office. He busted out a bottle of ketchup, and he was explaining the layers of plastic and why they're there, and all the details that go into it. And then he got out a hard drive, and showed this tiny little piece in the hard drive that blocks dust from entering, but lets air out for the fan, and I love these little tiny details. This is what I was really into. I don't need to become famous for creating the first of whatever. But I want to be part of these little necessities to get the technology to work.

And it was super inspiring. And I was like, this is what I want to study.

Aris Winger: We're learning on the fly with some of the conversations for this book, that these intro professors are fundamental in sparking these interests. We had someone else who was talking about how they sat in an Intro to Engineering class, but they were one of 300 people, and the Intro Professor still said, Here's what this is about, and gave these incredible examples, which is great. But then you had one-on-one, and your mom was there too.

Sibel Leblebici: I was in his office, my mom was there, and it was one-on-one. I could ask all these questions. I love that it was all very physical. When I went to learn about electrical engineering, much of it was algorithms and circuits and stuff, which I felt I couldn't really visualize. Whereas for the materials, it was, here's the thing that you made. It was easy to follow, and that's what I wanted to study.

Aris Winger: And that stays strong for a whole year in France. And you come back, now it's your 1st year. You know what you want to do. You pick the dorm that's not the engineering dorm. Go.

Sibel Leblebici: And then I'm taking that intro to material science class with that professor. And the class was great. He did all these hands-on things with us. Building unit cell models out of toothpicks and mini marshmallows. Learning about tempering metals by how you temper chocolate, how they're all very similar, and all the similarities between the steps. And then, you get to eat the chocolate, smell it, break it, and hear the sounds. And this is all the same stuff that you're doing in the preparation of materials. Chocolate is a material that, in all these ways, connects you with the material of the class. That was very memorable and easy to retain the material as you're learning it.

But it was also brutally hard. University of Illinois is known as a very rigorous engineering school, with your 1st year and a half, probably all weed out classes.

Aris Winger: And what's a weed-out class?

Sibel Leblebici: A weed-out class is where they're trying to get people to drop out of the program who they think cannot either keep up or are not interested enough to do all the work.

Aris Winger: How did you find out that it was a weed-out class? Did you hear ahead of time? Or did you get the vibe that it was?

Sibel Leblebici: I think you both get told by your peers, people who are ahead of you in the program, people who are sophomores, you're a freshman. The weed-out classes were not specifically in material science. These were the generic engineering classes that everybody has to take. The classes in material science were definitely not weed-out classes. The professors really wanted you to learn the material, and they wanted to keep you engaged. And there were only 75 students entering my class for materials science. It's a pretty small program, especially for a university that at the time had an undergrad population of 45,000 students total in the university. I don't remember how many were just for the college of engineering, but big school. The weed-out classes were hard. You also knew they were weed-out classes because of the way the curve was.

You would normally get a C if you got a C on your exam. That would be an A with the curve. It was really meant to make you feel you didn't know what you were doing.

Aris Winger: Oh! And did you feel that way?

Sibel Leblebici: And I studied hard, even in high school. I was really studious, and I liked to get straight A's. I liked to get good grades. That was very important to me, even though my parents always told me it didn't matter. It mattered to me. So it was hard to get these low scores on tests and assignments.

Aris Winger: Let's go there. You get something back, and it says 71 on it. How are we feeling?

Sibel Leblebici: Very emotional, crying, frustrated. Like I have to study harder. I need to spend more time in the library. I need to go to more office hours. I need to join more study groups. It's a lot of pressure.

Aris Winger: This is great because I want to go where the struggle is for our readers, who might be struggling. Are we calling anybody? Are we calling Mom? What are we calling about? Are we an internal person? The "I'll figure it out" type?

Sibel Leblebici: I'm talking to my friends, for example, one of my really good friends, who was in pre-med. She was taking weed out of classes, too. The classes are different, materials vs biology, but she also had weed-out classes, and we would talk about how hard it was. We would spend time going to the library together. And kind of bonding over the struggle, I would say.

But then, also, calling my parents, saying, "I'm gonna fail, I'm not gonna be able to do this." They tell me this is normal. These are big classes. It's what you'll see with the curve. You're gonna be fine. I think it was also hard, because I would get such good grades in high school, and it didn't feel hard. Then, going to college and not feeling like I'm doing well was an adjustment, and I remember some of my classmates would be like, 'Oh, I didn't even study, and I got an A without the curve.'

Aris Winger: Wow.

Sibel Leblebici: That was really hard, and I told my dad, and he was like, "They're lying. That's a lie. They definitely studied for that test, and they probably didn't even get an A." He was really trying to reassure me that it wasn't the case that I'd fail. That's what I was doing was the right stuff.

Aris Winger: And now the study group part. At some point, you're in class, how are you getting study groups? How is this happening?

Sibel Leblebici: Because the material science program was pretty small, it was a tight-knit group. And we would have our intro to material science and other fundamental material science classes. Then some of us would be in the same session of the generic engineering classes, math, physics, and chemistry. And because we already knew each other from material science, it was a tight group. Then it was, "let's meet up and study together." There were some classmates that I had who weren't in material science but were in engineering and were living in the same dorm. Sometimes we would study together. But yes, the study groups were crucial.

Aris Winger: Why?

Sibel Leblebici: I wasn't good at reading the book and figuring it out on my own. And honestly, at the University of Illinois, the professors weren't focused on teaching. It's a research university. Teaching was something they had to do. There are some professors who were really into teaching, but a lot of them weren't. It was just a part of their job that they had to do.

Aris Winger: What are you getting from a study group? What does a person get from a study group?

Sibel Leblebici: I think for me, the biggest thing was talking it out, verbalizing the material, and also if I understood something and then teaching it to somebody else, it was solid. I had that info and didn't need to study it again. Study groups were also important because you can find somebody who knows somebody who's going to get you that exam from 2 years ago, and the exam from 3 years before, because they're in some fraternity or sorority that has a whole bank of past tests. So getting access to extra material through study groups was also really important.

Aris Winger: Great. Then, you're pushing through. Does it get easier, harder, or do you get used to the rigor?

Sibel Leblebici: I got used to it, but it only got harder.

Year by year. And sometimes at the end of the semester, after finals, I'd go home, let's say, for Christmas. I go, spend time at my parents house for Christmas, and I'd be like, "I'm not doing this anymore. I can't. It's too hard."

And my mom would be like, It's fine. You can drop out. You can always go back. If you need a break, we can figure out something else for you to do.

I'm not going to hold my breath. Let's see if you go back next semester.

Aris Winger: And I want to be clear. What made it hard? Was it the hours you had to put in order to keep going? What was it?

Sibel Leblebici: It was the hours. Not especially freshman year. Making new friends was really fun, and the classes were hard, but they weren't terrible. I was able to manage them after I got used to the disappointment of seeing the grade on the test.

But then sophomore year, Junior year, the material got even harder. It was more difficult classes at once, and I had finished my Gen. Eds. And I also wanted to study abroad again in college, so I was trying to cram in some classes. That made it harder. And it was a lot of time not sleeping a lot. Going to bed surrounded by all my books in bed, and it was a lot of work.

Aris Winger: During this time, did you have mentors? Are you meeting people?

Sibel Leblebici: I had an undergrad advisor assigned to me. I met with him in my 1st semester, but there wasn't really a lot to talk about, and then I think I met with him in my sophomore year, and he didn't even look at me in my appointment. He was looking at his monitor. He's looking at my classes planned for the semester. And he said, "It looks like you are taking all the classes. You decided you wanted to specialize in electronic materials, so you're taking the classes. Do you have any questions for me?" It's impersonal and not helpful.

Aris Winger: What would you have wanted him to do?

Sibel Leblebici: To be more, "Do you think this is the track for you?" Or maybe, "You're taking extra classes, why is that?" Or, "You want to study abroad, I think that's gonna be good." Or, "I think that's gonna be bad for your trajectory." It was so impersonal that he literally didn't look at me. That was a huge red flag.

Then I was like, I'm never talking to this person again. I didn't even have any classes with him either. It was bizarre. And then I had a professor, Agnus Rockett, for electronic materials, and I had decided that I wanted to do undergrad research and see what that was. I really liked him as a professor. He was doing research on solar cells, which I was really interested in, clean energy kind of stuff. I started talking to him about, Can I join your group to do undergrad research? Then it naturally became that he not only became my research advisor, but also an advisor in general.

Aris Winger: I want to unpack naturally, because what does naturally mean? Did you go up to him at some point? Did he invite you? How does this happen?

Sibel Leblebici: I always went to office hours a lot with all my classes. I think it really helped having parents who are professors because you realize professors are totally normal people, and they're not intimidating. My dad was the department head of the Business Administration Department at the University of Illinois, and he would come home and be a silly person.

He has this big job at the university and is a normal guy. And to me, going to office hours wasn't scary or intimidating, or whatever. It's, "Oh, these people are here to help me. This is the time that they've allocated to help me. I'm gonna go." And I started going to his office hours when I was in his class, and that's how we got to know each other. And then, when I decided to consider doing some research. It's another thing to put on your resume that could help you get a job. And since I already liked the class, I liked him. I sent him an email, and I sent another professor an email who was doing flexible medical devices. I talked with that professor, and his research was cool. He ended up getting a MacArthur grant later, and he was very honest. I met with him in person, and he said, "This is the last time you're ever gonna meet with me if you join my group. I have a very hierarchical group. You'll be working with a grad student who'll be working with a postdoc who will be talking to me, and we won't have a mentorship relationship."

I'm grateful that he was super honest.

Because then I could decide, do I want to work for this super famous professor in this type of system? Or do I want to have more of a mentorship, and I chose the mentorship route.

Aris Winger: "I'm happy." You said that because there are plenty of people who pick the other one. But it's about which one you want for what you're trying to do.

Sibel Leblebici: Exactly.

Aris Winger: Powerful. Great other stuff from undergrad. How many internships did you end up doing?

Sibel Leblebici: I did the research one, and I did it over the summer. One year of this was with Professor Angus Rocket. He was my mentor. He also wrote a very, very good book on electronic materials. Very good reference. And then he suggested that I try working with a different professor in my senior year. He said you should get a variety of experiences. See what you want to do. And this other professor was working on lasers. He was in the electrical engineering department. It was not a good experience.

Aris Winger: Why not?

Sibel Leblebici: He wasn't super involved. He didn't give me a project. He kind of said, Go figure it out on your own, and I wasn't ready for that. I wasn't able to figure it out on my own.

I needed more guidance. And then I felt I was failing because I was supposed to figure this out on my own, but I don't know how. I don't know enough about the system. I needed to get access to the clean room and all this stuff. But I was like, what am I even gonna do once I get in there? I don't know what I'm doing. And the grad student who was supposed to be mentoring me wasn't really following up. That was frustrating. And then I remember being upset. I talked to my mom on the phone one day, and she said, Tell him you're not doing it anymore, you're not getting anything out of it. You feel you're wasting their time. You're wasting your time. So that was, and I did. I said I don't think this is helpful for anybody. And he was like, if you don't want to do it, don't do it. It's fine. Didn't even care.

It makes you realize you're in your head about things. Oh, I'm gonna be judged. And it's gonna look bad. And other people are gonna care that I didn't follow through with this, and then in the end, it turns out nobody really cares that much.

Aris Winger: Now, you're in your senior year at this point. What comes after that? What are you thinking about, future-wise? Are you thinking about going into the industry, graduate school?

Sibel Leblebici: I had talked to my advisor, Angus, about what I should do next. And this was 2010. It wasn't a great time in the job market, still feeling the 2008 recession effects, and all the jobs that I was seeing were kind of boring. It was to go work in a steel manufacturing company or make diapers 1% more absorbent, or I don't know. It was not what I was into. And I wasn't seeing a lot of jobs in electronic materials. I don't know if that's because Illinois and the Midwest are not known for electronic materials.

Aris Winger: But you were looking in the area.

Sibel Leblebici: It's because I was also going to career fairs and stuff, and most of the jobs that you are going to see advertised at career fairs are going to be regional.

That was something that was really helpful to learn. Go to school where you might want to work because you're gonna be able to find a job in that location more easily. But I didn't know that at the time when I started college, especially in electronics and tech stuff. It's regional, it's all California, or South Carolina, or Texas. But in the Midwest, you're not gonna really find anything like that. And my advisor said, You studied hard, and you got these really good grades, I think I had a 4.94 GPA. He said you should go to grad school. Otherwise, this kind of goes to waste. He also knew that I liked doing hands-on work in the lab. He knew that I might like doing research. And I decided I was gonna get a master's. I wasn't fully ready to commit to getting a Phd. I remember calling up my parents, saying, I know what I'm gonna do. I'm gonna apply for a master's program. I'm gonna get a master's in material science. And they're like, great, cool. Then I start looking at programs. And I realize, wait a minute. If I do a master's, I have to pay, but if I get a Phd, they're gonna pay.

Aris Winger: That's the secret right there.

Sibel Leblebici: So then I was like, I'm gonna apply for Phd programs. Cause why pay for this thing if I don't have to? I applied to a ton of schools. And I did all the visits during my last semester of undergrad. The visits are very cool, getting flown out to California and stuff in February, when it's miserable in Illinois. And you're flying to Santa Barbara, and you get to see dolphins, it's crazy.

Aris Winger: And you end up choosing?

Sibel Leblebici: UC Berkeley.

Aris Winger: How was the transition there?

Sibel Leblebici: It was easy, especially from an education perspective.

I had one professor who had taught my senior design class, and he was coming to Berkeley for some talk or something. And we met up for coffee. This was my 1st year. And he's asking, How is it going? And I was like, it's not very hard, almost all the homework that I have, I've done all these homework problems before. And he said, That's because we make our program really hard. I was Oh.

I was really glad I saved a lot of my old material from undergrad. Then, when I was in grad school, I could be 'oh, I've done this homework problem before,' and go get the old notes and work.

Aris Winger: That is fantastic. Then, the Phd. Time was also good? You picked an advisor there, also?

Sibel Leblebici: I spent a ton of time picking an advisor. I was probably one of the last people to choose an advisor. I came into Berkeley with a 1-year grant, a diversity fellowship, so whoever I worked for, at least for that 1st year, didn't have to pay for me because I was already paid. Then I ended up getting an NSF fellowship. That gave me a lot of freedom to choose because I had my own funding.

But I really spent a lot of time choosing my advisor. It was based on, of course, the research that they were doing. I had to be interested, and there had to be a project that I could work on, but also, are they gonna spend time with me? Am I gonna have a real mentor? I knew what didn't work for me before, from when I had that second research advisor at Illinois who didn't help me set up a project or anything, and I was kind of on my own. It wasn't successful; I knew I didn't want that. I also knew that I needed to feel really integrated into the group itself, because you depend so much on learning from other people in your group. For example, there was Professor Wu, whom I was really interested in his research, but almost his entire group was Chinese, and I didn't speak Chinese, and I didn't have any connection to the culture. And I was like, I don't think I'm gonna fit in.

I don't see how this is gonna work if they're all speaking Chinese in the lab. I'm not gonna learn random stuff every day about things like, oh, this evaporator tool! Don't forget to press this button instead of that one when you're doing this step, because it'll break.

I ended up choosing a researcher at Lawrence Berkeley National Lab to be my main advisor.

Aris Winger: I wanna ask you, as a slight diversion, about dealing with being around so many guys and men who tend to dominate the field of engineering. A young lady major is going through that. How in the world did you navigate?

Sibel Leblebici: A couple of things. One reason is that I didn't live in the engineering dorm; I made a lot of girlfriends who weren't studying engineering. I had close friends who were women. So I wasn't with dudes all the time.

The other thing is, there's a surprising number of women in the materials science program. Originally, when I was looking at what major to study, I mostly thought of electrical engineering versus materials science. I did have some classes in electrical engineering. I did notice that there were almost no women in the classes, and it was also a much bigger department. People were less social. You sit down in class, and I'm used to Oh, what did you do for lunch, and What are your plans for the weekend, whatever? And then I would go to these other electrical engineering classes, and all these dudes are quiet, and they don't talk to each other.

I was really lucky that there were more women in materials science.

Aris Winger: But there's something about you being able to find your group community somehow, some way.

Sibel Leblebici: The other thing, I should say, about my undergrad advisor, about Angus, is that he was really a proponent of, "yes, you're a woman in engineering, but you can do it all. You can have a family and be super successful if you want." He was very open to saying, "You can choose what route you want to go and what kind of life you want to have. And you don't need to feel stuck, because you're a woman in this field."

Aris Winger: Did you feel you needed to hear that?

Sibel Leblebici: I think it was helpful. Because there weren't that many female role models, he would give me examples, not necessarily from engineering. Still, I remember him telling me about a husband and wife who were both doctors, and she was super successful. She was affiliated with the university. He knew her. And they had 2 kids, a whole family, and they made it work.

He would say. Don't be afraid of success. You can have success and a family if you want to.

Aris Winger: That's powerful. Thank you for that aside. I wanted to make sure we got that out there.

Sibel Leblebici: I had plenty of girlfriends who were not engineers; it was great.

The other thing I would say about some of the men that I interacted with in class, that they had kind of this cockiness about them.

Especially because I'm from Champaign, Illinois, but a lot of my classmates were from Chicago, and they would be like, "I got into the best engineering program for material science. I got into the best school. I'm hot shit, and you're some girl from Champaign, a town."

Aris Winger: How are you fighting against that?

Sibel Leblebici: I think part of it was that it was what drove me to study hard. I'm gonna be really good at this. I'm gonna get really good grades. I'm gonna be really good at this. I'm gonna show you up.

Aris Winger: That's good to hear, thank you for that. Then, you finally pick your advisor at the PhD level.

Sibel Leblebici: Yes.

Aris Winger: And then from there, you have qualifying exams?

Sibel Leblebici: So at Berkeley, you do Prelims first, which is your oral exams, basic material science knowledge. And then do your qualifying exam in your 3rd year. That's specific to your topic. It's on what you're gonna research. That was stressful.

But again, a lot of groups help you. You invite people who are senior to you to your practice exams. They really give you a lot of good advice. And they give you advice about these people who are on your committee. These are the questions they are gonna ask you.

Aris Winger: Anything else about the grad school experience that you learn challenges?

Sibel Leblebici: When I talk to other people who are interested in going to grad school, I kind of give people a tough love attitude in general. And that's my way of giving advice. I tell people you have to be really comfortable with failure and rejection if you want to get a

PhD. Because you're pretty much gonna fail at what you're doing because you're doing something totally new. It's never been done before. You're going to fail almost every single day. And then you're gonna get one day out of 3 years, that's a success. And that's gonna be your paper.

And then, of course, you're gonna submit that paper and it's gonna get rejected and it's gonna get rejected by another journal. And it's going to get rejected again. And you have to be able to roll with it. And I think part of the rigor of the University of Illinois engineering, and getting all those bad grades, was realizing that it kind of set me up for being ready for all this failure.

Aris Winger: Do you do a postdoc? Or do you go into the job?

Sibel Leblebici: I did a fake postdoc. It was a job.

I applied. I was looking for a job in New York. My boyfriend at the time was living in New York. He was going to Columbia University for his PhD. And I was looking at jobs all over. I got an offer from where Kyle was working at the time.

But I had been applying for other stuff, too. But I knew I wanted to get a job. I didn't want to stay in academia because I didn't want to write grants. I wasn't interested in spending my time writing grants, and I really wanted to do more of the engineering work itself. I wanted to be able to make something that would go out into the world sooner than anything that I would be researching.

I applied for an NSF SBIR diversity fellowship postdoc, that's a mouthful, but any, at least at the time, any startup that had received an NSF SBIR Grant could hire a postdoc through that program, where the NSF paid almost all of the salary.

There was a startup in New York that was making micro LEDs for micro displays for augmented reality glasses, which was such a new thing at the time. I applied, but I don't think they expected anybody to apply. They were surprised because you have to go to a very specific website and look through all these entries. It was not simple. It's not something you're gonna find on Indeed or something. They interviewed me over the phone. I asked if I could go out and visit, and they had already offered me the job. But I was like, I think we should meet each other. I was only gonna be the 5th employee. Super small company.

But it made sense from a technical perspective, because all my research was done on solar cells. They were making LEDs, the same thing in reverse. All the physics and the material stuff are pretty similar.

Aris Winger: Now, going to the startup, how was that? What's that transition like?

Sibel Leblebici: I think the transition of moving to New York was a little harder than joining the startup. And before I accepted the job offer, my boyfriend broke up with me. I had to decide if I still really wanted to move to New York. And then I ultimately decided that. Yes, I wanted to have the startup experience. It was the time in my life when I was able to take this risk, and if it folded in 6 months, I was very fortunate. I have a safety net. My parents, I could move back in with them and then figure out what to do next. I was like, I'm gonna try it. I want to work at a startup. And it was small and new. This is really exciting, and honestly, my coworkers were great, and that's what I learned when I went there to visit them. They were open about what they were doing and about what's hard about the job, and it was a very physical job, all in the clean room. Physically, operating the tools in university clean rooms to make these very small LEDs.

Aris Winger: And then from there.

Sibel Leblebici: I worked there for 5 years. And then it was Covid.

Aris Winger: Yes.

Sibel Leblebici: Towards the end, we started to run out of funding. And at the same time, my then-boyfriend, who's from Ecuador, had to move back to Ecuador. And then I was like, this company is kind of falling apart. I want to be with my boyfriend. We need to figure out something else.

Sibel Leblebici: So I decided to look for jobs in Europe. Because that was a geographical location that was going to work for both of us.

I applied to tons of jobs. But it was a great time in the job market. There were many jobs to apply to. I got many interviews. And one of them happened to be with Meta.

Aris Winger: Got it. And now that you're entrenched as a professional, if you could go back to undergrad and add some stuff, any class you wanted, any curriculum you would add to help you day to day as a professional. What are some of the things that, when you started working at the startup, or in professional life. You're like, Why didn't anyone tell me this? Give me the skills, or tell me I need these skills? Why am I learning this for the 1st time now? What would that be?

Sibel Leblebici: One, I would say, especially for my 1st job, and the University of Illinois set me up. But I had a lab class that was required as part of my electrical materials program. I had to take a clean room class. I had to go into the clean room and make some basic transistors or whatever, but I had to learn what all the tools were, and how to do photolithography. What are all the steps: deposition, etch, litho, doping, etc.? And then what it's to put on a clean room suit and get ready to go into that space. And it takes a lot of the kind of anxiety out of it, because you've done it already.

Even if the processes that you're doing are different, it's at least a familiar environment you're in and not wondering, Why is this light orange or whatever. That was a really helpful class. And the other class that was really helpful, but it was horrible, it was such a hard class, but it was a lab class. It covered all aspects of material science. Some of them were labs on polymer length. How do you measure that? Some of them are labs on metal hardness. But you had to write up these really big lab reports. And then it was Oh, when you go to work, this is literally what I'm doing every day. I'm writing a lab report every day, that's my job, I do an experiment, I write a lab report, and even more so than doing a Phd, where you're doing this much longer study. But I feel at work, it's more like what I did in undergrad, where you're doing some work for 2 weeks, and then you have to write up a report, or you present it, or both. And I think that, really and there was a lot of rigor in what they expected from us in undergrad for that, how you plot data. Everything was about having legible axes, having the scale, having everything labeled, and having enough background information, how to present the data, and how to present your conclusions in a pretty concise format, which is what you need at work.

But I think what would be really helpful is project management. How to make a Gantt chart. I make many Gantt charts now, and I don't really know what I'm doing. How to use some project management software. I also think that at the time, Python wasn't a thing. But now I think it should be absolutely mandatory that you learn the basics of Python for data analysis, and that it should be used continuously throughout the curriculum. I was very lucky that I learned Python when I was in grad school. But I see people who don't know that I work with them. It's a setback for them.

Aris Winger: That's amazing. Alright. 2 more questions for you. One. What is it that you had to sacrifice to get where you are now?

Sibel Leblebici: Sleep. So much sleep. What else? And I still have a ton of hobbies that I do outside of work. And I'm about to start a family. I'm 5 months pregnant now.

Aris Winger: Congratulations.

Sibel Leblebici: I think a lot of people when they go to higher education. You sacrifice making money earlier. When I was working at the Startup, I wasn't making a ton of money, especially from living in New York City; I didn't have any retirement savings. And only now, once I started working at Meta, did I start putting money away for retirement, and I think I maxed out what I could put in my Roth IRA, but it's not really gonna do a lot in the long term.

I do sometimes tell people when they're thinking about getting a PhD. Think about it, unrelated to finances, yes, afterwards you can potentially get a higher-paying job than you can get out of undergrad. But if you were to get that job out of undergrad, you'd already be saving money. And by the time you're 6 years later, after this, when I'm going to be finishing my PhD, you might be making the same amount of money that I would be able to make. Sometimes I think about, oh, how much more savings and retirement savings I would have if I hadn't gone down that route? But I'm super fortunate now that I'm also getting matching funds from Meta for my retirement and stuff like that. I've been able to travel a lot, which is something I really enjoy even more by having gone the route that I did during my PhD. My advisors were both foreigners. They really encourage travel and going to foreign conferences and stuff like that.

I don't think I gave up that much.

Aris Winger: Good. Last question. Now, talking directly to the reader. If you could have any words of advice for a reader who's going through this now, who might be struggling, who might be doing fantastic... What would you say to them now?

Sibel Leblebici: Even if you're doing something that's really hard, you're really struggling through class, or you're struggling through some experiment during your PhD. And it's not going well, you still gotta have some life outside of school or outside of work. And I've really prioritized that work-life balance, and I know other people haven't as much. But to me, that's really what helped me get through those challenging times.

06 - Jesse Milliken-Callan

TAKE CARE OF YOURSELF

Pressure is real. It can come from others. It can come from within. It can be relentless. Pressure brought our next author, Environmental and Civil Engineer Jesse Milliken-Callan, to the brink of ending his own life. How did he recover? Through tapping into his support network, conversing with his mentors, and doing some intense self-reflection about what he wanted, instead of outside expectations, he began the process of an educational and life comeback. What you are about to read is an account of someone raised from humble beginnings who dreamed of being an engineer. It turns out that in the process, he discovered something much more important: his self-actualization and purpose.

*This story contains discussions of suicidal events and suicidal ideation, which some readers may find distressing. If you or someone you know is struggling, please utilize the resources at the end of the story for help.

Jesse Milliken-Callan

Water Resource Control Engineer, State Water Resources Control Board, California

MS in Environmental Health Engineering, University of California, Berkeley

BS in Civil & Environmental Engineering, University of California, Davis

Hometown: Vacaville, California

Aris Winger: Thank you for joining us, Jesse. Are you an engineer?

Jesse Milliken-Callan: Yes.

Aris Winger: What is an engineer to you?

Jesse Milliken-Callan: I feel it's been about problem-solving throughout the college journey and into life so far. That's kind of the point that has been hit repetitively to us.

Aris Winger: Who was saying that?

Jesse Milliken-Callan: By our professors in school. Our teachers, our advisors. You are the problem solvers of the world. Everybody comes to you and says, "Hey, there's this impossible task that we don't know very much about or know how to figure it out." You have very little information to figure it out, but we need somebody to figure it out, and our job at the end of the day is to kind of figure out what we can do and what we have to work with in order to come to some solution.

Aris Winger: I may be jumping all the way to the end of this interview, but knowing the Jesse that I met many years ago, to whom I am talking to now, how do you go from not feeling confident you can do that to that being your job every single day?

Jesse Milliken-Callan: I think it comes through the art of repetition. I might not understand how this problem works today. But what can I kind of gather within myself, and gather with the resources that I have around me, to ensure that I can answer whatever type of question comes up through the process. And I think it's a lot of trial and error. I think it's a ton of, I hate to say, figuring it out, going through the process of what is the very basis of the problem. What are the very basic concepts, structures, and parameters of what's involved? How can I use those to my benefit in order to create a solution? I think those things kind of give you, in some cases, informed decision-making. You want to, in a sense, really control the level of doubt within yourself. You want to be able to walk very confidently, knowing that you've overturned every rock you possibly could.

There's something that really stands out to me that Aris and I had talked about one time when he was tutoring me in math. I told him I felt

I deserved an A in the class because of all the work I put in. He said, "Deserve is a strong word. What makes you feel that you deserve that?"

Because if it's the very bare minimum of studying for the exam or doing the homework, that's what everybody is doing. You haven't differentiated yourself. What have you done to study the problem? What have you done to really understand all the different intricacies of each variable? Look and calculate this number. How did you get that number? Why is that number significant?

I think there's a real balance of trying to understand as much as you possibly can when it comes to that problem-solving technique. And it's a muscle. You have to work. It's not something that happens overnight. I think it's something that comes through repetitiveness and making sure that you're as confident as you possibly can be.

Aris Winger: Great. I love that response. Let's go all the way back to the start of undergrad. Where did you go?

Jesse Milliken-Callan: I went to the University of California, Davis.

Aris Winger: You and I met slightly before you arrived on campus. As you're going into Davis, how are you feeling?

Jesse Milliken-Callan: Growing up, I came from a smaller town, somewhat rural, with a little less resources at hand. We barely had any AP classes. The ones we did have, they could only find certain people to teach them, because not everybody has those types of degrees or background or knowledge. It's very hard to pull from sometimes.

I felt like going in, while I didn't necessarily know what was going to happen, I had a level of ignorance in myself to think that I was going to kind of figure it out, and then I felt as time got closer. I got to be around orientation and some of the people, and talking to them, I realized how small I was.

Aris Winger: Meaning?

Jesse Milliken-Callan: Meaning in a sense of…Everybody has kind of done their extracurriculars. Everybody has done the extra work. Everybody has been part of those things. And on top of that, people have been a part of programs, private schools, different things to where they've advanced their education to a level of... I had no idea what coding was before going into college. And then, all of a sudden, it's a part of my degree requirements. Some of these kids have been doing coding camps since they were in middle school. There are levels to those things.

Aris Winger: So you're already doing the comparison game. We're going to have some students, engineering majors now, reading this. Is the comparison unavoidable? What is your advice on comparison? How do we compare in a healthy way?

Jesse Milliken-Callan: Absolutely. Somebody who is going into competitive colleges, you're constantly going to be combating yourself against comparison. I always tried to remember within myself, and going into my faith base, is that comparison is the thief of joy, and that's reality. You can always find somebody who's "smarter" or who is more "gifted" upon a superficial view.

It's very important to yourself... I'm a very big sports fan myself. Kobe Bryant was one of my idols growing up. He would say it's about working on yourself. It's about trying to get yourself better. It's about trying to work within yourself. How are you being a better version of you? Because at the end of the day, that's what's going to really matter. Are you giving a better effort within yourself every day, which looks different in many ways?

Some of that could be studying, some of that could be going and putting in the extra hours, and some of it could be resting. That also should be a part of your scheduling. I think it's very important that in this process, even when you may be graded on a curve and forced into competitive environments that invite comparison.

Aris Winger: How many people are in a class?

Jesse Milliken-Callan: It depends. If it's an undergrad, general education, your general physics, your general chemistry, it could be up to a thousand students.

Aris Winger: You're taking classes in a stadium.

Jesse Milliken-Callan: Pretty much. It depends. They're a little bit less in the STEM field. There are rooms of four hundred to five hundred people. And looking around, you're… for one, as we understand Aris as a Black STEM student, you're looking around, you're saying. "I'm 1, 2, 3, 4, 5 of 500 students that are within this field to start."

But on top of that, you're thinking to yourself, there are 500 other people in this room, and they all come from different backgrounds. Immediately, for me, when it comes to that thought of comparison, it's how many are more well prepared than I am? How many are already 5 steps ahead of me?

Aris Winger: Are these thoughts that you actually had?

Jesse Milliken-Callan: Oh, absolutely.

In general, high school education, 30 kids is the number of kids you're gonna see in a high school classroom, 40-50 at the max. But when you walk in all of a sudden in college, there are 500 people. It's your 1st few days of college. It's a culture shock experience.

Aris Winger: Looking back at that moment, would you have tried to train yourself not to compare? I'm trying to understand. Should we compare? Is comparing going to happen, and do we have to fight it? Would you have wanted to not look around in the classroom and focus on yourself? How are we thinking about comparison in general?

Jesse Milliken-Callan: People can take that level of comparison in many ways. They can either do it in a positive way that encourages them to try to strive to be better. Or it could be in a negative way. I would say that in my personality, in particular, I took things in a negative way. I was thinking I am not of this class of people. I am not as smart as these kids. That either motivates us or puts a lot of pressure on ourselves, which I can expand on. But it puts a lot of pressure on ourselves to where they feel like they have to get everything right. I have to make things work.

I would encourage myself back then to focus on you, focus on what you can control. What you can control is how much effort you put in, how much time you put in. What you choose to focus on, what you choose to spend your time on, whether that's through school, whether that's through making sure that your mental health is at the forefront of whatever you're doing.

You can put a lot of pressure on yourself, and you can almost create a level of perfectionism. To accompany the self-doubt that you have within yourself, and that's a dangerous combination. That's a dangerous combination.

Aris Winger: Are you saying that you did have self-doubt?

Jesse Milliken-Callan: Absolutely. 100%.

Aris Winger: Imposter syndrome?

Jesse Milliken-Callan: That's the phrase I was looking for.

Aris Winger: How do we overcome that? How do we battle that?

Jesse Milliken-Callan: This is even before college. Walking up to you and saying, "Hey, I'm really not confident in myself."

Kyle, the first time I ever met Professor Aris, I walked up to him crying, which I'm sure was a very shocking experience. I had so much imposter syndrome. I was so scared of what I felt about not knowing if I'm capable of doing this.

I'm the first engineer in my family. There's never been an engineer before me. Nobody necessarily knows what this field is like. I don't know what I'm getting myself into 100 percent. I've only done what I've read. I researched as best as I could. But at the end of the day, I never had an experience like that.

What's really important about that self-doubt is that you find people who will lift you up in times when you doubt yourself the most. That's the key, for me. That's what helped me. For example, I had my mom in my corner and the friends I made quickly. Those are lifetime friends. I still talk to them to this day. I go visit them for family trips. We communicate very frequently, because we went through so much together, and we built each other up. It's important to find those people who see the greatness within you when you don't see that in yourself. That really helped me, because…

Aris Winger: And how did you find these people, the friends?

Jesse Milliken-Callan: For me, initially, being in many extracurriculars. I'm an introverted person, but I'm an outgoing introvert. It was very easy for me to kind of walk up to people in the 1st week of school and know that everybody knows nobody. It was very easy to kind of seek those people out. It was you in our scholarship area and seeking out your wisdom. I'm not the strongest person in math, to start. I need to attach myself to him because he's obviously a professor. That's important. But I think going into spaces where there are counseling centers or the extra office hours, meeting people, talking to them, getting to know these types of people. I think you'll figure out fairly quickly who is capable of lifting you and who is capable of tearing you down, because, unfortunately, both experiences are possible when going to meet somebody.

Aris Winger: Now you're taking classes. How is the content? Is it blowing you out of the water? Are you comfortable with it? Are you struggling? What's your relationship with the material, the speed, all of it in the classroom?

Jesse Milliken-Callan: It's funny. We were on the quarter system, and I did really well in the 1st quarter. That was because at my institution, they gave everyone the same first-quarter schedule. You can go from there after that first quarter. Most of them encouraged people to start slowly. Initially, I started with 12 units in the quarter system. I was able to focus on a few classes, and that really benefited me. Unfortunately, as every engineering student figures out, that's not going to get you graduated in 4 years. So you pick up classes a lot quicker than that.

It's funny, because in the 1st quarter, I really was there. You're in the dorms. If you go that path, you're in the dorms, you're focusing strictly on school. I got a lot of encouragement from my family to start slow, ramp up after that.

And then I started to add things, had to add classes, because, hey, I got to graduate in 4 years. After all, there's that pressure on me.

Aris Winger: Pressure from whom?

Jesse Milliken-Callan: I think pressure from the norm to start. The norm is that everybody should graduate in 4 years, even though I very much encourage everybody to do it if they can afford it, please don't do it in 4 years. If you can, do it in 5 to take that pressure off. You would ideally not. There's a different level of pressure when you have to take physics, chemistry, and math all together in the same quarter. You figure out slowly that you don't know any of what anybody is talking about. That really challenges your mental capacity. I always say, when you're able to break those things up, it's a lot better than having to squish them all together. And that's what I say there.

Aris Winger: It sounds like you're saying that if you're going to take some classes and not know a bunch of stuff, it should not be three of them.

Jesse Milliken-Callan: Correct. But I also understand the reality of people's situations. For myself, I was considered income growing up and stuff like that. I had 4 years of funding. After those 4 years, it's kick rocks. It's been nice to have you. Thank you for being a student here. We'll send you alumni reminders to donate after. Some people are within those timelines. If you can, cool; if you can't, I understand.

But I did well in the 1st quarter. In the second quarter, I didn't add too much. And then in the 3rd quarter I was… I'm also a working student. I have to work. I can't afford to live outside of that. I was preparing to move out because you're only guaranteed one year of housing in the dorms at my university. Thankfully, they changed that. But at my time, it was only one year. We all moved out to get an apartment.

I had to add working into the mix. I ended up getting a D in a class in the 3rd quarter of my time there, and that really… I didn't get the best grades either, necessarily. It really shook me. I was put on an academic support plan as well.

Once you have that level of pressure on you, that's a whole different experience. Because now it's…

Aris Winger: They're telling you, you have to do something or else.

Jesse Milliken-Callan: Not to mention, I was put on that in Spring, which means I had to think about it the entire Summer until I could prove myself in the Fall.

There was that level of pressure for what, 6 months? I had to kind of sit on that and think: Am I really cut out for this?

Aris Winger: And that D was in what class?

Jesse Milliken-Callan: It ended up being in math. There are a lot of things I could have potentially tried to do differently. I'm not going to sit here and say I was an angel in the class, and I'm not going to say that the professor wasn't giving me a hard time in the class, either. It was one of those experiences that really challenges you to figure it out quickly.

Aris Winger: We ended up taking it again?

Jesse Milliken-Callan: I ended up taking it over the summer. I was a class behind anyway, because I had to do a writing class over the summer going in. I failed the English placement exam. I had to take an extra English class. It helped me learn how to write in college, because I was a poor, very, very poor writer until I took that class. I didn't realize how poor a writer I was until I took that class. That also put me behind. I ended up having to take some summer courses to catch up.

Aris Winger: Do you want to bring up any seminal moments in undergrad?

Jesse Milliken-Callan: I think the first is going back to finding those people out who do believe in you. If I could give a level of advice is really to talk to your professors. They're people, too.

Aris Winger: Oh, give me one second. You're in a class of 504 people.

Jesse Milliken-Callan: Yes.

Aris Winger: And the professor is one of them. Class ends for the day. And you're saying that you're going to fight through that? Is it worth it to fight through hundreds of people to have this conversation? Tell me why.

Jesse Milliken-Callan: Yes, yes. I think it opens up a level of accountability between you and the class. I think it opens up the door to say, "Hey, this is my name." You're going to recognize my face every time you come to this class, and I'm going to make sure you do. My initial conversation with them on the 1st day is I walk up to them and say, "Hey, my name's Jesse. I'm a civil engineer, environmental engineer, and I'm really excited to get to know you and take your class." It can be as simple as that to start out with. It really puts a level of accountability because now they know your name and they know your face. They're going to see if you're in class during the allotted class time. That puts a level of accountability into your education.

It also opens up a level of familiarity and personality to the course. For example, you bring your own humanity into a course centered around Newton's second law. You might develop a relationship that may or may not blossom into an internship or referral to something later in your life. That wasn't my intention necessarily. I'm more about meeting professors because they've gotten to this position, and obviously, they know something I can learn about. How did you get to this point? I've had a lot of conversations with professors, and I learned a lot of valuable, even life, lessons in terms of getting to understand, having now been in the working culture, that is your Mini boss or your Mini project manager.

Aris Winger: Do you have an example?

Jesse Milliken-Callan: In terms of work or school?

Aris Winger: In terms of school, you, talking to professors and learning something by conversing with them.

Jesse Milliken-Callan: Absolutely. Office hours, you walk in, they respond with "Hey, Jesse, how are you?" all those different things. Almost every professor I was able to converse with would know me on a first-name basis, and we'd be able to talk. Through that, I was able to meet, in the very 1st quarter, Professor Jeannie Darby. She really helped me get my first internship, get my second internship, and then became a reference for the rest of my life. Meeting her and talking to her, she was able to give me…

Because I would be honest… I'd be "Hey, I don't understand a lot of things in your class, and I don't understand a lot of things about this college thing." She gave me a lot of confidence to understand that I don't have to understand everything when it comes to the conceptual level. She'd always tell me some things in the engineering field are common sense, and if you have really good common sense, you might be able to get by further than you think. That really helped me because I always felt that if I didn't understand everything, then I couldn't be a successful engineer. After all, we're "supposed" to know all the answers to the question.

Going back even to the beginning of the conversation… You can overturn as many rocks as you possibly can, but there are some things you might not figure out, and you have to be ok with that. What stuck with me during conversations was being ok with doing your best with an educated guess and continually working to figure out the different aspects of a problem through your conversations with your professors or project managers.

I didn't consider this. There are things that they give you that are important to consider, and can be little golden nuggets.

Aris Winger: That's powerful. At this point, your major is what?

Jesse Milliken-Callan: I was a double major. I was in civil engineering and environmental engineering.

Aris Winger: You mentioned Professor Darby. Who else are we talking about who was supportive and made a big impact?

Jesse Milliken-Callan: Professor Darby taught the intro to civil engineering course. She was really beneficial towards me, and then I had a professor called Professor Colleen Bronner. She was essentially the intro to environmental engineering. Both are still involved with the University. I still have conversations with them to this day. Both worked with me in terms of my imposter syndrome and my lack of confidence. They would say, "Hey, Jesse, you're in these office hours frequently. I think you're gaining some knowledge that you can't even give credit to yourself."

Having those important people around you to remind you, "Hey, I saw you at midnight, with the books open, writing notes. I saw you practicing problems. You have to trust that. Believe in that." Professor Bronner was one. Later on, when I went to grad school, Professor Mark Stacy... Many valuable conversations about graduate school.

Now, there are other cases where the other way around happened. There are other cases where professors aren't nice.

Aris Winger: Some professors weren't nice to you.

Jesse Milliken-Callan: On the flip side of things, other professors are there to just teach a class. My institution, in particular, was a research-based institution. Many of those professors are focused on research and research funds. They feel forced to teach a class. You have to be able to differentiate between the two. Some professors are there to be professors, and they love it. They absolutely love it. There are some professors there that are there because they have to be.

Aris Winger: I was wondering about the fact that both of the first two people you mentioned were both women, and they were both intro classes. There's something about a person who's teaching an intro class that understands their students may not be aware of things and is more apt to welcome students.

Jesse Milliken-Callan: Absolutely. I think the Intro classes are extremely important because those are the ones that essentially say, "this is what this is about, and we would love for you to continue on." These are the benefits of it. These are the struggles of it. On the first day of class, Professor Darby shows us the great successes of civil engineering and the great failures. She shows essentially what you're getting yourself into and how a professor portrays that is important, because they can really turn a lot of people off, or you can inspire a lot of people to say, "this is what I want to stick with for 4 years and the rest of my life after this."

Aris Winger: Ok, so you graduate from there and then? (Editor's Note: Notices more on Jesse's mind) Oh, wait...go ahead. What else do we have to know from undergrad?

Jesse Milliken-Callan: No. I want everybody to know, because I'm an open book. I always like to tell people that I did get into ruts in my college career. I ended up having some mental health issues myself in going into my upper division courses. I ended up 51-50'ing.

Aris Winger: What does that mean?

Jesse Milliken-Callan: I was planning to kill myself. I was planning to commit suicide. During my college stint, I got into some really… I had a lot of pressure on myself. Coming from a lower-income background, I grew up thinking that I had to get my mom into a better situation.

Aris Winger: Were you the golden child, the one who was going to save… You felt you had to be…

Jesse Milliken-Callan: I felt like that, and I was told that I needed to be. From a family dichotomy, very broken, in terms of different things that happened. I had a lot of family drama going on. I also had the pressure on myself that I needed to be able to get my mom into a certain situation, or get my family together and stuff like that, and it was going to be through my efforts in school.

I ended up putting a lot of pressure on myself. Overworking school-wise, work-wise, hardly sleeping, all those different things. I ended up having to take a quarter off, and kind of recentering myself and figuring out what I really wanted out of this in terms of my life. At that point, I didn't know what I wanted and what I really valued. I think there are different low points.

And the thing is, you think that it's you going through these different things. But there's a lot more than you going through these types of things. There are many people who drop out of their quarters for different reasons. I wanted that to be stated because this journey has different challenges.

I thought that the best solution through this experience, college, whatever, life, was to kind of stop at that point and move forward. I think it's important for engineering students, any student, but engineering students, who have that level of pressure on themselves, to realize that this is an option. Because it is a very pressurized major, it's always compacted. It's…

Aris Winger: It's competitive.

Jesse Milliken-Callan: Competitive always. There are different experiences that people may or may not have through the engineering track. And I just want people to know, too, that even in those dark spaces and dark timelines, it's ok to get help. It's ok to reach out to the people that you find and you need that will lift you up in those types of moments.

There's a real timeline where I didn't finish this degree. And we're not having this conversation. But there's obviously the timeline I'm living in now that where I graduated, and went to grad school. I graduated there, too, and I'm in the pursuit of my professional engineering license. There are different ways. I really encourage people to kind of reach out. Those professors I even mentioned earlier, I told them too. They really helped me get back on my feet, back on schedule.

At the end of the day, these are people's lives. These are students who are pursuing different things in their lives for different reasons. Some of them think this is the way out. This is the way that we're going to change the trajectory of our family, or to be able to live in a nicer space. Others are there to get a degree, because it's a part of what you're supposed to do.

There are plenty of different reasons. But I wanted to express my struggles as well…

Every day, I had to convince myself that I was going to finish. Every day, I had to convince myself that I was going to make it through this pressurized time and that I was worthy of doing that. I think it's important that everybody has that opportunity to tell themselves that they're worth the work that they're putting in and they're worth…

It's hard, even on a curve, to always consistently be getting D's and F's, or C's, or something. And then somehow, those turn into A's.

Jesse Milliken-Callan: That doesn't necessarily…

Aris Winger: You're seeing 48's and 37's…

Jesse Milliken-Callan: Class average is 33. You need to work on your mental capacity and what you can handle. Take as much time away from the books as much time as you put in, not to party or go crazy. But really give yourself time to work on that, because it's part of the process. This is all part of a process.

Aris Winger: First of all, thank you very much for that, for allowing us to hear that part of it. We're gonna hear many stories, and it sounds like you said something that needed to be said. That's a gift. And we really appreciate that. Somebody's life is going to be changed because you shared this story. That's the point. There are two things that are on my mind about what you said, which is a hidden part of success that I think we need to say very clearly. You said that part of the success is also being mentally ready, to be mentally prepared, and to be committed to your mental health also. What does that look like? In terms of practices, what would a person need to do pragmatically, week to week?

Jesse Milliken-Callan: Absolutely. I think it's important to realize that through the hours I'm making study plans and creating a schedule for myself. I'm a very organized person. Some people don't operate that way, but that's how I operated.

I have to hit 6 hours exactly of study time for this particular class, or I have to do this many problems and make sure that I complete all those problems. It's how my mental preparation works. I have to set these little goals within myself to ensure that I'm the most prepared that I possibly can be.

But I also think there has to be time for yourself to do things that you love and do things that you care about. And while I do love being an engineer and the practice of it, it's not all of who I am. There are other parts of who you are. Some people have different hobbies, whatever that looks like. That could be writing, watching movies, hanging out with friends outside the classroom, not talking about the classroom. Those need to be scheduled as well.

Those are integral parts to make sure that you don't experience burnout because it's very, very, very easy for you to get burnt out in this system.

When you feel you constantly have to be studying... and I had to battle this the entire time. I personally had guilt anytime I was doing anything that I felt was for me, because I could have been putting that time into studying. I could be putting that time into preparing myself better.

Combating that. It's an important perspective to see that you are resting. There is a difference between resting and not using your time wisely.

Resting is a part of the process. It is a part of making sure that you're at your best at all times.

Aris Winger: How did you overcome this guilt?

Jesse Milliken-Callan: I think it was very hard, and some days are better than others. I'm not going to sit here and tell you that I magically figured it out. I still deal with it to this day. Some people are able to ignore it. I'm not.

There's simple things that you can do. You can tell yourself affirmations. That this is part of my process. This is part of my daily experience. If you can't give yourself an hour to even exist in your space, I think that is a very telling thing. There's 24 hours in a day. I know that's not a lot to a lot of us. But you can't give yourself an hour to enjoy lunch?

I think perspective is everything with that guilt. If you can't allow yourself the perspective that I deserve at least an hour a day to do things that I like to do, I think that's that helps when it comes to combating that guilt.

It doesn't have to be hours on end, but you can give yourself an hour. Go on a walk, go exercise, do the things that you really enjoy doing. It's that bartering with yourself a little bit. Hey, I know we could put an extra hour into whatever we're doing. But how much more are you going to get out of that hour than giving yourself the opportunity to rest in your hobby? I think that's important.

Aris Winger: That's powerful. The second part that came to me was about this quarter that you took off. At some point you're off for a quarter now. There's a decision there where you decided to come back, or was that always going to be the case? You never had any doubts of coming back. What does this quarter off look like if you're willing to share? What did you do?

Jesse Milliken-Callan: I started that quarter and in the quarter system for those that don't understand how it works. It's the 10 week thing. You're essentially taking your midterms by week 2 or 3. I failed the 1st midterm. I said to myself that I am not where I need to be now mentally. I need to actually...

Funny enough, the quarter that I did step away was the quarter after the 5150. That came with many different things. You're hospitalized. You're in a facility for a little bit. You come out of that. All of a sudden, now you're on medication. There's a lot of different layers on top of that. I ended up finishing that quarter. I missed 3 days of school. It was the next quarter, because I had burnt myself out so much during that time that as soon as I didn't feel myself, as soon as I failed the 1st midterm, I said "I need to step away." I ended up stepping away.

I put it on that day. I walked straight to my counselor's office after getting that exam. And I said, "I need some time off." They said, you have two weeks to figure out if you want to restart in the spring, or if you want to restart the following year. At that point I didn't know. I didn't know whether I wanted to be off for multiple quarters, if I wanted to be off for a year, or if I wanted to never go back again. I knew I needed to step away for a second to gather myself. I went home. I sat down for a while and I really looked at myself. I said I need to get away from everything.

I end up hopping in the car. All my friends were in college so I ended up going down the coast of California and going to different colleges where my friends were at and kind of telling them where I was, the experience that I had. I was calling my mentors from all different walks of life, whether it was mentors from high school or mentors from UNCF. The mentors. I wanted to say everything that I was feeling at the moment. I don't want you to tell me what to do.

I essentially said, I would really enjoy hearing your perspective of where you think I... what you think I should... What my next steps would be, or what your next steps would be if you were in my shoes.

I took all of that information and made an informed decision. I ended up coming back the following quarter. Because I knew for myself that—and this is for me and might not necessarily be for everybody—but my situation in particular would have gotten worse if I had stayed away. I would have beaten myself up a lot in terms of...

Aris Winger: Because you wouldn't have finished, and then you would have been the failure.

Jesse Milliken-Callan: All of those things. But also, I wanted more for myself. I wanted it really bad. I think there's a difference... I think there's the realization of "Hey, this is not for me." And that's ok if people get to that point.

But I think that the important question is to always go back to your why. Who are you doing this for? Why are you doing this? And make sure that you're "who" involves you. It can't just be for everybody else. I think that was a very hard lesson for me to learn, initially. I think I got in for the reason that I can make a livable salary as an engineer, which is apparently in today's world "the goal." That's immediately kind of where my mind went along with the benefits of being a civil servant and being able to help more people.

But why did Jesse join the Major? Why did Jesse end up doing this? I think going back to it really helped me reprioritize. Am I doing this for me? Why am I doing this? Why am I putting much effort into this? Does it really matter to me? At the end of the day, it did it. It mattered a lot to me.

Jesse Milliken-Callan: It was about 10 days that you had to decide. On the 9th day I decided that I was going back next quarter. I took that time to sit back and really live with my thoughts, and the recommendations from my peers, my mentors and trusted people. This would honestly make me more upset, and maybe even put me in a deeper depression, if I'm sitting around and not using my brain or the things that I feel are important for me to keep working on .

Aris Winger: You come back. Is it smooth sailing between then and graduation? What is the journey from there coming back?

Jesse Milliken-Callan: I reprioritized myself in a lot of ways. What I wasn't doing that was creating a lot of initial burnout, was I wasn't prioritizing myself. That's why I'm preaching this. Really take care of yourself in this, because this is a marathon. This is not a sprint. The important concept that I took with me is you really need to start prioritizing yourself in this experience.

You need to make sure you're... For me, one of my nice, brainless activities: I love to go out, play video games, allow my brain to not have to be in ultra processing mode.

Allow yourself to do that. Allow yourself to go on walks. Allow yourself to go and have fun with your peers and your roommates.

Almost every Friday it would be

"Hey, Jess, you coming out with this?"

"No, I gotta. I gotta work. I gotta put the work in."

That was a space of unhealthiness. I think there's a saturation point. I think you're perfecting your craft... I don't even want to say perfecting because I'm not into the business of perfection, but improving your craft, improving your working capacity and then there's expecting that level of perfection out of yourself every day, which is unreasonable. When I got back, I really prioritized implementing the things within myself that made me happy, that I enjoyed outside of school. That really propelled me into a level of finding the balance of creating the time for work, creating the time for play, creating the time for yourself, those kinds of things. And then COVID happened.

Aris Winger: Oh, that thing!

Jesse Milliken-Callan: Then everything was thrown off track. It was a very interesting experience, because I remember...

Aris Winger: What year are you at this point?

Jesse Milliken-Callan: This is junior year. It was the whole time either way. It all meshed together.

We had an apartment with 4 guys, 2 bedrooms, and one bath. That was fun. It sounds like everybody's going to be virtual. We're all probably gonna go home. We all said, "We'll see in a couple of weeks, when all this starts to die down."

I said, "Yep." I didn't see my roommates the rest of my college years.

Aris Winger: Wow!

Jesse Milliken-Callan: It was a really interesting experience in that way. We all ended up being virtual, and we all had to learn how to be an engineer virtually, which is extremely difficult.

We are a profession that really does work a lot on programs independently. But our strength in engineering is through collaboration. That collaboration is enhanced in person. I loved working virtually as much as the other person. I will not complain about that. But I will say there is a level of being able to work with your hands in some cases. My profession in the civil and environmental realm, probably a little less than in the mechanical realm where they really are using their hands or using different aspects of 3D printing.

But for us in that realm, I think it really made us really focus anytime we did get that collaboration on Zoom to our time as wisely as possible, because you didn't have the opportunity to talk about the project over lunch.

It really forced us to kind of collaborate in an even tighter way as weird as that sounds, because none of us were together ever those really important times, especially.

It challenged us a lot to kind of collaborate as best as we could when we were together virtually. And it really opened the door for me to, as weird as it sounds, finish on time. I ended up finishing on time, because what else was there to do?

I ended up sitting around taking classes. I ended up taking 2 years of classes in one year.

I was in school for a year straight, and I pretty much did 2 years worth of college in one. That experience was a little weird, of course, but I think at the end of the day it really showed what your strengths were in a lot of ways, and what your weaknesses were.

Aris Winger: At some point you decide that graduate school is going to be the thing, getting a Master's. Why is that? What compelled you to do that?

Jesse Milliken-Callan: At this point, I've grown up my whole life, and either my family members have bachelors, or they were uneducated. I think for myself, I wanted in some ways to get that degree for the next generation so that they could look back and be proud of something. They could say "Hey, we have family members who have graduate degrees."

I think in some cases it's defying the odds as a black engineer. That in itself is something that is a revolution against the norm. Why not push that forward even more? Also, I wanted to make sure I'm somebody who loves to future-proof myself as much as possible. I think way too much ahead. I think it would open more doors for me going forward.

I had the opportunity to go to my dream college at that point, which was Berkeley, and prove myself there and create more connections. I knew going into freshman year that I was going to figure out how to get a Master's Degree. I didn't know how I was going to do it.

Aris Winger: Oh, you knew that from the beginning?

Jesse Milliken-Callan: I told myself, I want at least a master's degree. I didn't want to stop at the bachelor's. I wanted to move forward. It was part of my plan from the beginning. It continued to build up within me as I went through college.

I think there were many opportunities in undergrad. It's really difficult to stay in those moments for certain classes because you do have to learn the basics. You have to learn the building blocks of everything to get to your upper division courses, the math, the physics, and the chemistry. It's very difficult because at times it feels like you're doing things to get to where you want to be, but you're not where you want to be.

Once I was able to get into that space, I wanted to learn much more about the engineering realm. I felt I had to spend much time learning about math, physics, the general writing classes, and all those different things. I really wanted to really dive into the ideas of engineering. Pursuing an advanced degree would give me a chance to do that.

Aris Winger: Now, take me to grad school... What was that like? You spoke highly of an individual during this master's experience who was super supportive. What did that person do for you?

Jesse Milliken-Callan: I did have levels of: Am I ok to be here? Do I belong here? I decided to apply to all of the prestigious schools that I didn't get into for undergrad, Berkeley, Stanford, and so forth.

I got into Berkeley. I got into Stanford, and those opportunities had me thinking, "Whoa. I didn't even think I really belonged here," because of the prior denial that I had. I didn't feel I was at that tier of student.

I knew it was going to be very important for me to, as I had done in my undergrad experience, find the people who are going to lift me through the experience.

More so than undergrad, grad school really is about "What you put in is what you get out of it." It's really important to realize it's not something you just do just because. You should be doing it with the intention of really wanting to learn as much as possible. It really does give you an even deeper conceptual level. This gives you access to the possibility of being in this field for 40-plus years. This is what I want to understand on a daily basis. I really want to understand what I'm doing.

That professor, Mark Stacey, in particular, really helped me get through, in addition to helping with imposter syndrome, of course, the level of understanding that everybody here is just regular people like you. You are taught in California that Berkeley is the highest education you can possibly have in the state. This is the cream of the crop. At the end of the day, you're here, and there's a reason you're here. He helped me really feel like I fit in.

At the time, he was the chair of the whole department, but he was also my graduate advisor. We would have conversations about regular everyday things, about family, life, and things like that. He really helped me feel that this is a regular, everyday thing. There's nothing… this is a great experience, not saying this isn't special, but you're ok to be here. That level of welcomeness helped me really establish myself and really helped me feel I belonged.

The graduate experience was very, very interesting. Grades aren't necessarily the main focus. It's more about the idea of understanding the concept. Do you get what I'm teaching you? A lot of your classmates are graduate PhD students, as well. So you're mixed in with everybody, and everybody has a different idea of what they want out of the experience. That's the difference in a lot of ways. It sounds similar to undergrad, but it's even more personal in a way.

There are 40 people in this room. That's it. There are 40 people in this room out of all the applicants. They've handpicked you guys for a reason to be in this space together. I think it really is an honor in a lot of ways and pressure in some other ways. But it's an experience that we want you guys to succeed, not that people don't want you to succeed in undergrad. But it's very different. There's no weeding out.

Aris Winger: Tell me about the work that you do today. Is this your first job outside of the master's program? Where do you go after the Master's?

Jesse Milliken-Callan: This is my second job. My first job was a consultant for a mid-sized consulting firm. They work out of the East Coast, but obviously have offices everywhere. And it's your kind of atypical corporate design work. I did a lot of wastewater design for wastewater treatment plants, as well as some conveyance in terms of water pipes. You turn the faucet on, figuring out how to get your water there in simple terms.

But for me, I wasn't personally fulfilled. The main goal was to maximize profits and encourage shareholders, all those different things that you hear in terms of corporate jargon. I really felt unhappy with that. I didn't really feel I had a personal relationship with anybody at work or the clients that I did work with. It was very transactional, which is the idea of a consulting firm.

It wasn't for me. I wasn't very happy with that. I figured it out about 3 months into the job that I wasn't happy with, but at that point, I was married. Once you're in that type of commitment, there's a level of I can't quit my job and say, "Honey, I'm unemployed. Let's figure it out." That's not going to happen.

From the third month on – I worked there for a year and a half – I was trying to find a different job. But it was a good experience. It really was. It was a tough experience, but it really made me understand a lot. That transition from school to real life is different. I was not prepared for it. I was not prepared for it.

Aris Winger: What exactly do you mean?

Jesse Milliken-Callan: In school, you're around a lot of like-minded people. You're around a lot of people that share a lot of the same ideals and around your age range, typically, and you're around innovation and the idea of growing and changing.

You go into the workforce that is in America, and it's very much, in my opinion, the opposite. Where I was, I didn't work with anybody my age.

I felt there are certain standards that we all have accepted within the engineering realm, at least in the civil space, for good reason. There are certain standards, material standards, all these different things. There are certain things that you can innovate on, but not in the same way as in college.

When you go into the workforce, it's "Hey, I've been doing this for 30 years. This is how it works. Don't mess this up." It's very different. In college, you might breathe the realm of social justice and the ideas of being in an innovative world, then you go into workspaces, and they might have it in their company policy, but everybody on the board looks the same.

That is a very different experience. I think I was more... Honestly, I don't know what my expectations coming out of college were. The idea was that I had to get a job to start out with to figure out what's going on. You can only really experience your field in an internship to a point.

If I could go back and do it again, I don't think I would have changed much. Knowing myself, if I were away from school for that long, I don't know how realistic it would have been for me to go back in.

But if you're in a different experience, where you're, for example, not married, and somebody else is relying on you, then feel free to get your Bachelor's and hop around some jobs, and then get your Master's. Figure out what you really are looking for, if you have the capacity to do that. I didn't feel I did; looking back on it, I still think I wouldn't have changed much.

I need to get a job, and then we'll figure it out. I got a corporate job and was not a corporate worker. I really want to help people. I didn't want to be in a transactional position. Looking back on that, that probably would not have been my first job.

Aris Winger: Today, what are you doing?

Jesse Milliken-Callan: Today, I work for the State. I am a water resource control engineer. I initially started in the permitting realm of it, in the regulatory field of making sure that everybody is playing their part in environmental health, and making sure that things are up to standards for civil technologies with regard to water infrastructure.

The position that I'm in within this job is working with the State to provide grant funding to low-income communities in order to provide them with wastewater services. So anybody who's still on septic systems, for example, and is part of low-income communities can be served. Once those septic systems start to fail and they can't afford to keep up with them, not only does it become an environmental health hazard, but becomes a hazard to themselves.

We work with grant funding to provide infrastructure for those people to connect to city infrastructure or nearby city infrastructure to ensure that they can have wastewater processes that benefit them in their homes. So, preventing toilets from backing up into their house. They're not having to deal with playing in the yard, the septic system overflowing into the yard, and their kids playing in it.

Aris Winger: Is that meaningful work to you?

Jesse Milliken-Callan: Absolutely, 100 percent. I'm glad I found my niche. I'm very happy because I feel my work impacts communities that are marginalized and pushed to the side in a lot of ways. Whether that be through race or wealth. My work now applies more to what my heart desires, which is to help those who aren't really heard in a lot of aspects. That's what I do now. I'm loving it.

I also changed from the corporate realm because I had a kid. I'm a father now. Moving from the corporate world was important in terms of benefits and things like that. You start to think about those things as soon as you have that kid. But it changed my life. It changed my life 100%. I'm happy with where I'm at now.

Aris Winger: Excellent. Two more questions for you. What did you have to sacrifice to get to where you are at this moment?

Jesse Milliken-Callan: Everything. A lot. A lot. I had to sacrifice a lot of family events and what I wanted to do all the time. I love being in our field and working, and getting everything. But there are very few people who have the level of enjoyment of solving a problem multiple times for hours and hours on end. There are plenty of things I would rather be doing with my time. I love it obviously, but to a point, it is still work for me. In terms of sacrificing, I sacrifice time. It's the obvious answer. But in some aspects, in unhealthy ways, I sacrifice myself.

That's losing yourself and allowing yourself to get into those really deep, dark spaces. You change, as a person, once you experience those things. I lost some of myself in some aspects.

You put in so much work. For me, again, it was one of those things where, as soon as I get to this degree, I get through these positions, I'll be able to take care of my family. You do sacrifice a lot. I keep saying everything, but it really took everything. It took all that I had to do this degree, pursue a graduate degree, and pursue even beyond that with what I'm doing in my licensing.

Aris Winger: Is it worth it?

Jesse Milliken-Callan: Yes. Losing yourself, I wouldn't say, is worth it. Allowing yourself to get to those lost spaces, I don't think, is worth it if I'm being completely honest.

I would say, learn yourself in a better way, more positively. That's a better way of doing that. But was it worth it? In a lot of ways, it was because I gained friends that I will never lose. If I didn't have that experience in college, there'd be a lot of... My life could have gone a completely different way. I think it gave me a purpose. It gave me a blueprint for ways to solve and figure out problems. That in itself teaches you a lot about how to deal with anything in life, whether it's your marriage or how to be the father I am now.

There are tons of little problems and solutions that you're trying to solve for these different equations. All of that repeats itself in your life in different ways, if you allow it to. It taught me a lot, and that part is worth it. I'm forever grateful for that.

Aris Winger: Last question. Our audience will primarily be an undergraduate who's reading this. Now, this is your moment to talk directly to that person who might be in a class in their 1st year, second year, Junior, Senior, or about to go into the workforce. What do you want to say to them about the journey? Anything at all.

Jesse Milliken-Callan: If I can do it, you can do it. I don't mean that in a way that is putting down what you're going through now. What you're going through is real. You are in compacted classes that you're fighting to understand. You're in classes that you feel are impossible, that conceptually, really challenge you to a point of insanity. There's a lot of work that goes into figuring out how to be ok with figuring stuff out.

I would personally want them to know that it's going to take a lot of preparation from you, study-wise. Still, it will take a lot of preparation for you as a person as well to prepare yourself for whatever the battle is, your battle being the midterm, your battle being finals, your battle being juggling working, while studying. As hard as it is, I would encourage them to enjoy the moment.

Enjoy it as much as you possibly can, because you'll never get a space where you're allowed to fail. While there are consequences that come with that failure in college, you get fired if you fail in the real world. You will not be fired here as long as you don't flunk out, but allow yourself to be willing to fail. Because at the end of the day, it's how you respond to that failure.

Are you going to learn from that? I don't see that as a failure. I see that as you strive to learn, grow, and gain that success. I'd want them to know that you don't have to figure everything out and enjoy being in a space where you are allowed to grow.

Sometimes when you go into the workforce, people don't want you to experience those levels of growth. Enjoy the presence of your peers, enjoy the wonder, and enjoy being able to be in a space where the world is essentially your playground. You are being put in a space where you are allowed to innovate, grow, and change the world. Really soak that up. We lose that as we go on through life. Hold on to that as best as you can through this experience.

If you or someone you know needs support, contact the 988 Suicide & Crisis Lifeline. You can call or text 988 anytime, or chat online at https://988lifeline.org/. This service is free, confidential, and available 24/7.

07 - Katrien Herdewyn

You Can Do Both

Oftentimes, the world wants to box you in. It wants to easily define you. It wants to call you one thing. It wants to make you believe you can't be both. In the midst of doing graduate work in NanoScience, *Elegnano* Founder and Engineer Katrien Herdewyn learned about a new program in shoe design at the Art Academy, requiring more work on evenings and weekends. Faced with this moment when she thought she may have had to choose one, she chose both. Driven and diligent, this entrepreneur provides us with the story of a woman who, in the face of a world that at times doubted her, stepped into her own path of innovation and personal freedom.

Katrien Herdewyn

Founder at Elegnano, Belgium

MS in Nanotechnology & Nanosciences, KU Leuven

BS in Electrical Engineering & Materials Science, KU Leuven

Hometown: Wezemaal, Belgium

Aris Winger: Welcome, Katrien. Are you an engineer?

Katrien Herdewyn: Yes.

Aris Winger: Excellent. And what does that mean to you? What does being an engineer mean to you?

Katrien Herdewyn: That's a tough one. I think it's based on the fact that I got a degree in it. And I don't know if I use my degree; I think I subconsciously use it a lot, but it's not my job title, and I got the degree more than 10 years ago.

Aris Winger: We'll definitely unpack that because I'm excited about that. Let us go back to the summer, or any time that you think is important, before you head into undergraduate school. Do you feel you're ready to go into undergraduate school? Do you feel prepared? And how is this 1st semester of undergraduate schooling?

Katrien Herdewyn: I was always a very diligent person. For me, it was kind of the route. I personally wanted to go into art school, or something. Go for the creative side. But my dad was in academia, and my mom also did her full degree and got an additional degree, so there was no question. I had to go to university, and my sister was already studying medicine, and I had seen that, and I was like No, I don't think I want to do that. I don't want to have to learn many things by heart. I'm more intuitive when trying to solve problems and using my logic to answer questions or to study. And so for me, I did feel ready. There was no way I was going to quit after high school. Also, in Belgium, studying is basically free. So it doesn't really make that additional connection of, I need to really figure out what I want to do. Or, if I can live with potential debts or whatever that would come out of studying. Everybody who has a high school degree of a certain level goes to university. You also don't have to apply to universities. You choose the one you want to go to. So it's much more of an organic process where everybody around you goes through that and doesn't really question it. So, for me, I did feel prepared.

I studied 8 hours of math, which is a lot in Belgium in high school, 8 hours a week, and it was a natural transition to look for something in the sciences or engineering. And that was for me, I felt prepared. And as far as selecting engineering specifically for me, it became... My grandfather was an engineer. My uncle was an engineer. I knew I didn't want to do medicine, and the folder I went through all the different folders of all these different undergraduates, and the one of engineering said you had to be creative to be an engineer. And for me, that was it. I like the creative side, too. And that, together with the background of my grandfather being an engineer and knowing I didn't want to do medicine, and by elimination, I ended up studying engineering.

Aris Winger: And this 1st semester, how was it?

Katrien Herdewyn: I really liked it. In the 1st year and a half, you get all the general topics. We had analytics, algebra, physics, magnetism, all the specific topics. And I really liked it. But I also immediately realized that I'm not sure this job is something for me, but the contents of it. I love doing it. I loved solving the problems. I went to every single class. I was doing all the exercises, I really liked doing the content of it immediately, but also through the courses, which is, I feel, a big difference between engineering and sciences, is that in engineering they show you, even when you study real-world problems, like when we studied analytics, you get all the equations. Still, they also show you, this is how it's applied in the industry. Or this is how it works: this is the actual problem we're trying to solve. And I was never really... I liked solving the problem. But I wasn't too excited about what problem it actually was. I didn't care about optimizing a chemistry plant's performance or something like that. I liked the equations of it, but I didn't really like what you were trying to solve.

Aris Winger: How does that play out over the years in undergrad? At some point, do you realize that this isn't going to be your future career for you or how does this come about?

Katrien Herdewyn: I kept going, also, because again, I was a diligent person. And when I started studying, I always said, If I have to retake an exam. I'm doing something different; I'm not giving up my 3 months of summer to retake an exam. I don't know how it works in the US. But in Belgium, if you fail an exam in June, you get another chance in September of that year, and I didn't want to study over the summer.

I wanted my 3 months off, and as I went through, I always studied really hard, always went for the next thing, and selected my bachelor's. You have to select a major and a minor, and I went for 2 things that are purely based on, I like the contents of this, which were electrical engineering and material sciences. Most people focus on one thing specifically, and then study the basics of business or economics as a minor. I picked 2 engineering fields as my major and minor. But for me, those 2 are a very uncommon combination in majors and minors.

There is very little intersection there. But then, when I graduated with a bachelor's in Belgium, I always started a master's, too. It's kind of a continued process. You don't stop after 3 years, and nobody in the 500 students I studied with quit after those 3 years; everybody does the additional 2. And then again, for me it was kind of looking for exploring new things rather than thinking. What am I ever going to do with this degree? Which was the case, too, when I selected electrical engineering and material sciences, I didn't have in mind there were job opportunities there, or I could go work there. It was just, I'm interested in these two programs, let me just take these 2, and then in my master's. I picked nanotechnology for the same reason; there are still not many jobs in that field, especially in Belgium. But to me, it was Oh, well, I'll get biochemistry. And again, more biology. And that's all the new subjects. I'm interested in those.

I have no idea what I'm going to do with all of this, and I never did. I think in my last year, in your master's, they would invite you to all these job things, because engineers are sought after here, and in Belgium, even specifically, when they look for women more to meet their DEI goals. And you're very much sought after. They organize all kinds of events for you, and I went to a lot of them, but I always felt like I wasn't feeling that click with it. But it didn't really deter me from continuing. I was gonna get this degree from the day I really started it. So I had to finish.

Aris Winger: Did you feel you had a long-term vision as a student?

Katrien Herdewyn: No.

Aris Winger: Now, looking back, would you have wanted one? Would you have wanted to sit down with someone to plan out and say, Here's your path or plan?

Katrien Herdewyn: No, I think because I didn't, I focused more on what I was studying and learning everything than I would have been if I were like I'm going to do a career in engineering, or chemistry. I might not have explored so many of the other subjects. I feel today it serves me much better that I've had all these different, somewhat random, combinations of fields in engineering rather than if I had immediately said, I'm going to work in the semiconductor industry. Then I would have dropped a lot of other subjects that I have now. So, I don't think I would have changed it, no.

Did I miss it as a student? Sometimes, because I felt the people around me knew most people, most of my friends knew that this is the company I want to work for, or this is what I want to specialize in. But for me, I was always kind of like, "We'll see." But I was very high ranking in my year. I was really good. So, for them, it made it feel weird that you would be willing to study that hard and work that hard and get good grades, but then not have an intention to work towards something specific. So it was kind of a mixed feeling, but that working really hard came from how I was raised, and that's how you do it, and wanting to succeed, my inner person coming out, and not really of a long-term goal there. Which I think if one of 2 is missing, it might be problematic, if you're if you don't have an inner drive to do really well in school, and then also don't have a goal of: That's where I want to end up. Then I don't know how far you could get, but being one of 2 present for me was enough to keep going.

Aris Winger: And during this time, are there any seminal moments, important moments during the schooling that were impactful for you?

Katrien Herdewyn: No, I don't think so specifically. As I continue the story, I might throw back, like, "yeah, that happened when I was studying." But no, not at all.

Aris Winger: After the masters, where do we head then?

Katrien Herdewyn: I didn't know what I wanted to do. I attended a lot of those job fairs and dinners, etc, and I didn't really feel the same drive and energy as everybody around me was applying for jobs. And I was like, I don't really want any of these jobs. But I was doing a master's thesis at the Department of Solid State Physics and Magnetism. Because I did nanotechnology. You kind of get integrated in a lot of different departments, and I was doing my master's thesis in the department of Solid State Physics and Magnetism, because it was nanophysics. And I liked it there. And for me immediately. They were kind of if you want to continue your research and go into a PhD. There would be a position, mostly because there is also a lack of people wanting to do that. Most people just want to go into the industry and work. Every master's student asks for it, but especially the ones who are getting results and showing ambition. So they proposed that I could stay for 4 more years, and the University offered me a grant, so I didn't even have to apply for a grant. For me, that was 4 more years of buying time to figure out what it was going to do with my degree without diluting or making the degree worth less. There are still specific fields for which they would hire a PhD. But generally, it's considered not a degradation of your degree when you get a PhD. After I started it, but at the same time, I also decided, look, let's continue doing the research that I was doing in my master's thesis. Let's go on for 4 years. Here at the university was a magazine article that was about studying footwear design in part-time arts education. And it was possible to combine that with my job. I did have to get approval because, in theory, when you're doing doctoral research on a grant from the university, you're not allowed to find extracurricular activities that take up a lot of time, and definitely not another degree. But they approved it because it was on Monday nights, Tuesday nights, and then on Saturday the whole day, so it was possible to combine it with my schedule.

Aris Winger: I want to make sure I understand. Apply for what exactly? Let's step back for a second. You see a magazine article saying what?

Katrien Herdewyn: You can study footwear design specifically, shoe design at the Art Academy. It's an art and fashion Academy. But because it was still a very new degree at the time, it was still in a test phase for government approval. And it's not a fully installed course, meaning that it is in the evenings and on the weekends. So it's a part-time course, as it was established in Belgium at that time.

There are other countries where you could study it full-time. But in Belgium at that time. That was the only footwear design degree that you could take, and I'd always loved shoes, which goes back to my childhood. As a 4-year-old, I wanted to sell shoes for a living. I would build a little shoe store in front of the garage, trying to sell shoes. I was sitting under tables at 4 years old to watch people's shoes, not being distracted by everything else.

I always found them very, very interesting, and it continued. Yes, I bought a lot of shoes, but it went further than that. It was not just, ooo, that is cute. But also, how are they made? Because they seemed kind of 3D objects, kind of complex with lots of different materials. They carry your weights; it's mostly made from 2D materials. From a technical side, I always thought shoes were interesting, and somewhere between technical and little pieces of art. And when I saw that course, I was like, let's try it, I can combine it with my job. I'm not diluting my degree. I can continue on this engineering thing. But let's explore the one thing that I wanted to study out of high school, fashion or art, my parents said no to at the time (5 years earlier). But now that I have my degree, they can't really tell me no anymore. I'm gonna do it next to a job, they don't have to pay for anything. Let's do this as well.

Aris Winger: I'm gonna unpack this because this is important to me and someone reading this now. Someone who may feel stuck in the thing. They've been in engineering. And to your point, they have the family members, the grandfather, the heroes who say, do engineering. I want to go to this moment where, for some reason, you're not boxed in. You don't look at the ad and say, No, I'm an engineer, I can't, I can't. What is it? Because it also sounds like this has always been a part of… the fashion, the shoe piece, that has been a part of something you've been interested in for some time, and so does this ad awaken the possibility of that? Does it provide an avenue for you? Somehow, all the training and engineering doesn't hold you back and keep you in this box for some reason.

Katrien Herdewyn: No, I think one of the reasons that it was smooth was that I could do it in parallel somehow, because I did feel scared, being like, let's drop this engineering thing, which is a safe degree that will get me a job and a stable job that everybody around me thinks I should do. I'm also not bad at it. And even society looks up to engineers mostly, and to drop it for a creative path. Generally, people are a little bit skeptical about what you are doing with your life. Where is this going? But the fact that I could do it in parallel, or figure some stuff out in parallel, made it somewhat of a safe transition. I don't think that if I hadn't had that option, if it were, let's not work for another 4 years, because the footwear design degree is also 4 years. I'm not sure I would have done it. But because I had that safety, I was let's try it. And like I said before, I'm naturally somebody who's always doing a bit of pros and cons and risk analysis. It was like, there is not that much that can go wrong doing this. It's also year by year. If after the 1st year, I notice this is really not for me, or I'm really bad at this, or I can't combine this with my job. And my job is at risk. I'm at risk of losing that or my position at the university, but then I can always stop it.

Aris Winger: That's helpful. So now you apply and you get accepted. And now you're doing both at the same time.

Katrien Herdewyn: Yes, and that was a very rough 4 years, because that was my whole life. Everybody who's ever done research at university. It's a lot of work. They also expect a lot from you. I also had to teach because there was a shortage of teaching assistants. There were many different things. I had to do measurements for companies. There were many different things on top of my research. Full days, definitely full days at work, and then in the evenings and on the weekends, at night, I was learning how to make shoes. Which is also the designing part of it, but also the physical part of it. There is also sanding that comes into it, and using hammers and nails, etc. I've literally had blood, sweat, and tears because of it.

My fingers were bleeding on many occasions, not because of my research, but because of what I was doing for the Art Academy, but maybe because I didn't have much time outside of it. I think one, when you do research in the university, you kind of stay in your environment, that is the same environment as studying with your friends who are all close, everybody lives close. You don't have to put that much effort into maintaining your friendships because most people still live in that city, and you bike everywhere. So there is that University town vibe that you have. It's not that I did not have a social life. My social life was happening over lunch with my friends who also worked on campus. But then, the pure focus on those 2 only, and not having any more distractions. I would hardly ever go on vacations.

4 years of only being in that really marinated me into 2 fields, and they immediately kind of started intertwining in those years. And I think it's mostly because that was my focus the whole time. I immediately really loved footwear design, but my engineering degree immediately came into my footwear designs as well. The 1st shoes I designed, I had a book full of sketches, and an equally big book full of calculations of the heel's angle, shape, and geometries. Experimenting with how far we can go so that you can have dynamic and static stability.

I was immediately using that, also in the materials that I was trying to use, experimenting with things that were really not made for shoes, and still using them in footwear. It immediately came together. In my research, I guess it didn't come together or didn't flow over as much, except for the fact that I was doing a lot of microscopy. But at the atomic scale, atomic force microscopy and the images that I was seeing were more than once an inspiration. Because for me, yes, there is science there, and you're trying to figure out what it is, and you're trying to create a certain structure at the nanoscale. But it's also just pretty. And even on many occasions, you create something that wasn't supposed to be there. But it still looks very pretty. So a lot of those images ended up being an inspiration for some of the designs that I was making to work in both directions. Less literal in the directions from the shoes towards the science, than from the science towards the shoes, but they definitely immediately intertwined, and it only grew over the years. In my 3rd year, at the Art Academy, which is also the 3rd year of my research. My collection was literally about how different elements, like oxygen and carbon, etc, how they manifest in different forms, as you go to different structures, like the hexagon ring or diamonds, and then use all of those, combine all of those structures in a footwear design. I had different elements like germanium, silicon, oxygen, and carbon were the 4 shoes in that collection I used as an inspiration.

Aris Winger: And how are the people in the Art Institute? Are they engineers? You're bringing engineering there? How are they reacting when you're bringing engineering over there? Are they receptive? Are they like, what are you talking about?

Katrien Herdewyn: Both. They're definitely like, I don't get this at all, but they also think it's fascinating. I feel a lot of what some engineers lose is that feeling of magic because you're trying to figure everything out, and you don't look at anything anymore as, that's magical. People in art, most of them, really love science. Most of them don't understand it, but they find it magical and very interesting, and they try to understand it. But it's nice being between the 2 fields, because they still have that sense of wonder, and I feel artists, even more than people in most jobs, are very curious and wonder a lot. So having the 2 feeling something, that's normal to me. And then experiencing them, like Wow, that's very interesting. Or they ask questions you might not ask yourself anymore because they come from different places. So, they were definitely encouraging towards it. Obviously, when there was the whole book of calculations, they had no interest in looking into that. They wouldn't open it. They didn't even try anything there, but they appreciate the end result of it coming with a heel that doesn't look like you can walk on it, and then you can walk on it.

Aris Winger: That feels magical.

Katrien Herdewyn: Yes.

Aris Winger: After these 4 years, then what?

Katrien Herdewyn: I loved working in the 2 fields and wasn't ready to give up either. After those 4 years of studying footwear design, I learned that I did not want to be a footwear designer.

Aris Winger: What would have been missing if you had gone in that direction? What would you have missed that you couldn't let go of?

Katrien Herdewyn: Not wanting to sound degrading, but it's a pretty monotonous type of cycle. It's a very fast cycle, the fashion industry. You have to gather inspiration, gather materials, and then you design, which is usually about 10% of the time. And then you go defend those designs, you take in trends, etc. So for me, it wasn't challenging enough, knowing that you have to do that cycle at least twice a year. In most places, it's four times a year. You're going through the same thing over and over again. While definitely when you're in school, you push boundaries, once you go into a commercial setting, you need to make things that are for everybody, or that adhere more to what's been on trend and what will sell.

For me, it was less exciting. I like fixing problems, solving problems, figuring things out, and experimenting with new materials. I didn't feel the job market. There were a few companies that were doing fun things, but even their commercial part of it always takes over. So, if I only did that, I knew I would miss a part of the research, engineering, or science. I already noticed that I loved working on shoes when I was studying. But I also liked stepping away from it and focusing more on fixing problems or creating stuff, being in the lab and making reactions rather than creating shoes.

Also, when you work in shoe design, obviously, the practical part, you're not physically making anything anymore. A factory is doing that. It would be mostly drawing, designing. So I knew it wasn't really 100% what I wanted to do.

Also, realizing that I'm glad my parents made me first do university, because I think it would have been a lot less likely that I would have studied footwear design and then gone on to study engineering, or something else. It was definitely the right order for me. But also not wanting to give it up completely, I was very fascinated by the potential of science and engineering and everything that's been developed in that industry. That impact is still developing. The fashion industry doesn't pay a lot of attention to engineering developments early on.

We also have to make a historical shoe at the Art Academy, and you notice that shoes have been made the same way for a hundred years. We've replaced some people with robots and natural materials with synthetic ones, but overall, the construction of a shoe, the way it's made, is pretty much the same.

Then, working in and having a background in nanotechnology, you work in the future, the next 30 years in semiconductors always felt like a little weird combination. I felt there was a lot of opportunity. The rest of the world might not have seen it that way, because fashion techs didn't really exist at the time, but I really saw opportunities, plus I didn't want to have to give up either. It made me decide to either try to find a job in it, which was really hard, because there are very few companies. I think if I had grown up in the Bay Area, I might have gone into that field. But in Europe, and Belgium specifically, but in bigger Europe, nothing was moving in fashion tech at the time (2014). There were no real job opportunities. That's when I decided, let's just try this and start a company that combines the two.

Aris Winger: Let's stay here for a moment. You're recognizing that you're in this intersection. You may be the only one in this intersection. Tell me about the emotions behind it. How does that happen? How do you start a company?

Katrien Herdewyn: I think I have a backup plan similar to my earlier thoughts. I have a degree in engineering. I also have a degree now in footwear design, which offers more freelance opportunities. If this doesn't work, I still have options. I have very little debt. No responsibilities. Not married. Don't have a house. Don't have any children. I have a lot of freedom at that time to take the risk and see, and if it doesn't work, I have a foundation that I can fall back on, which I know is a big luxury that not everybody has.

I decided… It was pretty impulsive for me, not being the most impulsive person, but more seeing… If my contract with the university hadn't ended after 4 years, it would have been harder, too. But I didn't have a job anymore. Your contract just ended. I knew I didn't want to stay in Academia. I wasn't going to do a postdoc to drag this out. I have my degree in footwear design. It's really at the point of either you go apply for a bunch of jobs or you start your own company, and both of them sound equally hard to do.

During my four years at the university, I noticed that I can work really hard if I love something, but if I don't, I quickly move into almost burnout feelings of not seeing a reason to do any of it, feeling like a little cog in a big wheel.

So I knew my best chance was to work passionately. I've also always been convinced that it's very important that what you do you absolutely love, and what you love should be what you spend your most time on. Doing that in a job is not always easy. You can do it on the side or find a combination of the two.

But for me, as a twenty-seven-year-old at the time, I was still naive enough to give it a try. I was going to find that passion in what I do every day. That's why I started the company. It didn't need that much. I needed quite a lot of money, not compared to Bay Area standards, but in general, I needed about 120k to survive the time between starting a company and having my first product on the market. I used a loan and the money I'd saved over the four years of working to start that. I felt the financial risk was fairly limited.

Aris Winger: And what was the goal of the company? What's the mission?

Katrien Herdewyn: I started out because I specialized in nanotechnology and footwear. I wanted to first create a footwear label that integrated nanotechnology, but also other engineering. We wanted to engineer a shoe 2.0, not for athletic wear, but for shoes that we wear day to day. I started with women's shoes, mostly stilettos and heels. These are shoes where a lot of discomfort has been around forever. It's very hard to find people who enjoy wearing heels. They don't have to be that uncomfortable. I started with solving those problems, for example, using nanotechnology in the leather of the shoes to make them water- and dirt repellent. We integrated the lotus effect in the shoes. That's named after the lotus flower, which stays immaculately clean even in the dirtiest pools. You add tiny little pillars on a surface, and in the case of leather… The problem with leather is that it's like our skin. It absorbs water, and you can put a bunch of sprays on it and treat it, but the sprays wear off, and water in the form of rain, snow, or mud ends up damaging the leather. We're not really evenly protecting the leather with those sprays. The places where it's sensitive, which are at the bottom of your shoe, where the leather goes under the outsole, or where the leather flexes when you walk, those wrinkles, that's where your leather is extra soft. If you put layers on top of it in the form of a spray or coating, that's where they break. That's where the water and everything that's dissolved in it will damage it more. Over time, it makes your sole come off the shoe.

I wanted to use nanotechnology to put those tiny pillars evenly over the surface. We attach them covalently to the fibers, and they are close enough together that water can't really get to the fibers. It constantly stays/balances on top of the pillars. And you create a hydrophobic surface that way. But the pillars are positioned far enough apart on the leather fibers that your fibers are still elastic, flexible, and breathable, which are good leather qualities. It's used in construction. It's used in airplane toilets, in the car industry. It's a well-known and studied phenomenon. It's even used on fabrics. But the challenge with leather is that every skin is different. It's not just every skin, but even across the skin. There is no uniformity. The places around the neck, the paws, the back. It's all different. It was really an optimization process, together with the tanning process, to get the amount of active groups at the spacing, then at the pillars, and an extra step of the tanning process, to then have leather that would withstand rain and snow and all those kinds of stuff, and still be soft and flexible.

But another reason why I wanted to use it is that I could use much softer leather. Traditionally, we use quite hard leather in shoes, and then it's covered with layers. It protects the shoes from rain. But that's also why you will get blisters when you put a lot of pressure on your feet. The material you place your foot in is hard and causes friction. You will get that feeling when you break in a shoe, which you shouldn't have to feel, because of all the layers that are there to protect it. When you break in a shoe, you are forcing all those hard layers to shape to your foot, using your foot as the mold.

With nanotechnology, we could use glove leather. The reason normally glove leather isn't used is that it doesn't survive the production process. The shoe production process. It absorbs too much of the oils and the glues from making the shoe. But now, because of those pillars, we could avoid those absorption problems and use much softer leather to make the shoes, resulting in much more comfortable shoes. Other examples of re-engineering shoes: our patterns are algorithmically optimized to reduce the amount of waste that we have in the leather. Or our heel for the stiletto is specially designed. It is always positioned perfectly; you can walk on a stiletto, but it feels like a big heel. We went through a complete redesign of the shoe, and I wanted to do it that way because in the four years that I studied, I've realized in the fashion industry that if you want to create improvements, you have to show how it's done. I see a lot of engineering companies already at that point, coming up with really cool materials, and I was trying to use them in shoes. But you can't convince most fashion houses to use things if they haven't seen it in a product on the market being sold. For me, that was the strategy. I always thought further than a shoe label. But I felt a shoe label was one good way to work with the factories, the same factories that also work with brands Hermes and Chanel, Dior, etc. It is in that same high-end fashion where they do investments in those types of things.

But at the same time, show it in a real product, and not try to convince them that they should use this heel because it's better than what they're using. It made me learn much more about the process as well.

I think what I experienced during both engineering and footwear design is when you have to do/use it yourself. You can create almost anything on paper. You can create whatever you want, and you can make it work. But it's not until you put it into practice, and you try to create it yourself end-to-end. You get to limitations. I think that was also an important step, or a feeling. I need to go through this process myself to figure out if I can do it, if possible, before I can try to push this on a larger commercial scale or expand it further.

But the idea was always a fashion tech company. The name of the company is Elanano, which is the words elegance and nanotechnology smashed together. It was broader than this is a footwear label, or this is my shoe label. But starting with a specialization in footwear or elegant products in general, and then nanotechnology, because it was more my specialty, I felt that doing things at a small scale at the time was very nice to integrate with fashion. Fashion is a very visual industry. People are not waiting for moving shoulder pads or shoes that light up in certain conditions. It's a cool gadget. But I was interested in fixing problems within the industry, and I felt nanotechnology as a field was good because it's pretty invisible. You can still change the properties of the material at that scale. Now we do much broader than Nano, but it's still a very small part of it.

Aris Winger: Now that you're out of school and operating day to day, if you could infuse your undergraduate training with some of the skills that you need to operate every day, what would you have wished that you had learned, or that you have been taught?

Katrien Herdewyn: It's a difficult one to learn, I think, but it is a skill that I feel myself and the engineers that I work with struggle with. They teach you how to think in a certain way, and it's a great way to think. I think that's the biggest skill you get as an engineer. It's the way.

Aris Winger: What way is that?

Katrien Herdewyn: The way you approach problems. The way you learn how to reason, try to solve it, break it into smaller problems, and go into each of them methodically, no matter what the field. You're attacking a problem.

I feel I also do it on the business level. I also do it on a personal level. And I notice the engineers that I work with do the same thing. I think most of us engineers already have that naturally, and then it solidifies as you go through your studies. But most people do not approach problems that way, and don't think that way, especially in what I do.

I need to work with a lot of people who do not think that way or do not work that way. When I work with engineers, it's super easy to work with them, because you're thinking in the same way. But it's such an important skill to learn to communicate, and follow the thinking of the people who don't work, or don't reason in that way. I think that's a skill that is not about explaining your problem, because we get plenty of assignments that require a good presentation, laying out how you're doing this.

It's more problem-solving together with people that do not think that way, because we've very much made the world into engineers being the ones who are solving the problems that other industries have. But we may not understand the problem in the same way they do. I usually combine designers, fashion designers, and footwear designers with engineers, and you very quickly see that they're not understanding. Designers, footwear, and fashion designers ask good questions, but the engineers do not get the questions. They're not interpreting it in a way to then come to the solution. You're communicating on different wavelengths.

Finding a way to have engineers venture into different fields, more from during their degree. Have them work with lawyers, have them work together with arts majors, etc, to learn more about how to grasp problems from other industries and try to come up with solutions themselves from that problem, not when it's already completely digested for you. Digest it yourself. Try to ask the questions to people who do not think the way you do.

Aris Winger: You're dialed in a hundred percent at your company? There's nothing on the side?

Katrien Herdewyn: I'm starting a second company, but it's in the same kind of space, and now it's still under the umbrella of the 1st company.

Aris Winger: What does the next ten years look like? Do you have a vision now for the company?

Katrien Herdewyn: I have to say… The world is in a lot of flux, and I feel I've always operated in a field that moves a lot. You can't really predict necessarily how things are going to go or what new things will be developed. And with Elegnano, I've really set up a company that's inherently flexible. The first 2 years were pretty normal in establishing a label. It was mostly focusing on getting that rolling and making sure that it was running itself, working with the factories. But after that, I started working more and more with other companies to innovate, to work with both tech companies and fashion companies, where we would do projects to combine the two. And that's been moving forward more and more. The company is now 10 years old, and about a year ago, one of those ideas kind of turned into We should create a separate company focusing on that. That's, for me personally, an additional step.

I think it's very much my personality and my engineering background that I want to constantly work on new things and create new things. My goal has never been to make a footwear label and then try to sell it in every single store across the world. I want to improve on that product. That's also what we do, even the shoes that we have, we treat them as tech products. We take the data back, we improve it. And we put new versions of that same shoe on the market. It's keeping that mindset alive that has given me a lot of freedom, and keeps me engaged and excited about what I do every day. It is a little bit of a puzzle to do that and be profitable at the same time, because you have to make money too.

For me, moving forward, I think what's mostly come in is the sustainability aspect. I think learning from being in the industry for so long, working with factories, seeing everything that's happening, being a little bit frustrated with how the industry has responded to the COVID pandemic, when they really had a chance to reset and didn't do it, went straight back to their old ways. I feel there are a lot of opportunities there. I think initially, it was combining fashion and tech. The last 2 years, it's been more and more for sustainability reasons. How can we use tech to make what we wear more sustainable? We don't do projects for fast fashion companies. Those became values, the sustainability aspect. We don't want to contribute to making the problem even worse. That's also a major focus: improving, creating new materials that we can use in the footwear industry, supporting efforts into setting up experiments, optimizing those materials, and seeing where we can make some of the research that's being done sometimes for the military or athletics. We can bring that into day-to-day footwear. How would that look? How can we improve that? That's been the focus more and more. Now, I go to fashion week each half year, and that's also the focus every time, the materials we look at and experiment with in our prototypes. How can we integrate electronics for optimization and new materials? This is the main focus.

Aris Winger: Excellent, there are three more questions. Tell me about stepping into being the leader, the one, the visionary for the company. How easy was that? Was that something that you were passionate about? All of a sudden, you look around, and people are looking at you for what to do next. How did you step into being the leader?

Katrien Herdewyn: I think it grows gradually. We're still only 15 people. So it's not like it's a big team that I need to lead. I think one of my problems in the early days was that I didn't really... At the time, I was 27. I'm also a woman who dresses in skirts, and I am not what people envision when they think, Oh, that person has started a company. Or that person has something to say.

I noticed that often when entering a room or attending trade shows and conferences. People were always asking who is in charge here, or treating me as the secretary.

But the transition into more of a leadership role really started when I came to the United States in 2017. I received a grant from the Belgian royal family, with which you can go anywhere in the world as long as it's outside of Europe. And that's how I ended up here. That's how I know, Kyle. And it's really here that I was pushed towards stepping into a leadership role. One, because I moved here by myself, and then I was placed in a culture that is much more open and "loud". In Belgian culture, it doesn't matter who you are or what age you are; you tend not to speak unless you're given the word. People ask you a question, and you answer that question. You don't volunteer to say something. So even in meetings with clients or going after business. I was a leader, but I was a leader in that framework of what society or culture accepts from you and expects from you. It was working, but it wasn't very effective. Doing it the way you do it here. If you implement that in Europe, it will open more doors. It does get you further, you can manage being the nice, in your place person, but it is definitely more effective to go out, sometimes rub people the wrong way, or make them realize things on the spot. And so I definitely learned that here. I don't think my personality necessarily changed. But the way I communicate and the way I bring it out changed a lot, and that helped me in Italy, doing business there, here, doing business. I don't think I would have been able to even do business in the United States with my Belgian mentality.

People wouldn't have responded to it at all. So I 1st had to learn that, and then notice that it does work across. So that's more, a leader to the outside. As far as being a leader to the people that I work with. I feel I'm still somebody who doesn't really lead through authority… I want to surround myself with people who know more than I do and are better than I am at stuff, to get whatever they need to fix. I want to know enough of something that I understand what they're doing. But I don't need to be a specialist on something. I also don't like being the specialist on something. I want to know it to a certain level of depth. And for me, that has worked. The people that I work with respect me, but they also know they can say anything - there is room for their own ideas, but I'm also not positioning myself above them. I am positioned among them, and I know that it is possible because of the low number of people, too. I know, once you get to a very big company, hierarchy becomes much more important, or you need to create that structure. But I created the company in a way that it doesn't really need it that much. I hire people who are very passionate about what they do. I think that's a pro of being in the field that I am, and what we do is that there are so few people in it, and the people that do, like, nobody is doing this because they know there are a lot of job opportunities in it, or it pays well. People are doing it because they love doing it. So it's easier to find people who work in it who are really passionate about it. If you get to work with passionate people, it's very easy to be a leader of people who are very passionate about their job.

So I think my main qualities as a leader are finding the right people and knowledge, understanding people, having a good gauge of when I meet somebody, if this will be a good person to work with or not, or if somebody who would work. I think that's my main talent as a leader.

Aris Winger: Thank you. Lots of what you said leads into my other question about navigating men in general in engineering, a male-dominated field. And we imagine again, there are some young women who are reading this now who are in a class, and there are very few women in this class with them; it could be hundreds of students. They're in study groups, or they're in projects. And they're surrounded by men. And what men bring, good and bad. And so how is it? What would you say to them now about navigating men in general? And you've already responded. Now that you're in control, you can navigate and get away from the types of things that can happen when men show up. And what would you say to them directly at this point?

Katrien Herdewyn: I wish I could say it gets better, but it doesn't.

Aris Winger: Ok, let's just tell the truth.

Katrien Herdewyn: You always will be one of a few, and I think it depends on your personality, and I guess most people that I know and me personally as, I went from just blending in and not wanting to rock the boat and not saying something when something happens to you, or they treat you in the in the not good way. To become more vocal about it. Answering. And for most people, the realization is you should answer, fight back, or when you see something or something happens to you, initially, you might freeze up, which is also what happened to me. But over time, you need to build the muscle to respond to it, or you can decide to completely accept it. But in my experience, the ones who completely accept it end up leaving the engineering field.

Obviously, try to find the ones, because there are plenty that are not a problem at all. Obviously, try to find the ones. But we also know that, I think it's called a negativity bias, but if one person treats you poorly, there can be 200 that don't. It's the one that treats you poorly that will leave you stressed, and it's the story that sticks to you and will make you feel insecure, or whatever, as a result of it. Definitely try to focus on the good ones, because there's plenty of them. It's a very fun field to work in. I love working with men as much as I do with women. There is no reason to choose one over the other, and that's not merit-based. It's a personality thing, and there are as many good things in both genders.

But learning how to live with it, or how to respond with it in a way that you can live with it, and for me, that is calling it out and putting them in their place. Usually, with a little bit of humor, a lot of them will not accept it, and it might not solve the problem. But you need to learn to live with it yourself. So for me, that's become more important. For example, I stopped working with a client because of the way he responded to messages… I couldn't attend a meeting with him personally, and I had to send one of my team members, who happened to be a woman, to him, and I knew she might be strong enough, but I didn't even want her to have to deal with somebody who says and does those things. So once you get the choice, you can avoid them. But I did work with him for 6 years, and accepted it for that long, and always felt bad about it, and answered, but a lot of people don't learn either. It's not your responsibility either. I think that's the last one that I want to say. It's not your responsibility to raise people properly that treat you poorly, but focus on the good ones. Try to find companies or jobs where it's clear that it's not tolerated.

I think, then, the other aspect is feeling that you are just as good, or could be just as good. I noticed in my 1st year of study, and even afterwards, I said I was considered the secretary in many contexts. They are like, you should be the one who does the report and does the writing because you have nice handwriting, and that makes the presentation because you… And if you like doing that, by all means do it, but always reflect on yourself: Am I doing this because I want to do it? And is this for me, a growing opportunity? Doing something you're good at and being cut out of the things you want to learn is not a good way. In the first, let's say, 10 years of spending as an engineer, you should constantly try to learn more, including your studies.

Aris Winger: I appreciate that. Alright, 2 more questions. To be where you are right now, what have you had to sacrifice?

Katrien Herdewyn: I don't know if I would call it a sacrifice because I knew it going in. But I definitely don't have a life that is congruent with a typical… What most people aspire to have in their lives. I still don't own a house. I'm still not married. I still don't have children. I don't want any of those things. So that makes it easy. But I understand that for a lot of people, that is something they want in life. So in that sense, I might be a bad example of what you could achieve, and that you could have everything if you want as a woman, an entrepreneur, or an engineer.

I don't feel I had to sacrifice... I've definitely spent less time with friends. I spent less time traveling for vacation, but I also find, for me, not doing it in those contexts not living that typical life has learned me to give a lot of appreciation for things, like I spent 6 weeks in Italy last summer, and that was traveling mostly for work, but being in the same place for a long time, sure I haven't visited all I could. In the 6 weeks, I could have gone to 6 different countries, but my ambition is more to dive deep in one specific spot. And I think that's what I'm doing for my career. That's what I'm doing as far as traveling goes. It's what I'm doing, as far as friendships go. Yes, I've lost friends over the years because I didn't have time or spent my time in 3 different countries for my job. But I also feel that the friendships that are really worth it will stay, and the same for relationships. And yes, it's a sacrifice, but it's also by elimination you find what's really good for you, and quantity is not needed; the quality is what's there.

Also, I think, sleep. But I've always been a very light sleeper, so I don't feel I need that much sleep. But other than that, I can't really think of something I sacrificed.

Aris Winger: The final question. There are going to be lots of young people reading this. This is your opportunity to talk directly to them. Some of them might be struggling, trying to get through their degrees. They think they're in a box. Some of them may be seniors who are about to move on to the next thing. Whatever advice you want to give them, this is your time to talk to them directly.

Katrien Herdewyn: Obviously, I'm one person, and it worked for me. But I do believe, standing strong in your own values is key, and you may not know them. Honestly, I did not know my values. I took my time to figure out what I thought was really important at the age of 22 or 23 when I graduated. And it's good that you can do that in different environments. Expose yourself to a lot of different things while you're studying and in the years after. But it's always possible to switch gears.

I feel it doesn't matter what age you are. I do think it's a combination of finishing what you start, I think it's a good one, but also don't be afraid to switch gears. If you take the route that is laid out for you for 10 years, 15 years, it's much harder to get back. It's still possible at that point to get back, but the more you go along with following whatever's thrown at you, the harder it becomes to step away from it. I did that during my studies, and I did it 4 years after my studies, and I do that now, still, in my company. I wonder every single year, it's usually around December, I'm kind of wondering, what have I achieved last year? And is any of this me? Did I do this because society wants me to do this, because this is how you were a good person, leader, or engineer, or did I do this because it's me? It's because I really want it, and I care about it. And you need to find a balance between the two. But I feel that doing that from early on is a good strategy. Making sure that you can have a long career and be happy in it and feel fulfilled at the end of it.

08 - Cooper Whiteleather

SOCIALIZE WITH INTENTION & CULTIVATE RELATIONSHIPS

A person is not an island. How we succeed in the world is necessarily tied to how we relate to others. Process Development Engineer Cooper Whiteleather was keenly aware of this from the start of his undergraduate education. Making connections from day one, he built a large network of people whose support and crowdsourcing helped him navigate the challenges and questions that naturally arise along the path. He leveraged the skills needed to make these connections beyond the classroom and into a blossoming and bright career. In reading Cooper's story, you'll find it is emblematic of the Hidden Curriculum, a set of skills and ways of being that we all need to be the best problem solvers, but are never taught while sitting in a classroom.

Cooper Whiteleather

Bio-Process Engineer at Mycoworks, South Carolina

BS in Materials Science & Engineering, Virginia Tech

Hometown: Geneva, New York

Aris Winger: Welcome, Cooper. Are you an engineer?

Cooper Whiteleather: Yeah, I guess so.

Aris Winger: What does being an engineer mean to you?

Cooper Whiteleather: I guess to me it evokes ideas of problem-solving through technical and logical means. Every career involves a degree of problem-solving, but it's especially STEM-focused in engineering.

Aris Winger: And so when did you feel like you became an engineer?

Cooper Whiteleather: Oh, I don't know.

Aris Winger: Was it recently, or did you feel like one in undergrad?

Cooper Whiteleather: I don't know. It feels like you're earning your ability to call yourself an engineer, because, I guess, I've also had days at work where my title is engineer, but it doesn't feel like I'm doing engineering.

Aris Winger: What does it feel like you're doing?

Cooper Whiteleather: Like pencil whipping or documentation, or sitting in meetings and making sure people are all on the same page, feels different than what you picture.

Aris Winger: And what did you picture?

Cooper Whiteleather: I think doing a lot more math and design, and I guess decision-making around mechanical or scientific ideas. But I guess it is entering the real workforce. It's clear that most things are not just a problem of is the yield strength is enough for the application. Right? There are a lot of other factors that seem to get left out of the undergraduate experience.

Aris Winger: That is exactly why we are here talking, because there's somebody who's learning about the yield stuff you just mentioned, and it's just like, Oh, that's what it's going to be like. And you will have these deep insights into how it might be a little different. Take us back to the summer before 1st year. So you finished high school. You're about to go to Virginia Tech. Why did you choose Virginia Tech?

Cooper Whiteleather: They had a well-ranked materials engineering program. And that's what I'd kind of set my sights on doing. They are one of those 1st year general engineering programs. We don't choose our specific track, so it was kind of a gamble if I got into it or decided to do it. But they had a good reputation there and a very active undergraduate running club, not the Varsity team, but a competitive and social group of runners.

Aris Winger: Well, how'd you know about that?

Cooper Whiteleather: Social media. They had a super active YouTube channel at the time, and I guess, like Instagram and stuff, were just starting to have importance. And that was something I wanted to make sure I continued doing when I was looking at other schools. I was also curious, you know, if there were groups who were doing that.

Aris Winger: So you get to Virginia Tech. How was the transition? Course content, class size, culture, socially, the whole thing.

Cooper Whiteleather: Socially, I think, was easy because of the running club thing. I essentially kept my same schedule from high school. Study, work out with friends who all enjoy the same sort of sport, and then go study, do homework, and stuff academically. My 1st semester was my lowest GPA, which I think was indicating that I was trying to figure out how to do it, because it's a lot more self-directed, right? You meet for class a lot less frequently than in high school. And I guess that 1st year had some of those stereotypical "weed out" classes.

Aris Winger: What do you mean by "weed out" classes?

Cooper Whiteleather: I got to skip most of them because I took APs in high school, but there was a sense from the undergraduates that there were certain classes that were almost intentionally difficult. Even if the subject matter wasn't necessarily super important, or all that cognitively difficult. Just the structure of the class made it that way.

Aris Winger: Give me an example. What do you feel like was a weed-out class?

Cooper Whiteleather: One of ours was certainly intro calc for engineers. So I didn't have to take it because of calculus in high school. But it was essentially self-taught through these online modules, where you'd watch videos and then practice. And it seemed like it was a huge investment of time for those who had to take the class. And then there wasn't a lot of actual support from human beings to help the course. It was like grad students walked around a computer lab. So it seemed to be a mix of either you intuitively understood the material, and you didn't need to study that hard, or you had the grit to study and figure it out entirely on your own. Those are the kinds of people who passed, and if not, you have to go into a different major.

Aris Winger: Got it. Any feelings of imposter syndrome 1st semester, 1st year, like you might not be able to do it? You're in the wrong major?

Cooper Whiteleather: I think in my second year, I had some. I guess. I wondered if I was studying the right thing. So I looked into what they called sustainable biomaterials. And then I had some hard decision-making around what to minor in. I was really interested in fermentation. I had done some of it in high school, when we had a viticulture class. But I knew it was gonna be a huge investment of time to do that, because it didn't overlap at all with my major-required classes. And so it was a lot of conversations with parents and classmates about, like, why am I considering these other things when I have a path set out in front of me.

Aris Winger: Yeah. So, what was giving you the idea to maybe think about something else? What were the challenges?

Cooper Whiteleather: I think, reading course descriptions for courses that were outside of my major and being like this is so much more interesting than what I'm doing right now. Which is a little bit of the grass is always greener on the other side. Sort of so when you're near the throes of Diff-EQ, or something which you can't possibly imagine using. That biomaterial looks more interesting.

Aris Winger: Yeah. So I wanna talk about these throes just a little bit. So you're in it, and you're in a class. Diff-EQ, how many people are in it?

Cooper Whiteleather: Probably like 15 to 20.

Aris Winger: Okay, that's not bad. And you're like, what is the point of this?

Cooper Whiteleather: Yes.

Aris Winger: Okay, and then that means that like, wait. Maybe I could do something else?

Cooper Whiteleather: Yeah. Or it's just spending lots of hours doing theoretical things. They have no application, like it's not like you need to do this in order to unlock the ability to go do this other, more interesting class.

Aris Winger: Right. So okay, got it. But at some point, you're just like, let me just go ahead and knock this out. How many classes were there like that for you?

Cooper Whiteleather: It's a good question.

Aris Winger: Percentage-wise, were like half the classes were like that?

Cooper Whiteleather: Probably like 5 to 10% of the classes, to be honest. But it was in that critical sophomore year where stuff is actually starting to get hard, and you're not past the point of no return, like you could switch. And still graduate on time. And so when all of those hit at once, it's all the math classes that feel pointless at the time, and then maybe, like a hard lab, or something like that.

Aris Winger: I'm glad you said that, because again, we can imagine 1st years, and maybe sophomores, reading this. Unpack the, when things start to get hard, piece. What does that mean? Does that mean more courses are happening, and they're at a higher level?

Cooper Whiteleather: Yeah, I think some of it is probably imposter syndrome. Like you mentioned earlier, that's when things get really hard and you're actually starting to be challenged.

Aris Winger: Does that mean that you're hearing material that you haven't heard of before, or is it just a lot at one time, or all of it?

Cooper Whiteleather: Yeah, probably all of it. Maybe it's a huge assignment, and it's gonna take you several hours to complete, even if it's easy. Or maybe it's really just 2 or 3 questions. But you're going to have to pore over every inch of your notes and work with classmates who took better notes than you. And that can be daunting when you start to worry if you have the right skills. Which I think, having gotten through it. It's like, of course, you don't have the right skills. That's why you're taking the class.

Aris Winger: Yeah.

Cooper Whiteleather: Yeah, and then adding on to that is, if you have friends who are in different majors, *and you should try to have friends who are in different majors*, and if they're not also going through the same crucible at that time, and they're able to go to more sporting events, or go to the movies, or, do more social things… It can be very, you know, either jealousy or you start logistically considering, Would it be better for me to go into some other major, that my friends make look objectively easier.

Aris Winger: Because they make the grass look greener for sure.

Cooper Whiteleather: Yeah.

Aris Winger: Yeah, sure, they're smiling and having a great time in a different major.

Cooper Whiteleather: Yeah.

Aris Winger: Okay, so you mentioned something. I wanna just make sure I understand, you had mentioned these classmates that you were working in working groups with. I wanna unpack that. Talk a little bit about working with other people. How helpful was that? Might you even say that having other classmates working in study groups was necessary? You could have done it by yourself. But how much easier did it make it to have classmates and study groups?

Cooper Whiteleather: I think it makes it, certainly easier from getting the work done standpoint. Not to say that you're cheating or dividing questions. The ability to bounce ideas off of and make sure that if my logic for this problem makes sense to the other people, we probably all got it somewhat correct. Then even if you're getting the answers wrong, at least emotionally, you have people to commiserate with. Right?

Aris Winger: How do you find these people? How did you find your study groups?

Cooper Whiteleather: That's a good question.

Cooper Whiteleather: No matter what method you use to do it. You have to take the social initiative, or at least be willing to say yes, if somebody invites you to study. I think in very few cases was it structured where the university was telling you to study with certain people. But yeah, I mean, you do it like they were friends from clubs, or like the running club specifically, who are also 1st year, second-year engineers, and we were all in the same class. So it's when you meet those people and you're already friends. And then you happen to have something which you're all struggling with on a different topic. It's easier to come together. I think the harder thing is getting from just directly from the classroom to a study group.

Aris Winger: Yes. And have you done that?

Cooper Whiteleather: I have, but I don't remember if it was like the person I'm sitting next to in class, and it's like, Hey do you want to study on this day, or if it was more so, like, we worked on a group project last semester so we had a tendency to be more social with one another.

It wasn't the school saying or structuring a means for you to study with other people. You kind of had to figure it out on your own, but I don't know that I would want the school to prescribe that, like, would it end up with the same development of your social skills if it was just like, here's a group of 4 people? Go do your homework with them.

Aris Winger: Yeah, I don't even think we're suggesting that a school would do it. It's just that a student needs to be aware of these types of skills. You need to socially connect.

Cooper Whiteleather: Yes, certainly important.

Aris Winger: Okay. So, now you're rolling through sophomore year, things start to get hard, and then, is there a moment where? After which you're just like, Okay, I'm finishing this thing. Is there ever any smooth sailing? What are the challenges that are happening for you in undergrad?

Cooper Whiteleather: Yeah, I think after the big Gen. Ed engineering stuff was complete, sophomore second year-ish. By then, I'd spent at least a year with the same people in my classes, because we were now assigned to the same major. My major had about 70 people in each graduating class. And so then it became a lot easier. You'd have group chats. We had a Discord server for specific classes. So it was a lot easier to propagate advice or information from the study group that went to office hours and talked to the Professor about this question that everybody's been wondering about. Now, like clarification from that, it has now bubbled through the entire cohort. So certain logistical things like that, and understanding how to study, and which of your study spots on campus were the most productive for you. That starts to get figured out and ironed out.

Aris Winger: How is it that you learned how to study? Is studying different from high school?

Cooper Whiteleather: Yeah. High school was a lot of just doing the work right. You have to read a book chapter for English class and then fill out an assignment about it. Versus what it felt like in college was that a lot more of the actual discovery of the knowledge, or internalization of the knowledge, had to happen outside of the classroom.

Aris Winger: Yeah. And so, how did you end up making this switch transition?

Cooper Whiteleather: I guess it was like a necessary evolution of if you don't figure out how to use your notes and the textbook to answer homework problems and like test problems. Then you probably didn't make it this far. I don't know if that was tips from other people, or if it's kind of natural that if you don't know the answer, you flip open the textbook to that chapter. And I guess. Yeah, I'm not quite sure how you learn that if that was structured or not.

Aris Winger: It feels like you're amongst this community of common majors running 70 deep. So are you all competing with each other or not? Does it feel competitive to you?

Cooper Whiteleather: It didn't feel competitive at Virginia Tech. At least not in the majority of the classes, I think, like senior design, we were actively competing, but that was much later. But no, it didn't feel competitive, really.

Aris Winger: Okay. So then, you're getting close to finishing junior year and senior year. You're thinking about the future. What's happening?

Cooper Whiteleather: Yeah. What was going on there…

Aris Winger: Don't act like it was that long ago.

Cooper Whiteleather: It was such a blur. At least in my program. By the time you hit your 3rd year. You've gotten most of the pure math, science, and that sort of stuff out of the way. So, being in material science, we had specific classes, distinct courses of materials or metallurgy class, and a polymer class. So Junior year was typically when you worked through all of those. Which I think helped people dial into what they were interested in. Once we hit between your 4th semester and your 6th semester, people had started to segregate themselves into, like, these are the people who really enjoy metallurgy, and these are the people who do ceramics, so that even more greatly kind of subdivided the cohort into groups.

Aris Winger: And you were coming into which identity?

Cooper Whiteleather: I knew I didn't like metallurgy. But I was interested in polymers, and I was also taking green engineering as a minor and so I was kind of mixing those two ideas a lot, and I think that was a really good way to kind of push a progression. You went from general engineering to material science to a certain class of materials, and then by senior year, you had to have a senior design project figured out, so that it was an application of a certain class of materials. Which made a lot of sense both in the moment and looking back, like, that's probably the way you should do it.

Aris Winger: So there was something that you had mentioned about getting support, resources from your classmates in one other group. But you hadn't mentioned direct mentors. Are there any faculty members? Anybody who was helping you along the way that you could point to?

Cooper Whiteleather: Good question. We, as a department, had a departmental lounge with tables, and people would go study there or sit in between classes because it was closer to the lecture halls than the library was. And occasionally, professors would wander through there. But that was also where our advisors had their offices. So if you had a question, that was like a very easy place to go. And they tend to know, like when the big historic assignments are coming through. Professor 'A' is really hard. The Second exam is like, Oh, it's almost time for that. You guys really need to study, and it's also.

Aris Winger: Oh, wow! That's useful!

Cooper Whiteleather: Yeah, or like getting mixed in with folks from other graduating classes. The juniors and seniors are all there if you're in the lounge as a sophomore.

Aris Winger: Okay. Good.

Cooper Whiteleather: I don't think that there was a form of direct mentorship past freshman year unless you sought it out yourself. There are certain people who are always in office hours, or they're working in undergrad research on the side, and the Professor knows them better. We did have a freshman mentorship program at Virginia Tech, which you could opt into. You get paired with a second or 3rd year engineering student, and they would essentially force you to create a study group weekly. You had to meet with a bunch of other kids, and you talked about how classes were going and things along those lines.

Aris Winger: Got it. Is there anything you would change or do differently about the undergrad experience? You would do more of this, less of this. Would you do it any differently?

Cooper Whiteleather: Yeah, I should have gone to office hours more frequently.

Aris Winger: Why?

Cooper Whiteleather: I think, now, looking back, that I have not as many relationships with faculty as I could have if I'd intentionally cultivated that and spent time with them.

Aris Winger: But what did you miss out on in those relationships? What do you think you didn't get?

Cooper Whiteleather: With the few that I did build relationships with, I was able to ask them for career advice, junior and senior. Or asking about courses I should be looking to take, or certifications after college, as well as sometimes more candid feedback about a project, or an assignment you did. And instead of the transactional kind of here's a lecture you take notes on. You give me an assignment. I give you a number back, and you know, back and forth until you get a grade. So I should have been more intentional about relationship building, which is another one of those social aspects that is not as emphasized as it should be.

Aris Winger: Was this because you just hadn't considered it, you didn't need to, or because you were nervous to do it?

Cooper Whiteleather: I think a lot of it was that I didn't feel I needed it to get the grades I was comfortable getting. So if you enter it with a mindset of I'm here to get a certain GPA I'm proud of and get a diploma and leave, you're missing a big part of it. And I think I did miss some of that experience.

Aris Winger: That's good. No, that's powerful. So now you're in senior year. Are you applying for jobs? And do you know what you want to do? Or you're applying everywhere? What's happening there?

Cooper Whiteleather: Yeah, I'd had a couple of internships, which now I don't think are representative of real work after college. But at the time, who knew? Oh! And I remember feeling, Senior year, that I had kind of boxed myself into having to work in the manufacturing industry, because all of my internship experience was in manufacturing. And I had not cultivated relationships with a heavy R&D Professor, or done a true undergraduate research and development project, or anything like that. So it felt like I'm technically sound. But I've only worked in industry. So my best bet for full-time job applications is the industry.

Aris Winger: Got it.

Cooper Whiteleather: Which, I guess, if you know in college that you definitely want to do a certain thing, then you don't need to diversify, but I think it may have been wise to build my resume in a more well-rounded way.

Aris Winger: And so they have different types of internships?

Cooper Whiteleather: Yeah, which sometimes is out of your control. You know you can't build a well-rounded resume just by what you apply to. It's what you get accepted to, but I certainly could have tried harder to do maybe one summer, instead of working for a company or a lab at Virginia Tech. But yeah. Who knows? Maybe I would be in the same position, saying, I wish I had, you know, intentionally focused all on one thing right.

Aris Winger: Right. Okay. So then you get the job that you're working at now.

Cooper Whiteleather: Yes.

Aris Winger: Okay, and what do you do today?

Cooper Whiteleather: Today, I am named as a process engineer for a manufacturing company. And what do I do? I essentially own the execution of the process for a certain portion of the company. But the process and design for the value-added steps are determined by someone from more R&D or process development-focused groups.

My responsibility is largely to execute those things and ensure they happen in a cost-effective and manpower effective fashion.

Aris Winger: So now we're here. What do you wish Virginia Tech had taught you that you're discovering today? If you could dream, and the answer to this is probably tied to when you're just like, wait, I wish I had been taught this..

Cooper Whiteleather: Yeah, I think again on the theme of social stuff, which is maybe both difficult to teach, and nobody is teaching it, like the study groups that you cultivate yourself. You are all essentially doing the same work, like it's 4 people. So you have 4 times as many man-hours occurring while you're studying.

Aris Winger: Yeah.

Cooper Whiteleather: But in the end, you've just produced 4 relatively similar copies of the same thing, right? It's still homework number one, with the same 10 questions. And maybe my work looks a little different. But we probably checked that. The formulas we were using are the same in group projects that are assigned to you by the school. There's a little bit more diversification of workload, right? It's like, maybe this person is writing the intro to the research paper. And this person's doing a certain calculation and writing up that, and doing the conclusion, and whatever, but you still all have the same goal and usually share the same grade.

Suppose it's a group project for entering the working world. You still have to work alongside people in a group project or a study group. But your goals are almost never the same, and I guess, like the end result of completing that work together is not equally distributed. If that makes sense, you could have several meetings about executing a project in your company. And half the people in those meetings will have no actions or like work to do.

Aris Winger: Oh!

Cooper Whiteleather: Right, there'll be an action plan. And it's 90%, all for one person.

Aris Winger: Oh, okay. Have you been that one person sometimes?

Cooper Whiteleather: Yes, yes, yeah.

Aris Winger: Okay.

Cooper Whiteleather: Which is fine. Suppose you intend to be the executor of things, because that is within your skills or experience. But it does create a different dynamic when you're working with those groups, right?

Aris Winger: Yeah. So I just wanna make sure. You're in a room with 8 other people, and they're all talking about something that's 90% You?

Cooper Whiteleather: Yes, and I guess the way we would phrase that would be like. If you're the person executing a project or an experiment, you have to do the majority of the actual physical, intellectual work. But you have to make it work for all the stakeholders of multiple departments. And that is not practiced in the classroom setting.

Aris Winger: Even in the Senior year, the design course, even that senior year course. They didn't do that.

Cooper Whiteleather: Even then, I think it felt a little more balanced, I guess, like we had an advisor who was one of the professors. But he was both like our supplier and our main stakeholder. What they are providing by way of "funding" is advice, and what they expect of you is the project result in June.

Aris Winger: So even for that, professor, who might be reading this, they might wanna just go ahead and bring in 3 or 4 other people just to make it feel like it's a real thing, right?

Cooper Whiteleather: Yeah. And maybe it's outside of that specific professor's control, like our group was. And our work was entirely based on the ideas of the students, and we had a deliverable that you had to provide to the professor. Still, I know there were other research groups within our major and outside our major, who are actually working with like an industry stakeholders. Where it was like, you're essentially gonna do some calculation or modeling, and they were gonna use it in their factory or R&D department. Probably a more realistic experience, though probably still tame for students.

Aris Winger: So I wanna go back. At some point, this happens the 1st time, right? Like, you're sitting in this space, and you have the stakeholders around, and they're talking to you about your work and what they want from it. How are we feeling about it? Are you like, Oh, this is a lot, or I can do this, or is there any imposter syndrome now at work coming into the job?

Cooper Whiteleather: Good question. I think a lot of it at the very beginning was feeling maybe lost or a little disoriented, where it's like, I'm not sure what I'm allowed to do without explicit permission, versus what I need written approval in order to do. If it costs money, usually you need some form of approval from other people, whether it's just writing something or asking another employee to do something. What level of checks and balances exists there, because a lot of those checks and balances are either non-existent or they're very systematic and uniform in school, right? With the due date, this assignment is the same for everybody. You know what the circumstances are. You're expected to turn the homework in at the end of the week.

Aris Winger: Now, we should mention that you're working for a startup.

Cooper Whiteleather: Yes, yeah. So some stuff is more chaotic than it likely would be at a well-established company. Yes, that is true.

Aris Winger: Cause I wouldn't hope or imagine that there would be more structure in some places where you would get some guidance on that type of stuff.

Kyle Clark: So, along those lines, with these assignments that are given to you, assignments in school are homework projects. A professor is asking something of you. Now you're at work. You are effectively given an assignment, something that's asked of you. Is it still clear? I mean the clarity of when somebody says, go to Chapter 11 and do the even numbered problems from 2 to 16. That's pretty straightforward. But do you get the same kind of clarity on what you're expected to do after you receive 5 action items in the work environment?

Cooper Whiteleather: That's a good point. I think we all know the answer is no.

Kyle Clark: So then what do you do?

Cooper Whiteleather: I think when you're 1st starting out, or if it's the beginning of a project or working with a new stakeholder. It is harder to understand precisely what the next steps are. You might need to ask follow-up questions or ask someone who's been in the role longer, or something along those lines, to get clarification of what precisely exists within the demands for this action item. Then I guess the remainder of it is probably context clues and historical experience. Right? Like, you're asked for a summary of a certain kind of data, and the 1st time you do it, all you do is pull the data up in a spreadsheet in the next meeting. And people look to you for that and ask that the next time, you need to come with a chart instead of just an Excel sheet? And so that sort of trial and error and learning, whether by failing when you present those results, or by bouncing ideas off of other coworkers, is how you start to figure it out. But you're right. It's a lot more general in most aspects. Executing your assigned tasks usually involves pulling in people who weren't in that original meeting. Right? You're assigned an action item. And now, in order to get this done. I have to go talk to safety and quality and supply chain to make sure they're now aligned to the thing that I was assigned to do by these other 3 people. And I don't know how we could mimic that in the educational environment.

Aris Winger: Right.

Cooper Whiteleather: It would cost a lot and take great effort to simulate a work environment in the classroom.

Aris Winger: Now, will some of the things that stakeholders want feel like they're in conflict with one another?

Cooper Whiteleather: Certainly. Yeah. I think one of the things I see most often, which is in conflict, is like the deadline versus the volume or thoroughness of data or execution that's desired. Where, if you have a super short timeline, the easiest thing is just like a quick and dirty prototype, or like a really short experiment, which might not have a huge sample size, but gives you some early looks. And the alternative is if they need a huge sample set or a really thorough examination of some problem that's going to take more time. So if neither one of those things is willing to flex. You're probably gonna be working some overtime, or you're gonna have to just say I'm not gonna be able to deliver.

Aris Winger: Okay, so what is it that you're still trying to learn these days about being a professional? Something that you're trying to figure out?

Cooper Whiteleather: One of them is how to get coworkers or colleagues to perform upstream actions, which enable me to complete the things that have been assigned to me.

Aris Winger: So there's something about there being a lot more interdependency.

Cooper Whiteleather: Yes, certainly. I mean, interdependency is a really good word for that. In the academic environment, it's very typical for a professor to have students create an assignment. It goes straight back to the professor. Versus work is a giant chain of Somebody up here said this needs to be done, and it funnels down through several layers and branches out in order to actually complete that thing.

Aris Winger: Have you been sitting waiting for someone to finish something before you can do your part?

Cooper Whiteleather: Absolutely. Yeah. And I think the thing I'm trying to figure out how to learn is like, can I do that through social capital and like just asking alone, or at some point, is it just fundamentally necessary to go up the chain of command, or find, a means of accountability and documentation to chase people to get things done. And then that balance of where it is sometimes just more valuable to just get it done yourself, even if it's something that falls outside your role. But you are capable of doing it. There's a break-even point in there somewhere. So it's definitely one thing I wish I were better at at this moment. And then I think the other thing is like learning how to say no to assignments or projects, or I guess the inverse of that other thing. How do I get people to take action? And then also, how do I effectively dodge actions that even if they do apply to me, I don't have the bandwidth to do this at the moment?

Aris Winger: What makes that difficult? Why is that hard to do at this moment?

Cooper Whiteleather: I think it's a balance of if I want the business to do well, and I understand that this is an action that would support the business. There's a feeling that I should do this and get it done. But then you have to temper that with, if I take on this additional item, will I be able to get the other things done, which are also important for the business?

Aris Winger: Now, you brought up this whole business piece, and where does that come in? Where does allegiance to, or commitment to, the business show up? Is that from day one? Or did you figure that out? Or because there's something about you being an engineer and being successful? But now you brought up, oh, I want the business to succeed. So where did that show up? And how quickly?

Cooper Whiteleather: I guess, jumping back to my undergrad. I knew I didn't want to work at a widget factory. I wanted it to be either really interesting or important to the world or some community. So I intentionally did not apply to companies that made things that I either didn't understand or didn't really care about, and while those things are all fundamentally important for the most part, someone has to make them. But it wasn't interesting to me. And that, combined with my green engineering minor, I wanted a focus in sustainability. I have historically found it hard to work hard and be passionate about things that I don't understand the value of. And so, if the company is something I believe in, then I want to support it. Whether that's sustainability or improving the quality of life for some group of people, or lowering the cost of a very necessary product for people. So I think those are the inherent motivations, aside from just getting stuff done.

Aris Winger: That's good. But when did that feeling become clear?

Cooper Whiteleather: I think, for this company specifically, from the beginning, I was motivated by a potential sustainability aspect, and it being novel and interesting to work on. And at present, after building basic relationships with coworkers and the people who work here, they have a strong desire for the business to succeed for their benefit. As a startup, if we fail, there are people who are going to be out of a job. And I'm to some degree motivated by that. And then I think the other piece, the less selfless piece, of finding it hard to say no to action items is the personal benefit aspect of if I show I can get a lot more done. Does doing this extra work mean I get a promotion, an increase in compensation, an increase in social capital, or something along those lines? Or, if you really hate it there, it's another item for your resume, so that you can get that next job.

Aris Winger: Yeah. And so, how many no's have we said so far?

Cooper Whiteleather: Very few.

Aris Winger: Right. I know. I asked a question that requires a number, actually.

Cooper Whiteleather: Oh!

Aris Winger: Yeah, is it 1, 7, 3 out of 50? Can you count them on your hand?

Cooper Whiteleather: Yeah, probably, and then there are even ones where you say no. And the company still says, Yeah, okay, that's gonna be a yes.

Aris Winger: Right, you're under pressure, or is it fleeting? Tell me about pressure.

Cooper Whiteleather: I think a lot of it is self-imposed. And then once people see that you are putting yourself under pressure to succeed, they're willing to put more on you because they think you will get it done is one of my assumptions, and the other one is because they think it is one of your maybe personal goals.

Cooper Whiteleather: Yeah, I guess, closing up on learning how to say no to things. I think it's both learning when it's appropriate for me as an individual to say no. Like when I have too much on my plate. I did the same thing in college. I had too many clubs, classes, minors, and stuff, and you get overextended. And then, also once I've decided it's a No, how do I make that? Say no, and make it in such a way that people can't force me to take on an additional project. Neither of those is something you can negotiate in college, right? The professor decides there's a homework assignment. It's pretty hard to beat that.

Aris Winger: Right? Yeah. So it sounds like you're trying to figure out strategically, how that works? So you answered the piece about pressure. Moving forward. What are you looking to do? Do you feel like you have a plan? You want to be here for a few more years, or you're just getting your feet wet, or…?

Cooper Whiteleather: Yeah, I think it's dependent on how the next couple of months turn out, and yeah, it's gonna be a balance between Could I do better elsewhere? And then also, what does better mean? And that's some formula between compensation, learning ability, and upward mobility.

Aris Winger: Tell me about this ability to learn. How big is that for you?

Cooper Whiteleather: I think it's big now. I acknowledge there are lots of things I don't know how to do, both from a genuine technical point of view, and then also from the how-to-navigate-business point of view. In manufacturing, there are several languages that people speak in terms of continuous improvement. And I don't speak any of them right now… Things like Kaizen, Six Sigma, 6W-2H, etc, all these acronyms and different tools people use. And they're super similar between companies, because you can use the same tools, whether it's a metric wrench or a standard, they do the same thing. They're just solving problems with different dimensions. And I've not been professionally trained on any of those things, which is difficult.

Aris Winger: So these concepts were just thrown at you at some point.

Cooper Whiteleather: Yeah. And I think it's also the company figuring out what tools they want to use.

Aris Winger: Got it. Got a couple more questions for you. So, for you to be where you are now, what have you had to sacrifice?

Cooper Whiteleather: Oh, wow! What have I had to sacrifice? Most of the friends and connections I built over the last 5 years in college are geographically very far away. That's because I chose a job based on what I expected to be doing and what the company was doing, instead of prioritizing relationships and being geographically near the people who I cared about, which wasn't a factor I thought was going to be important, but I think is important.

I sacrificed the whole, making it hard to say no to things. Certainly, like health and sleep, you sacrifice a little bit, which is funny because it's the stereotypical thing to do in college, where it's like, you make bad decisions, and you work really hard. And now, in the real world, it's like, Wow, that work-life balance is a little more important.

Aris Winger: Why is that? You're like feeling it more, or cause it's why is it more important now than before?

Cooper Whiteleather: I think, because in college it feels like it's a giant community of people who are largely doing the same, where the schoolwork truly never ends, right? You just choose when you're gonna do your homework or study. And now in the "Real World", there are people who have, either by chance or by strategic alignment of their careers, gotten a better work-life balance than I have. And that seems advantageous in multiple ways.

But what else have I sacrificed? I guess those are kind of the 2 big things. Life outside of work and then geography. And now I realize I should have done that differently.

Aris Winger: Alright. Lastly, as you know, we're gonna have some people reading this who are all over the place, undergrads reading this, taking classes. You're now talking directly to them. What would you say about the engineering process? How to get through it? Being a professional? Whatever you want to tell the reader right now, get after it.

Cooper Whiteleather: Hmm… in professional life, I've kind of talked about the difficulty of saying no, and that has drawbacks to work-life balance, and being able to fully devote yourself to certain valuable projects. But I would encourage you in your undergraduate years, if you're still there, to say yes to as many things as you can. If somebody invites you to study with them or invites you to join a club, start a minor, take an extracurricular class, or something like that, say yes. Then assess, maybe after the 1st few weeks of taking this elective class or hanging out with this particular group studying, if that's something you want to do. But if you don't say yes, you don't get to make that decision later. So I think. Say yes to lots of things. The more experience you get there, the more accurate you'll be with making decisions in the future. So I highly encourage saying yes to stuff.

09 - Anthony Hinojosa

THE BEAUTY IN ENGINEERING

It only takes a moment to change your life. We can't predict what that moment will be. For Construction Engineer Anthony Hinojosa, his moment was initially annoying. Waking up to the loud noises of a new dorm being built too early every morning can rattle anyone. One day, though, he looked out of the window and saw something else: His future. In an uncompromising account of engineering as service, his story reminds us that engineers have the capacity to provide great utility in making buildings while simultaneously providing great beauty in the form of the purpose those buildings provide to communities.

Anthony Hinojosa

Project Engineer, Dustin Construction, Northern Virginia

BS in Construction Engineering & Management, Virginia Tech

Hometown: Annandale, Virginia

Aris Winger: Hi, Anthony. Are you an engineer?

Anthony Hinojosa: Yes.

Aris Winger: What does it mean for you to be an engineer?

Anthony Hinojosa: It really means being someone who is collaborative, who can problem solve, and really try to come up with innovative ideas that can try and change the way something is done. That can be something that's already been in place for many years, or things that are new and up and coming that can better somebody with either a disability or somebody who is living a normal life.

Aris Winger: What type of engineer are you?

Anthony Hinojosa: I am a project engineer for a small general contractor in construction.

Aris Winger: You mentioned this word collaborative. Tell me more about that. Tell me how collaboration shows up. Why is it important in what you do?

Anthony Hinojosa: When people think of engineering, people think about the math and the science, which it is. That is part of engineering. But you're not only doing math and science. You're not one person that's in a cramped room, that typical office space, crunching all these numbers and all that. You're ultimately collaborating with a team of people. That team could be your boss, or maybe you're the boss. You're the one who's managing this team, and you all are trying to reach whatever goal you're trying to reach.

From my earlier example, if you're making an invention for somebody who has a disability to improve normal day activities, you have to collaborate with a team because everybody is contributing to this pot, which is the goal of making that product.

Aris Winger: Take us back to the summer before you went to undergrad and your 1st year of undergrad, and how it went. How are we feeling about going into undergrad at the time? Do you feel prepared, excited?

Anthony Hinojosa: I graduated in May of 2024. I entered college in the fall of 2020 during that weird COVID period. Things were going online. I was super excited. I was ready to get going. I entered Virginia Tech as a general engineering major. I was leaning more towards the computer engineering or computer science side.

But then, after taking some general engineering courses, which helped me really understand what engineering is, I realized that computer engineering isn't really cut out for me. I knew I wanted to be an engineer. I knew I wanted my work in the future to be something that I could change and help better the lives of other people. But then, after taking a few courses, I didn't have a feeling of belonging in this type of engineering. I decided to take one more semester to think about it. It wasn't for me.

Aris Winger: Two things here. You spoke of some intro to engineering courses that gave you an idea of what engineering was about. What did those courses say? What were they? What did they cover? You're sitting in there at some point, and somebody says, Engineering involves this, and something clicks. What was that?

Anthony Hinojosa: Virginia Tech has two intro to engineering courses that you have to take, one in the fall and one in the spring.

I had the same professor, who helped me continue learning what engineering is. But the first engineering course was really going into the super basics of this is engineering. And then kind of trying to research all these engineering disciplines into what you really want to go into.

There's an assignment which was, "What are Hokie engineers?" And then in that assignment, you're supposed to explain what engineering means and then research three disciplines. I don't know how many disciplines of engineering Virginia Tech has. I believe there are eleven or twelve. You're supposed to research at least three and give yourself an evaluation.

Then the next year, it dives into a real project. It explains the engineering process that typical engineers go through when trying to accomplish goals. There is an eight-step process.

Aris Winger: Is this where you realize, oh, not computer science?

Anthony Hinojosa: During the "What are Hokie engineers?" class is when I decided computer engineering is not for me. Computer science isn't for me. And I was also taking the intro to computer science course, which I wasn't wrapping my head around.

Aris Winger: Got it.

Anthony Hinojosa: There's something else that happened during that time. During that time, I lived in a Virginia Tech dorm, and they were building a new dorm outside my dorm. It was outside my window. Every day, I would wake up to construction noises. Hammers were banging. All these different things. I would look outside and say, "Oh, can you guys please shut up. I'm trying to sleep. It's 5 am. What are you guys doing?"

But then, I grew an appreciation for it. It was my built-in alarm. I would look at it throughout the day and see the progress. There's a moment in my life where I looked outside, and it was the exact time when I was writing this, what it is to be a hokey engineer. I looked outside and saw something that would change my direction in life and what I wanted to do at tech.

What I saw was: there were people on the roof, they were doing these dangerous things, and they were doing it safely because they had personal protective equipment. But they're there. It seemed awesome. There are people on the ground. They were commanding the workers to really problem solve. They're communicating with each other. There's teamwork. And they're all doing this because there's that common goal at the end. And that common goal is something that's beautiful. They're producing this product that will better the lives of someone. That's how I view construction.

Yes, there's the bad size of construction. You can hurt the environment. But through that engineering, you can find different processes that can help with that. Also, construction is about creating community. That dorm is now finished. I believe they finished it in 2022. Now hundreds and hundreds of people gather there. They're making friends in that building. They're coming together. There are classroom spaces there. They're doing all that. It's the product you produce that's impactful. That's what I find beautiful about construction. That's what I find beautiful about engineering.

Aris Winger: Is being a construction engineer to you a form of service?

Anthony Hinojosa: I believe so. I am a project engineer with two jobs now. One of my jobs is at a park in Loudoun County, Virginia. My other job, which I spend most of my time on, is at an elementary school. It's a mosaic elementary school in Fairfax, Virginia, which is currently a renovation project. We finished the additional portion of the project. Now, we're moving on to the renovation. The reason for that is that it's an occupied school. We're working around the students, and keeping the students safe is our number one priority.

Every day, I see the students come in. They're small. They're wearing their backpacks. I see them come into this new addition we built every day. And I'm like, "Wow, I'm building these buildings that these little kids are developing, not only learning. They're making these friends, I'm sure."

That's the beautiful moment of engineering. Yes, it's stressful. Yes, there are times when I feel "Oh, man, this sucks." Why can't the kids go out somewhere else while we build this? Because they're seemingly an obstacle to what we are trying to do in building the addition.

But that's where the problem-solving of engineering comes in. The owners are making us do these extra steps. But again, that problem-solving, collaborating with a team, and producing this end result makes engineering beautiful. You're doing the service for somebody else, whether that's a younger person who's 5 years old, somebody who's my age, 22. Somebody who is 50. Who knows? You might be building a retirement home. It's all a service to people.

Aris Winger: Thank you for this. How would you characterize your first year at Virginia Tech? Were you online the whole time?

Anthony Hinojosa: There were some in-person classes. I took five classes in the fall and five classes in the spring. I believe two of my classes in the fall were in person. I took 3 online, and then the two others in the spring were in person. It was a mix of both. You had the option to do it all online.

But because of COVID, I was alone from March to August. I was feeling lonely, and at the time, I was ready for this new chapter of my life. I wanted to be in college, meeting new and different people from different backgrounds. This is another thing I think is beautiful about engineering. You're put in these teams of people that you don't know from the beginning, and at the end. You become friends with them. They bring whole new perspectives. They're from areas that you've never visited before. Sometimes they're areas that you've grown up with in your backyard.

Aris Winger: Take us through the years. How's the rest of college? .

Anthony Hinojosa: Freshman year, I would say, was a very good year for me. I made a lot of friends, but then in the second year, it became apparent who the people were that you will be spending time with the most.

But the second year. third year… Now you're diving into the fact that I need an internship. I need to learn all this whole engineering…

Aris Winger: Why? Why is that? Why are you feeling this need? Where are you getting this need from?

Anthony Hinojosa: It was because in order to get a job, you need some experience.

Aris Winger: But how did you know that as an undergrad? Where did that come from?

Anthony Hinojosa: Well, my brother is 4 years older than me. He's one of those mentors. He's given me advice as we go, particularly in life. With regard to internships, he advised me to make sure I had one, because once you have one, you can learn. Then you could use that to get another one. Use that to get another one.

Aris Winger: What does your brother do?

Anthony Hinojosa: He's an accountant for KPMG. But I would say for all majors, landing an internship is important in your undergraduate years, because it gives you that idea of what you're going into in the future.

What's my life after college? It gives you a taste of the work you're going to be doing.

Aris Winger: So you start getting this need to have an internship. How do you get one?

Anthony Hinojosa: Luckily, in construction, there aren't a lot of students who want to go into construction.

Aris Winger: Just to clarify, do you want to start construction after this first year class, after looking out the window? At the point you are sold?

Anthony Hinojosa: This is interesting. I was researching it for my Wannabe a Hokie Engineer assignment. You're allowed to pick three areas. I said to myself, "Let's have a wild card. Let's throw it in there."

Then I kept researching it. Even after I turned in my assignment, I was still searching for what construction engineering majors do throughout the day. What jobs can you go into? What do those jobs entail? What's a day-to-day? I'm searching up all these videos, reading all these different things about this major, and after college life. Then I realized: This is what I'm doing.

Aris Winger: When is that?

Anthony Hinojosa: That is the fall semester of freshman year.

Aris Winger: Now we've got you dialed in. Now we're searching for internships.

Anthony Hinojosa: Yes.

Aris Winger: Got it. How do we end up finding one? You were about to say that you don't have that much competition.

Anthony Hinojosa: Virginia Tech's a little bit weird about this. They have a construction engineering and management major, which is what I graduated with. Then there's a building construction major, which is outside the college of engineering. We take similar courses. But it's not all the same. I would say ours is a little bit more math and science-based.

But in construction engineering management, my class had about 60, which was the largest we've had in that school program, and then building construction had another 62. It was around 120 total.

Virginia Tech has different kinds of career fairs, and they're run through the colleges. They have a business career fair. They have a college of engineering career fair. They have an environmental career fair. Within the College of Engineering, they have an event called Expo. It's a career fair for the College of Engineering.

I went to the first one in the fall of my sophomore year. I went to it and I did my research. Most of the companies I was looking at were in aerospace, electrical engineering, and computer science, all these different ones that don't really apply to construction or even civil engineering. Out of about 200 companies that went to that career fair, I would say only ten of them were actual civil engineering or construction-based. I wondered what was going on here? I went and talked to the companies. I wasn't really feeling the vibe from most companies, except for this one, which I did end up getting an internship offer from.

But besides the College of Engineering, or that expo career fair, the School of Construction had a separate career fair. Those companies are all construction-related companies, and about 150 were there. But again, 150 to 120 students are going. Your odds are pretty good. Each employer should talk to 120 students, and the students have 150 companies to talk to.

I was motivated to get an internship and do something.

Aris Winger: I want to take you to when you're about to walk into this room. There are 150 tables. What are you saying to yourself?

We might have some readers who are shy and introverts, who aren't outgoing. What are you saying to yourself? What are they supposed to say to themselves before they step into this room? They might have a little bit of imposter syndrome. They don't even know how to talk to people. What are we saying? How do we get them ramped up for going into this room now?

Anthony Hinojosa: I would consider myself a pretty outgoing person. But, of course, there are always those nerves. I always have these nerves in these moments.

My main fear was that I'm gonna say something stupid, or these employers are gonna ask me a question, and I'm going to be shocked and not know what they are talking about.

The employers are going to hand back my resume, even rip it in my face, and say that I am too dumb to work for them. Those are the emotions I was going through before, a week before this, and even up until the day of.

I told myself that today is about putting yourself out there, number one. Number two, practice talking. It sounds stupid because you've been doing it since you were in kindergarten. But practice talking to these managers who come in for the career fair. Practice talking in these high-stakes environments.

Luckily, I've had people give me advice on how things will be. I had an idea of what to do when I walked up to my 1st employer, give them my 1st resume. This is what it's going to play down to.

My advice to other people would be to find that older person who has gone through this. I know professors would have gone through this. Your classmates who are upper-class people can help.

Aris Winger: You didn't know what 150 companies did, though. How did you select which ones?

Anthony Hinojosa: What I did was I researched at first. I got the list and saw the big-name companies in construction, or at least the companies that most graduates go to. I had a list of 20 different companies.

As a sophomore, I was optimistic and naive, thinking all 20 of these were perfect. I'm going to talk to all 20 of these. I tried to do it at the career fair, but I didn't end up talking to all 20, because some of them I ran away from because I was too scared. Some of them I did end up talking to. But before talking to those 20, I talked to other companies that had emailed me ahead of time. I was going to use them as practice for the major 20. It would help me break the ice at the career fair because this is my first one.

I talked to the first company to break the ice. Sometimes I did find myself freezing up. Sometimes I do find myself being a little bit scared, and I've had to do some quick thinking. But then, once I felt I had it down, that's when I finally talked to the major companies. I really wanted to talk to you. Over time, I've had to do less ice breaking because I've felt more confident as years progressed.

Aris Winger: Is this where you end up finding the internship?

Anthony Hinojosa: You do one for the fall and one for the spring. Most people, of course, since it's the fall semester, are trying to find a summer internship. The fall semester is really where everyone, everyone's going after it. The spring one is where people who didn't find the company in the fall, or didn't end up getting lucky the 1st time around, that's when the spring semester career fair comes into play.

Aris Winger: How did you end up finding the internship?

Anthony Hinojosa: I didn't really get the vibe from most of the companies that I wanted to talk to that first semester. I thought I was going to get the vibe from them, but I didn't. I ended up getting two internship offers, though. I was jumping. I still thought something was missing.

I decided to go to the spring career fair. I was going to make it a priority to talk to those two companies to keep that connection and relationship going. I also planned to talk to more companies, because I felt there was more out there. There has to be.

Aris Winger: How long did you have to turn them down?

Anthony Hinojosa: I told them about my situation. I want to talk to more companies. I believe they took it well. They extended the offer and kept in communication with me, trying to make sure I wasn't ghosting them. I thought they took it well.

Fast forward. Now, I'm at the spring career fair. I got an email. I got three emails asking to talk. One of those emails was from the company that I've interned with for the past three summers and winters, and now I'm working for that company. It wasn't even on my radar at the time. It wasn't something I was going to pursue. I didn't even know who they were. I did a quick little research to find out more about them. In all honesty, they were one of those icebreaking companies I was going to use to get comfortable.

Talking to that company at the fair, I felt, number one, a great vibe with them. I love the work that they were doing. I liked how their internship program was structured, how their internship makes you feel you're not the young guy running around getting these upper management people coffee. You're not this one guy holding a clipboard, writing down whatever your manager says. You're somebody who is a part of the team. You're learning throughout from experienced people. That's what really got me, and why I wanted to pursue this company in the future.

Aris Winger: I want to unpack the vibe. What's being checked off that's sending you the signals? You mentioned a good one about that. It looks like you're going to get credit for your work. Well, you're doing meaningful work. It looks like they're going to give you meaningful work to do. It looks like they're giving you credit. You were also mentioning this vibe piece when you're talking with them. What does that mean?

Anthony Hinojosa: Construction, I would say, is a people business. You're constantly talking and working with people. You're working with the people on your team and with people as your clients, too. What a good vibe means is when you're working with these people, you want to make sure you have matching personalities.

From talking to the Human Resources director, these people match my personality. When I'm not doing the work, I can talk to these people and relate to them. I think that's an important part of engineering, too. It shouldn't be all work, work, work, work, ideally. You should always have these downtimes, because team chemistry is everything in engineering. If you don't have team chemistry, you're unable to talk to each other about anything… Really, people who have team chemistry, who can match each other's personalities on off hours, they're the ones that produce results. There's Google research about how this team chemistry produces more results than teams that don't have it. I remember that article being shown to me, I believe, in Intro to Engineering Spring.

Aris Winger: You've been vibing with them a while now. From year to year, you go back. We've talked to some other people who have espoused "Try something else. Go somewhere else. Do another internship. Try this in all these different areas, different companies." Why is it that you stayed with the same one? Did you ever get the temptation? Did everyone ever say, Shouldn't you go somewhere else?

Anthony Hinojosa: I still don't have a clear answer. It was that gut feeling. But this is what I can make out of my emotions and why I did it.

Freshman year, I went to the career fairs, too. Of course, most companies, not even engineering companies, don't really hire freshmen. I went in there being optimistic. They have to take at least one, and I feel I can be that one. I was a little cocky then. But I kept getting turned down. But I talked to that one company that I told you about.

They said they don't take freshmen. They took upperclassmen. I felt like "Oh, man, come on!" I wanted for my summer to at least get something. Fast forward to May. Classes are starting to wrap up. I reached out to that company. They left that impactful moment on me. I was asked to join the summer to work the labor. Can I at least get my hands dirty? Can I at least watch what's going on?

I'm still at least part of this team.

So, back to the question. They, number one, gave me an opportunity, which I'm grateful for, because then I was able to use that opportunity to talk to different companies.

People realized I was willing to do anything to advance my career. He's shown that he has this initiative. They gave me that opportunity. Number two, they have very experienced people. I would say that they have a high retention rate. Most of the people in the company have been there for 10 plus years. That shows me this is a great place to work if somebody's working there for so long. During my 1st summer, I kept talking to these people, learning more about their personalities, and learning from them through the career lens. I could tell that they're very knowledgeable.

Let me come back next summer. When they did hand me an internship opportunity for my Sophomore summer, going into Junior year, I wanted to learn from these people. I would say it was their experienced staff and their work culture. Moreover, it's a third-generation business, so it has this family element also. It has that family feeling, and that's always a great place to be, because when you leave to go to work. You don't want to go to work. It's not a job. It should be a career, which is what most people say. You should feel happy to go to work. That's another reason why I kept going back, is that family vibe.

I kept talking to other companies, but there was that pull that company had on me. It wasn't until Junior Year that I really started to contemplate working with them three summers in a row. That's when I talked to other companies. These other companies were paying me more with a lot of the same benefits as the other company. I really don't know why I came back to this company when all these different companies were offering me the same thing. It's weird to me.

Aris Winger: Would you do it differently today?

Anthony Hinojosa: For the experience, yes. I see my classmates talking about their past experiences. It wasn't jealousy. But I do wonder what would happen if I didn't do an internship with this company for 3 years. I'd want to go back and do it for the experience. I was missing out on something. It's always in my mind… I'm always playing these games: what if I took this road instead of this road? If I could go back, I would do it for the experience. But I was super lucky with how it turned out. Now I like what I'm doing with my current company.

Aris Winger: Is there anything before we leave undergrad? Is there anything in undergrad that is challenging?

Anthony Hinojosa: Two things, the 1st thing, I was in the Sigma Phi Epsilon fraternity at Virginia Tech. I became President. Being a part of that fraternity and within that President role, I learned what it feels like to run a company and that company structure. It really helped me with my transition. After college, I was able to draw these different parallels. This is how you run an effective meeting. Let me try this within my own organization. As president, you have to do the legwork, and you have to please your stakeholders.

My recommendation for people who are reading this book is to join an organization. It can be anything. When you step into these environments, you start to draw these parallels. You're able to see how operationally they all function. Learning that from a lower stake environment in Virginia Tech organizations, you can transfer that knowledge to higher stake environments and companies.

Aris Winger: This leads to my second question, which I should ask more clearly, now that you're in the professional world. What is it that you wish you had been taught? It can be anything. It doesn't have to be content. It could be skills, any skill at all. This should have been a class on this, or you would have loved to have had a class for.

Anthony Hinojosa: I love how Virginia Tech prepared us for content and how to problem solve, but I really wish there were more specifics on how the industry works. I'm not doing differential equations in my role or linear algebra. If I want to change my career path, I might use it. But for now, what was all this knowledge for? I'm not doing anything really that they taught me.

Engineering classes really teach you how to problem solve and how to do it individually by yourself, or if it's a group project, they teach you how to collaborate within your team. But that's one of my things in engineering. Now, of course, you need that knowledge, because sometimes they tie into different classes. The career path I chose isn't the same career path that somebody else is going to take.

I will say at this job, being there about 9 months now, that the first couple of months were rough, as they didn't dive in mainly into what I'm supposed to be doing, or they did, and I wasn't seeing it in the beginning.

Aris Winger: You weren't seeing the big picture?

Anthony Hinojosa: I would say I wasn't seeing the big picture. But now I do after kind of talks with my project manager and my executive. It's a small company. I'm able to talk to the Executive Vice President, the Vice President of Construction. After talking with them, now I get it. In the past 2 to 3 months, I get it now.

I would also say that I wish we spent more time in school focusing on how important collaboration and communication are to engineering. Communication is really everything, and I wish they put more of an emphasis on it. If they did, I didn't see it.

I'm talking about updating your team, communicating with subcontractors, and with your stakeholders. I think the school could have done a better job in that preparation. A course on teamwork and communication, or at least putting the two together, explaining how an effective team should run.

I thought I had it. I thought I had it with the organization that was in. But stepping into that new role, it was... There are some different parts that I wasn't navigating well.

Aris Winger: Couple more questions. To be where you are at this moment, what have you had to sacrifice?

Anthony Hinojosa: Sleep.

I am thinking more about what people sacrificed for me. My parents sacrificed. They sacrificed for me to get to my internships, because they really cared, coming from a 1st generation household or being a 1st generation student. They sacrificed for me to be in this position, whether that was driving me or giving me the food I needed every day to think properly, and all that. They definitely sacrifice for me, and there's a toll that.

They're doing so much for me. And now, what am I doing for them? What am I sacrificing for them, because they sacrifice so much for me? What am I doing? It's something that I think about.

Most of my friends are out of my area. It's harder to keep in contact with all your friends. My daily schedule is now waking up, working, cooking, and eating.

Aris Winger: Now is your chance. We might have some people who are undergraduates and some others who are reading this now. This is your time to talk directly to them. What do you want to tell them about becoming an engineering professional? Some of them might be struggling. Some of them might be a little lost. What do you want to tell them?

Anthony Hinojosa: Don't sacrifice your mental health for the money portion. I love what I'm doing. That's because I know the definition of engineering. This is what I want to do. But if you're doing it for the money, rethink it. Engineering isn't about the money. It's trying to make a community better.

I see a lot of students, a lot of friends in freshman year, who switch out because they were doing it for the money.

Secondly, you have to think about your why. Your why is going to keep you driving, keep you moving. If you don't have that cemented in the ground, you're going to be asking yourself all these different questions.

For me, this is about giving back to my community. It's what keeps me going. I get frustrated sometimes with my team and with clients. But it's my 'Why' that really kept me going. If you don't have a why, you're really going through the motions. You shouldn't be going through the motions in anything.

One last thing. Surround yourself with friends or a support group. Engineering is not one of those things where you can go through it alone. Most people need this support group. You need some people who keep you going. I was telling you the story about my switch from computer engineering or computer science to construction engineering management. After receiving my 1st test grade in college, which wasn't hot, I was bawling my eyes out. I had to call my brother because he's 4 years older than me, but he took 2 extra years to graduate. I called him up first. I told him I wasn't sure if engineering was for me.

We talked it out, and he helped get me clear on my why. It's important in college, and even after college, to have your support group. Who are those people that you can count on and call if you're emotionally down? Who are those people who will celebrate your wins? Surround yourself with people who can support you, and surround yourself with people who you want to be.

10 - Ariel Leslie

DO IT SCARED

Imagine it. Imagine spending years working in an area, majoring in it, and getting the highest degrees in the land in it. An opportunity comes along in another area that's similar but just different enough to make you nervous, to question whether it's the right path. What would you do? Systems Engineer (and Ph.D. Mathematician) Ariel Leslie made the decision that she could fulfill the requirements that Lockheed Martin proposed. That was just the beginning of an account that emphasizes a lesson we all need to heed: We may not always know it, but oftentimes we have everything it takes to succeed somewhere within ourselves. A whole new world can open up once we decide that we are qualified.

Ariel Leslie, PhD

Systems Engineer, Lockheed Martin, Dallas, Texas

PhD in Mathematics, The University of Texas at Arlington

BS in Mathematics, Texas Southern University

Hometown: Dallas, Texas

Aris Winger: Ariel, are you an engineer?

Ariel Leslie: Yes, by title.

Aris Winger: What does it mean to you to be an engineer?

Ariel Leslie: Honestly, I love this question because I think an engineer is just someone who can think well and work well with others in order to solve a really large problem in an incremental fashion. I don't think I ever thought I would ever be a person as an engineer or an engineering title. But once I got into this role, I realized everybody can be an engineer in a sense. This is not to diminish those who study engineering, because that particular training, getting that kind of degree, is monumental, in my mind, because I don't know how people do it. I work with aerospace, electrical, and mechanical engineers daily. It blows my mind. So that's my definition of an engineer. It's just someone that can solve a problem in an incremental fashion and learn how to work with others in order to do so.

Aris Winger: So, as the reader very well knows at this point, we have asked, and we are going to ask every person this question; you are one of the few people who actually, in the definition, have talked about working well with others.

Can you talk about that piece? Why is that a part of your definition? Why is that part of being a good engineer?

Ariel Leslie: I don't think an engineer is an isolated role, even though I didn't study it. I've never seen an engineer just work by themselves, even if it's just, you know…

Maybe they have that one particular part. But there's always a section of their role that is understanding why they're making what they are making, understanding why they're coding whatever they're coding, if they're a software engineer, and that means working with others. So you have to communicate in some fashion. You have to understand the larger project you are a part of, and there's no way to do that unless you're working with others.

And so I think that's huge, and it's not just isolated to being an engineer. I think that's for any job you have. You must learn how to communicate. Well, I think this is just props to my current team. This is probably the best team I've ever been on, and all they do is communicate.

They're just really good at saying, "Do you understand this?" Or "Hey, let's talk about this," or "Hey, let's meet." And "I noticed you did this." Keep in mind this and this and this, and I'm like, Oh, thanks, thanks! Or do you want to? They'll openly ask, Do you? Do you need help with that? Or would you like to come to our meeting? I usually accept because I am naturally a secluded kind of thinker. I like to think by myself. And then I open up when I am stuck.

I've had to rearrange that working process. And so I don't know... I think maybe that this role has just opened my eyes to the fact that engineers work really well with other people.

Aris Winger: So I'm thinking about the 1st or second-year student who's reading this, who thinks they can work alone. But you just said, No engineer works in isolation.

Ariel Leslie: No.

Aris Winger: So in lots of ways, the quicker you can get into groups, the better.

Ariel Leslie: The better you are, honestly. And it's not just this role. It just makes you a better team member in general, I believe.

Aris Winger: Now I am struggling a little bit because I am a mathematician also, and we lost you somehow. So you started off in mathematics as an undergrad?

Ariel Leslie: Yeah, yeah. I was a math undergrad. And I was a math Phd student. So it wasn't until I started my career that I started to kind of make a new path for myself. But yeah, I started an undergrad as a math major. I studied health studies as a minor because I've always been interested in math being applied to something else.

And then I matriculated to a Phd program and studied mathematical neuroscience. So that was probably like my first introduction to working with engineers because I had to work with some engineers during my dissertation work.

And then I graduated in December. So instead of waiting eight months to get a job, I started in the industry, and my first job just happened to be at Lockheed Martin. And I've just kind of matriculated through. I started out as a data analyst. My second job was as a data analyst. And then, now, I'm a systems engineer. I still do a lot of data analysis, but in the context of systems engineering. So it's just really how different systems come together. And I'm probably preaching to the choir with this because you guys probably already know these things… But

Aris Winger: No, no, you're talking to students.

Ariel Leslie: Yeah, you're right. You're right. So systems engineering…I don't know how to say this in the proper way. And I probably should know the best definition for it. But it's really just a culmination of different areas coming together for a mission system. So I particularly work on the F-35 program on the developmental side. So basically, we develop different capabilities that will go on to the F-35 fighter jet in the future. Right? So these are things that are being coded. They're just in software development at this stage. And then it matriculates onto the next stage. So basically, as a systems engineer, we are overseeing communication between the systems engineer, the design engineer, the test engineer, and the integration of everything. And so…I don't know how I got on this path, but…

Aris Winger: Where's your role in that?

Ariel Leslie: What we call it on the inside is called a capability lead. So as a capability lead, I'm tracking how well we are breaking down our features. So we do a lot of things in Jira. How are we doing with this program increment recorder? How well are we breaking down what we call anomaly reports, which are things that we have…We make room for mess-ups, and then, when those mess-ups are larger than the room that we allotted for them, we call them anomaly reports. And so I track how that is broken down. I'm tracking how well the programs are saying that they can get work done. So that's my job is just looking at the data over time, making sure to…I don't want to say this rudely, but basically keeping people honest, like, "Hey, in retrospect, you guys really don't do this much work in this amount of time. Let's, you know, kind of put things in…"

Aris Winger: Are you an auditor? In some sense? You don't wanna call it that.

Ariel Leslie: I don't. I don't because it's technically not. But I basically just try to help work across all these different domain teams or software teams. And making sure that the capability is on track.

So a lot of that is just looking at data, making sure the teams are getting done what they say they can get done, and making sure that our team is tracking that because it takes one person to make sure that their team is doing well. Then it takes another person to make sure that the data matches up with what they're saying is going on. And so I'm on the data side. I hope that makes sense.

Aris Winger: That's great. I'm wondering. So at some point you were doing data analysis, and then at another point, it comes to you, either the opening or somebody comes to you directly and says, "System engineer is open to you."

Lots of us, including some of our readers, we'll look at something that has a title that we don't think associates with what we have done. It has a list of things, and we say to ourselves, "Oh, I can't do 80% of those." Some of us still apply. But most of us don't. So how is it that the title, this new thing, which seemingly seems out of your range on paper, you decided, "I'm gonna give that a shot."

Ariel Leslie: Great question, because that's literally what happened. Backstory. I always have a mentor at my job. So I was speaking with my mentor and mentioning, "Hey, I'm kind of getting used to what I'm doing. I want to do something different. I was kind of yearning for that."

I don't know how to say it, but I want to be uncomfortable again. I guess that may seem really weird, but I just felt like I wasn't pushing myself. And so I started going out and looking at different roles. And what you said just kind of pointed it out to me...I don't think I would have ever applied for this role if it weren't for my mentor, and I do believe sometimes you just have to try it, anyway. So...

Aris Winger: What did your mentor do?

Ariel Leslie: So he is actually on the data analysis side. At the time, I was in the global supply chain area. And he said, "You know what? You have the skill set. Maybe you should try being closer to what we call the production floor. So everybody who's ever had any type of leadership role at the company has had some type of dealing on the production floor. I've never done that. And I thought, why not branch free and try it out?

Aris Winger: One second. Why not? Because you might fail. It might not work out. All sorts of reasons for why not. And it's also not easy. What made you continue to...

Ariel Leslie: I just wanted to do it scared. I was scared of the role and thought, "Let me just try it." And I thought, "What else could go wrong?" They could say no, or I could not learn something, which I knew would never happen. I just didn't want to be stagnant in my career. And I could see it coming where I'm gonna be doing the same thing every month, every quarter, and I would..

Aris Winger: Did you feel like you had maxed out?

Ariel Leslie: Basically, and do I think I could have probably revamped myself in the role? Yeah, probably. But I didn't want to do that. I knew the same thing was gonna keep coming towards me. So I just thought, Let me try something else. I don't know what I'm doing. I kid you not... this job description had four bullet points, and I probably.

Aris Winger: Was that good or bad?

Ariel Leslie: Probably bad. I probably would not recommend someone applying to a job that doesn't have that much detail. But they couldn't put that much detail because of the classified side of the job. They can't say everything I get now, but I didn't get it then.

So what really kind of pushed me was "I'm just going to try it. I'm just going to do it. I don't know what's going to happen."

This was probably the only job I got a pre-screening for, where somebody called me first, talked to me, and asked me, "What do I see myself doing? And I think that was the only time I've ever had someone in an interview or pre-screening ask me that in a genuine manner. And so that was kind of cool.

But then I didn't hear from them for 2 months. So I thought, "Oh, well, that's my answer." And then they reached out to me again. So I think that probably was the turning point for me; they actively sought me out. They saw something that I didn't see in myself. So I thought, "You know, I'm just gonna go for it."

Aris Winger: Let's go back to the mentor. You're having a conversation with them, and they're just like You've got what it takes. What are they saying exactly?

Ariel Leslie: They knew my data analysis skills. And they knew my communication skills. And so he was just like, "Why not try something different. I think you could…You should try to…" Oh, okay, so let me give some background again.

Every time we met, it was based on our first meeting, which was a plan of how I see myself in 5 years and 10 years. Either I will go the individual contributor route, or I will go the leadership route. And so he would just kind of ask questions: How are your communication skills in this route? Would you be okay with taking this training? What did you learn from that training? Okay, so maybe look at this job. And then he was the one who said, "Don't close yourself off to engineering roles or things of that nature, because I didn't know what that meant. I only had, up until this point, analysis roles that had some type of data in the name, so I was very apprehensive. But he was the one who looked at the job, knew the team, kind of, meaning there was the name of the team, and he knew what that meant, so he explained it to me.

He said, "I think you'd be great. You're going to be pushed, and I think that's the way you want to go."

And at the bottom line, he said, "The only way for you to know if you are a leadership type is to try it out." So I said, "Okay, I will try it out." I don't think I would have applied if it wasn't him saying that because I just struggled with... I wouldn't even say past tense. I would say present tense. I struggle with seeing my gifts in leadership or seeing my gifts in math in general, and how they can be applied elsewhere, even though I got a Phd in it and all the things.

I think this was a good working relationship for me to kind of push myself into the unknown. And honestly, it's worked out beautifully. I have been pushed into uncomfortable spaces. I've learned a whole lot about engineering and a whole lot about myself.

Aris Winger: You said something that I want to come back to. You said that I've always had a mentor. When did you realize that you always needed to have one? Who are some of these mentors? What do they do for you?

Ariel Leslie: I think it began in graduate school. Of course, I had my advisor, my phd advisor, but I always had someone outside of the math department that I could go to and talk, to ask about career guidance, and even just guidance within my Phd. Studies. How should I tackle this type of research? Or is it okay to have a co-advisor? You know, things of that nature. I always wanted someone with a bigger picture view rather than just my advisor, because it just helped me see how, outside of grad school, this lesson will help me in the future.

Aris Winger: And how did you find this person?

Ariel Leslie: While I was in grad school? One of them used to be a math professor and was now in the Provost's office. I was a member of the LSAMP Bridge to the Doctorate Fellowship, and so I acquired two more mentors that way. So that's the main way I met them.

And then once I started at Lockheed, I literally would just pay attention to the people who were at the different meetings, or who I met in person. And I would say, "Okay, I'd like to meet with that person." And I literally would just cold email people like, "Hi, I was in this meeting. I really enjoyed your talk about this," or something like that, or their perspective on things, or how they led the team. So that was probably like my first two mentors.

Aris Winger: But did you ask them in this email?

Ariel Leslie: Yes, I would say, point out that I am looking for mentorship. Would you be open to it? Would you be willing to set up a call?

And most of the time, these people are really high up. So they had Admins. I would just reach out to the admin. It was my responsibility to put myself on their calendar. So I reach out to them, put myself on their calendar, and I would probably keep a mentor for 6 months. I would just do like 6 months at a time, probably take like a month off, and find a new one. And then at my job, we have this program that you can go and look through and see different mentors, and that was the first time I used it for my latest mentor.

So that's how I would just literally cold email people and say, "Hey."

Aris Winger: And you weren't afraid?

Ariel Leslie: Oh, I was scared. I'm very scared, very nervous, even though I was on a computer. I said to myself, "When should I send this?" And I would just send it. And most of the time, people were very genuinely excited about being a mentor. They were gracious. They would say how they were so excited that I reached out to them. "I would love to be your mentor." I would give them my background and all of that, and just make sure it aligned with what they thought would be productive to their career as well. You know, sometimes you can reach out to someone, and they could be unsure. And I had to be open to that, thankfully. It has not happened to me yet, but not saying that it won't.

Aris Winger: Okay. So I got a scenario for you. Here we go. I want you to help out one of our young people reading this now.

Let's say they are taking the intro to environmental engineering course. They are one of 400 people in the room. They are sitting. This wonderful professor lady comes up and says, this is an intro to environmental engineering and proceeds to just blow that students away in what this discipline is, what it can do, how it impacts the world. And this person's like "I've got to get to know them. I want this person to be my mentor now." But this person again looks around the room and sees that there are 399 other people. These office hours are going to be tough to get their attention.

So convince the reader right now that they should still go ahead, send the email, go to office hours, pull them aside, even when it feels like there's no way that person can have the bandwidth for them.

Ariel Leslie: Do it anyway.

Aris Winger: Why? What are they going to get?

Ariel Leslie: First off, you're going to get the confidence to keep doing it. Number two, what's the worst they can tell you? No. Okay, great.

Your next question will then be, "Do you have someone else that you would recommend?" I'm sure they know someone else who's great, but that's the worst they can tell you. So.

Aris Winger: But the possibility of a Yes has so much upside.

Ariel Leslie: Yes, yes.

Aris Winger: What do they get with a yes?

Ariel Leslie: Yes, you get the confidence of "You know what? I can ask these questions. I am not the only person who has the same questions. Number 2. I have now increased my network. I've now met someone who is way smarter than me, way more experienced than me. There's so much to learn. So now you have increased your network, increased your bandwidth to learn, and you now have someone who will potentially be in your corner for years to come. You have someone you can ask questions about, not only their career, but also the subject area you're interested in. Given that you're a first or second-year student, you have a better outlook on what this degree means for you. You have a better outlook on how you can use it in the future. So you have a better outlook on what type of classes you might actually be a better fit for. You probably are going to be privy to research groups that they know about, research experiences that they know about, for the summer internships that they know about, or even during the school year. They probably know other students who are like-minded as you. So now you have a study group. You have people who are also learning the same subjects as you, and can tell you about their experiences in certain classes or just tips and tricks to help you get through that year. There's so much more.

Aris Winger: The whole world opens up.

Ariel Leslie: Yes, everything opens up with that. At some point, you have to turn off that "no" part in your brain to be able to send that email, or just go up there and speak to them. If you have the opportunity to see that person and shake their hand, go. Say a few words. Do it anyway. Just go do it. I promise you. That person is expecting someone to come and speak to them. They want you to go and say hello and ask them questions. Yes, they're busy, but they're not…

If they're a good mentor, they're not too busy to stop and say something to you because they want to pour into the upcoming generation. They will always stop and say something to you.

So I think that's the biggest thing, just get it out of your head and get out of your own way.

I'm saying this because I did. I had to tell myself the same thing because I struggle with that. But at some point, you have to tell yourself: "I'm not going to learn more. I'm not going to see all the things and opportunities that are available for me, unless I just do it scared."

Just do it scared.

Aris Winger: Thank you for that. So you're in this discipline every day. And you're working with other people. Now, did you already have these types of skills for working on teams? Or did you have to build them on the fly? How did you become a good teammate?

Ariel Leslie: I think it's a combination of both. So I do think I honed my good communication skills while I was in graduate school, because you're spending so much time learning this material. You're spending so much time researching.

At some point, someone else has some type of information that you need, and it's usually your advisor, who will say, "Hey, go talk to this person." Maybe you should go reach out, or go to this research talk, or go to this meeting.

That's how I met people. That's how I learned how to present my information. That's how I learned how to present who I am to a certain person. And that's how I learned to send concise emails. It's cool now because we've got ChatGPT. But back then, you know, you needed to, just, you know, get straight to the point. And so that's how I honed my skills on how to speak to people in person and via email.

So once I got to Lockheed, I was already… my first job on a team. Then, eventually, I was leading that team, and I was leading interns. And so that really allowed me the opportunity to break down larger concepts, larger projects, in an incremental fashion and learn how to delegate.

So the first role I learned to delegate. In my second role, I learned the skill of advocating for good projects. So, not always does leadership think that this is a good idea. Well, that's your job to put something together and persuade these people to say, "Hey, no, we should look into this. This is actually really important." My second job was the first time I advocated for myself, got a project, led that project to leadership, and it moved forward.

And then my current role, this role I've had to learn the skill of communicating and learning things on the fly. I will say this job gave me a whole new appreciation for those in the military. I've had to be briefed on things, and in that 30-45 minutes, I am now responsible for all that information I just learned.

I failed miserably the first time that it happened. But eventually, you learn to pick up on information. You have to know this stuff immediately, and you have to know how it affects the next person. You have to know how to use this information in your data analysis. You have to be learning to speak to people, learning who and who not to speak to about certain things.

So I think that's what I've learned in each role: a different type of communication, a different type of capacity that I've had to learn to work within.

Aris Winger: There are some of our readers who are in very competitive environments. And yet when I listen to you, I hear no ego. There's no time to be trying to be better than somebody else.

Ariel Leslie: My 1st thought is, I have to put myself in their shoes, right? So, as a first- and second-year undergrad, I understand. I get it. You feel like you have to be on your P's and Q's, and you should to…

Aris Winger: Stand out.

Ariel Leslie: Yes, to stand out in order to get to those research experiences, you have to fight to get into those really good research groups that you may have opportunities to get into. I get it. I get it, as you should. I did the same thing.

But when it comes to being in the industry, your ego has to be checked at the door. Everybody has the same bottom line: Get the product out the door. If you know a better way of doing something, speak up if you have some experience in doing XYZ. Speak up. We are all on the same team. We want to get the same job done, and we want to do it well. We want to be the best at it.

A company is very competitive in that in that realm we want to be the first, best at things, and only the only way to get there is if everybody is doing the same thing on their everyday job.

So I get it, in that mindset. But you have to switch it off once you get to…

I feel like if you're in the right place in the right company, the right company will want you, will want everyone to be their best, and you're only at your best if your ego is checked at the door.

Nobody wants to work with someone who's a know-it-all. Let's be honest. When your team dynamic is good, your work is great. If your team dynamic is "let me get at their throat," somebody, somewhere, some product, is not good, and we won't name names, but we've seen companies mess up.

So I credit my team for saying, "Hey, we're all here. We need to get the job done. Let's bring our best selves, our whole selves to the job, and you get it done."

So yeah, I check my ego at the door. I don't really think I have one, but maybe it's ego to say you don't have one. I don't know, but I think that the biggest thing in having a good team is to let people know, "Hey, I've done that before. I think it's better to do this. Okay, great. Let's do it."

Aris Winger: I want to ask about study groups in general. When you were an undergrad, how did you find them?

Ariel Leslie: I was a standout in undergrad, so finding people to study with wasn't hard. People usually flock to me, saying, "Hey, you seem like you understand this."

And sometimes I was, and sometimes I was not. And so I needed the study group to do that. I'm gonna have to take a step back. I was in study groups in high school, so I was used to that.

I know I work well… I do better in classes when I'm able to ask questions, or I'm able to teach what I know.

So I did that in undergrad. I made sure to always have somebody I could study with while I was an undergrad, and that was my selling point for going to UT Arlington for a Phd. That was my selling point for UT Arlington, because the grad students always worked together. They were always together. We shared notes. Older grad students would just pass down notes from various classes and say, "Hey, this is what I did. You can use this," and I did the same thing. I would just keep passing it on. I think that's really helpful to be able to be in a group where you are not only learning, but you're also teaching, because it helps you to learn more.

Aris Winger: Can you talk a little about what the major challenges you faced were?

Ariel Leslie: I kind of said something like this before, but really just getting over myself…I have always struggled with having confidence in the gifts that I have. I never wanted to be that show off, but I knew I needed help. So it was just always being able to speak about it. "Okay, I'm struggling in this area. Who else is struggling in this area?" And I think the study group helped with that.

Another thing is, I went to an HBCU for undergrad, and I think in HBCUs there's always this open door feeling… like everyone is together.

And not saying that UTA wasn't completely like that. But it was different. It's just a different feeling. And so I struggled with that.

Aris Winger: Struggled with what exactly?

Ariel Leslie: Not as much as an open door feel. In undergrad, I could literally just walk into the math department, and anybody would have their door open, and I'd be like, "Dr. So and So, I need da da da" or "Doctor so and so, can I come?" Because I was there all the time, they would say, "Oh, yeah, we can go to this or go to that and take this class."

In grad school, their doors closed. Do I knock? Are they there?

Should I wait till office hours? I'll just send an email. There were so many barriers that I wasn't used to. And so that was a struggle for me to go hopping over that barrier. It's just different. It's a different system. You need to communicate via email. You need to come during office hours. I didn't always have to do that in undergrad. It didn't matter if it was office hours or not; their door was open. You ask a question.

Grad schools aren't like that, you know. There are boundaries for things, and I get it. You know, they are professors at a top research institution. They have different things going on. There's a lot. So that was a struggle for me.

I'm grateful that I didn't have any financial struggles. I always had something there, meaning my school was paid for. I was able to teach when I was ready to teach. So I'm grateful for that. But I will say the struggle came when going from not teaching to teaching and having a similar workload.

I struggled that first semester of teaching my classes, and my study patterns had to change. So I struggled with my first couple of tests in that semester. But eventually, you know, I had to get with the program and learn how to re-prioritize my schedule.

Aris Winger: As you're thinking about what you do today, if you could go back and list some things that you had to figure out in the engineering world, even in the data analysis world, that had you saying to yourself, "Wow! I have to learn this now? Why didn't they teach me this in undergrad?" What are the things in undergrad that you wish they had taught you about where you are right now?

Ariel Leslie: Especially on the data side. But you also see it in engineering.

We have really nice, beautiful, laid-out data sets in undergrad. That is not real life.

I spend so much time in what you call the ETL pipeline, the extraction, the transforming, the loading. There's so much data you have to filter through. Make sure it makes sense. You are extracting what's duplicate or whatever is duplicated, making sure to merge information that wasn't in the first data set. Does that make sense? Did you then transform into a way that is helpful for this team? But then you need to transform in a different way for this team. I wish there were a class specifically just on messing with ugly data sets. That's real life. It doesn't look pretty. It's not pretty, ever, ever, ever, ever. So that is number one.

And then I think, number two...I don't know how this would be a class...

Aris Winger: Let's do it. Let's dream. We're dreaming.

Ariel Leslie: I think you always have to be a lifelong learner. You need to learn to always be reading, learning *something*. Once you have acquired one thing you have to learn, you've not acquired everything. Okay? I think sometimes... And maybe it just is me. Maybe this is just an Ariel problem. Do you think you got the degree, or you've taken that class, that you have now gotten the things you need? No. I am consistently and always asking someone, "Okay, what does this mean? Can you send me to this website? What class did you take? Is this training? Okay? I need to read that." File surf, that's what we call it. I'm reading this folder. I'm reading through these files. Okay, I need to learn about this. There are just so many things… and engineering and math are very similar.

I liken it to the universe, like you. You've got this continent over here, this continent over there. That's your realm of study. And this was my realm of study. But there are often overlaps, right? There is a term: avionics: aviation, and electronics. I never knew that existed. And in my role now, I have to know all about it. So I was digging up things, learning things here. It's just… I don't know if this is a class… I don't know, but just learning how to identify the major points that you need to know for every aspect of your role.

And I think over time that happened. But if I could have learned how to realize what I need to read and how I need to read, and how to outline myself for learning this aspect, and then moving on to this part of the role.

Maybe that's a time management class. I don't know. Just really understanding that you've never made it. You're not there. You have not acquired it at all. You still need to learn this.

Aris Winger: So that the end of school isn't really the end.

Ariel Leslie: Never.

Aris Winger: So this feels like a theme. Do get stagnant.

Ariel Leslie: You have to go.

Aris Winger: Let's break down your avionics experience. At some point, you're sitting in a room, and the topic just keeps coming up over and over and over again, or at some point, something comes under your purview. You realize that you need to know more about this. And so what happened there? What did you have to do?

Ariel Leslie: I just remember reaching out to someone on my team. Who… I don't know. Maybe he was just the only person that was in his cube at the time, and I was like, "Hey, this avionics thing! Do you have any training that you would suggest for me?" And he was like, "I have all the things." So he sent me this folder of Unending files. I said, "Thanks. That's exactly what I needed."

Aris Winger: Okay, but wait. That look on your face is not going to translate to the book. So you say that with sarcasm.

Ariel Leslie: I did. Because I looked at this folder… What is this? It was just so…

Aris Winger: There was no "Introduction to Avionics" file, right?

Ariel Leslie: No. It has all this terminology, and I'm sure aerospace engineers know all these things, right? They've seen it before. Me, as a math person, was like "What?" So I'm Googling what this term means. I'm Googling what this means. And then they come back with, "Oh, yeah, make sure you look at this website as well." So it was just…

I was inundated with so much information. So I had one day where I said, "I can't read anymore. I'm done." So I stopped reading.

I got up and went to the next person I could see in their cube. And I just started asking questions. And that's when stuff started clicking. I just started talking to people. "Okay, how does it work for your capability? So what does this mean? And which team does this? Okay, what does their team do? Oh, okay, so you do this. And how does that work with this person?"

Ariel Leslie: It's just really I had to ask for help. Number One. In that moment of asking for help, I got information. I got too much information, so I had to stop myself from being overwhelmed.

I got myself out of my comfort zone. I went out and talked to someone else. Mind you, I was on this team for maybe a week, so I didn't know anyone. Yeah. So this is a completely new team.

I knew no one at all. So I'm learning their names. I'm learning what they're the lead of. I'm learning what their background is. I'm learning how avionics is pulled into their capability or their role.

They suggest someone for me to talk to. We pretty much divide into 3 separate groups what we call electronics, warfare, or weapons sensors. And then communication, navigation, interrogation, all these different routes. And avionics is different in each of those 3 categories.

I would talk to one person there in navigation, all that stuff, then they would tell me, " Oh, go talk to this person. They're in sensors." And I'll respond, "Oh, yeah, you should meet this person. They're in weapons."

So I'm asking everybody basically the same set of like 6 to 8 questions so that I can kind of get a feel. What I will say is one skill that I guess I acquired over time, how to ask questions. I would just always have a list of questions with me, and I would just take it with me to everybody I talked to. And so that's how I learned.

I just had to tell myself. Okay, this book has to close at some point, and I have to see how it's actually used in real life. I have to see how these different domain teams are using it, how they're using it to code things and how these people are using this for this capacity in this realm. I needed to know. And that's how.

Aris Winger: The questions were the vehicle for which this would happen.

Ariel Leslie: Yes. I think that's one major skill: Learn how to ask questions. The only way to do it is to ask the questions. You have to learn how to read information, pick out some of the main themes, and formulate a question around that.

And then just really being a people person. I think when you lead with ego, or you lead with: "I know all of this…" I'm pretty sure I would have had a different outlook or dynamic on this team if I came at people like "I have a math Phd, I know all of this, you should tell me this."

Aris Winger: Right.

Ariel Leslie: I don't. I don't need to prove anything. I am the one who doesn't know anything. So, asking the questions, coming at this in a manner of like, "Okay, I'm here to learn, and you know more." It changes your perspective.

Aris Winger: Any regrets about missteps in the undergrad space? Things you would do differently if you could?

Ariel Leslie: Great question. I don't think I had any missteps. I think I would have taken data courses earlier. Just getting an eye for how a computer works. I would say I don't know that I would take all the engineering courses because I didn't know that I would end up here. But I will say to my undergrad self, I wish I had gone to more engineering talks just to see what that's like, because I find that math and engineering overlap very often.

I think if I had just gone to a couple of talks, just to learn how math is used in engineering? What is engineering in general? What are the different types, and what are their roles, and how do they all work together? I think in general, knowing that information would have opened up a whole new world earlier.

Aris Winger: So you had mentioned that engineers are tied to problem-solving. So when a new problem comes your way, what is your problem-solving process like? What do you want to do? What are you thinking about?

Ariel Leslie: It's a great question. I get this often. My team lead asked me a lot to look at different things. So my first tool…I guess you could say that in my tool belt is, I ask questions. I'm asking, what does this mean?

Who is the person that you're pointing me to talk to? What is their role and what is their role in connection to your role and my role? And how do they fit in the big umbrella? I'm asking what data is available.

I'm asking about the timeline. When you're in the industry. You need to know the timeline. So I quite often ask, When do you need this information? And who's the audience? Do you need this in a formal or informal format? Do you want me to make the team's page so people can see the information I have accumulated and the results I have found? Do you need me to make a website? Do you need me to put this into Tableau? This does need to be a dashboard, that kind of information, because then that tells you what kind of reader you're gonna have, and it also tells you what the reader is looking for. If your reader is a technical person or a non-technical person and then what they're looking for. So the questions that they need answers to, you need to make sure that that information is obvious.

Aris Winger: Yeah.

Ariel Leslie: And then I just kind of fill in the blanks as I go right cause that kind of helps me.

I don't know. I kind of imagine a number line. I've got my first point and my last point, and I probably have a midpoint. So I'm just gonna fill in as I go, and in between filling in, I get feedback. So I'll do something and ask a set of questions, beginning with "Hey, does this make sense? Could you find this? Could you see this?"

So that's kind of how I think when I'm approached with a problem. I want to know the timeline. I want to know my audience. I want to know who I should be in conjunction with, whom I need to be talking to. And then I need to know the major points. What do they need to know, and how do I need to present that information?

Aris Winger: Yeah, so there are some people who are at some institutions that don't even have an engineering program wanting to be an engineer. Kyle was one of these people. Getting degrees in non-engineering disciplines. And so how did math work? What were some of the skills that math brought and helped you as an engineer today?

Ariel Leslie: That's a great question. I think, in any realm, math brings a very logical approach to problem-solving. We're very much like this, then this right? So I'm looking for all of my assumptions. I'm looking for all of the things that I know need to be true in order to get to the end goal. Right? So I obviously think engineers are great problem solvers as well. I just think we have a very different approach. We're more of the exact approach, right? Also, something that I think as a math person that I have learned is learning how to ask questions. I know I've said that several times now, but I think through undergrad and grad school.

Because I knew I was applying math to other realms. I needed to ask these people these questions. For example, I don't know how the brain works. So I need to ask you a question, Neuroscientist. I don't know the passageway… I'm just making up stuff… from the thalamus to the frontal cortex. What happens in between there? I need to ask you those questions. So being able to ask questions is, I think, an invaluable skill, and just being able to communicate well, right? So that's probably the overarching thing: being able to communicate. And I think as a person, I had to reach out and learn how to do that. In math, we can communicate, but it's through math. But that's a person. There's a person on the other side. So I needed to learn how to reach out to that person. And I think doing research talks and going to different meetings and all that stuff really helped to do that.

Also, I am a huge proponent of like research programs, summer for all the things that you can do in summertime. That's how I was exposed to different things. And so, being in those different programs, I learned how to work well in a team of people with different strengths and backgrounds, and I'll put it out there… like different ethnicities, different cultures like all of these things are real life. I think learning to do that early on has helped me now. Now I can relate to someone from a different ethnicity and culture in different ways.

You have to learn to do that in a way to respect others. It's a way to invite people to bring their full selves to the team and the job.

Those are, I would say, some of the major things.

Aris Winger: Two more questions for you. First, what did you have to sacrifice to be where you are?

Ariel Leslie: Time.

Capacity. I am married and have a child, so I sacrifice time with them sometimes, and I don't always like it.

Yeah, I think especially while I was in grad school. I felt like a lot of friends that I have are out traveling, doing anything. Don't get me wrong. I travel to go to research talks, but like it's a different type of travel, right?

So, just doing the things I think I would have really enjoyed. You sacrifice relationships. And that's probably not even a negative. I feel like people who fall off during those times probably weren't for you, anyway.

I will say just as being a mother, I sacrifice different career opportunities, and I don't really see that as a negative, because I prioritize my family over my career.

So…and that's not true for everyone. And that's okay. That's your choice. And you shouldn't feel bad either way if that's what you want. I want a family. I want to be an integral part of my family. So there were lots of opportunities that came about, and I just said, "No."

But on the flip side, there are opportunities like this job that I currently have, that I naturally probably would have said "No" to, because I was just terrified of it.

And my family encouraged me to do it. So there's the opposite side of it. It's like, you know, really pushing yourself to do things. So I sacrificed my ego in that realm.

So, yeah, those are my sacrifices.

Aris Winger: Final question: now you know who our reader is. This could be a young person reading about you and your story who is inspired by it. Just take the time, say whatever you want directly to them about succeeding, getting through challenges, overcoming… anything you want to tell them.

Ariel Leslie: First things first, I would say, "Congratulations." You've made it to this point, and kudos to you for taking the time to read about other people's stories.

You see something yourself, or you see something in someone else you like for yourself, and you're looking to expand and grow. So kudos to you for doing that.

I think it's great to celebrate your wins along the way, and I think it's great to take accountability for the not-so-great wins along the way to really understand what your path is and your career journey, and to understand that your career journey is not the next person's.

So figure out what works for you and enjoy it. Enjoy every year, every semester, every month, and find something to enjoy. It's not going to always be fun. I hated some parts of grad school. To be honest, I hated some parts of undergrad. That's okay because I learned from it. I learned more about myself.

So take the time to learn more about yourself. Take the time to learn more about your craft and your area of study. And take the time to push yourself.

This is the best time to push yourself to do things that you would never choose to do. This is the best time to find a mentor, find someone new to study with. Take a class that you probably thought you would never be able to take. Learn to code, learn how to work with different people of different personalities or different backgrounds, and also learn how to check your ego at the door. Learn it now, because you will be humbled later.

Enjoy yourself and enjoy engineering. Enjoy whatever background you are in, whatever area of study you're in, and ask questions.

I would just say, just enjoy every part of the journey, and kudos to you for making it to this part of reading more about others, and hopefully, you learn more about yourself.

11 - Seth Fortuna

THERE'S MORE TO IT THAN A GPA

There are times when we have the urge to go beyond the surface level. We might be investigating something that we know is profound, but through no fault of our own, be relegated to completing rote tasks about the topic. It can be frustrating. Principal Staff Engineer Seth Fortuna found this unbearable. Working as a technician in his first job outside of school, he realized that he wanted more autonomy to explore ideas at a much deeper level. Cue his return to school for graduate degrees and now his role in Research and Development at Sandia National Lab, where he works on innovative ideas and projects. His experience there has made him realize that a great GPA is a marginal indicator of what it means to be a good problem solver. The engineering path of Seth Fortuna is the story of a man whose great GPA got him a job he didn't want, and forced him to re-evaluate what it means to be great at what he does.

Seth Fortuna, PhD

Principal Member of Technical Staff, Sandia National Labs, Albuquerque, New Mexico

PhD in Electrical Engineering, University of California, Berkeley

MS in Electrical & Computer Engineering, University of Illinois Urbana-Champaign

BS in Electrical Engineering, Penn State University

Hometown: Harrisburg, Pennsylvania

Aris Winger: Welcome, Seth. Are you an engineer?

Seth Fortuna: Yes.

Aris Winger: What does being an engineer mean to you?

Seth Fortuna: I guess someone who designs and makes things does some function. So that's if I just had to explain it in one sentence. That's how I would explain it. But obviously it's a lot more complicated than that. Usually, you have to design something and make it so that it does this particular function that you're interested in, but in reality, sometimes it's hard to know what that function needs to do. So a lot of your job is figuring out and understanding the problem. Working with customers who need a particular problem solved, because you're often not just making stuff that's gonna go into a vacuum. You're gonna make it for a customer, or you're gonna make it for a very specific function. And even understanding what that function needs to be, which seems to be the easy part, but is sometimes the hard part, because often the customer doesn't know what they want. So a lot of the job is managing expectations. Making sure that there's clarity and what you're setting out to do between yourself and the folks who are interested in the work that you're doing. There are other sides to the work. A lot of time is spent just managing personnel, like setting work priorities for people who are working for you or doing work for you, and managing conflicts. The actual engineering part of your engineering job probably takes a smaller percentage than maybe you would like. So there are a lot of people management as opposed to technology development and technology management. So there's all of that, too.

Aris Winger: We've asked this to everyone. But you're one of the 1st people to actually mention attending to the customer. And so I'm wondering about how that shows up. And is the customer a wide-ranging group of people? Could that just mean your boss? Could that mean someone who has someone in the private sector, who is the customer? And what is this relationship with the customer? What are these conversations like?

Seth Fortuna: So I come more from an R&D environment, and so the concept of customers may be a little bit more nebulous, but, generally speaking, for me, the customer is going to be who's paying me to do what I'm doing. So I work for an FFRDC, which is a federally funded research and development center, and so we charge time to projects like a lawyer does. So every week I gotta fill out a timesheet and say, I worked X hours on this project, X hours on that project. So it's very clear who's paying my salary. But diving into a little bit more detail there. So my customers have people from other government agencies who want something delivered. And so it's very clear that they have this widget in mind, or it could even be like a model or something, and they have expectations of that being delivered by a certain time, certain date, and so forth. But I also have R&D customers. So I have maybe a level one or level 2 managers who are managing a pot of money that's just meant for General R&D, and so they have this idea that they're gonna need something 5 to 10 years from now. They're not exactly sure what that need looks like. But they have a sense that, okay, in 5 to 10 years, we need something in this area, and so, I might propose to get some allotment of that money to do a project. But it was very nebulous, like 5 to 10 years from now. It's really hard to know exactly what that problem looks like. So you try to work with your customer. In this case, the customer is often a project manager who has a sense of the problem. And I guess what I'm trying to say: It's a very kind of an open-ended thing. It's more abstract. It's not a concrete thing that needs to be delivered. We're just trying to work towards an overarching goal. But maybe we're not exactly sure what the problem is gonna look like 5 to 10 years down the road.

Aris Winger: Alright. So take us back to the summer before you head to undergrad. So you're going into undergraduate school at Penn State.

Seth Fortuna: Yeah, this is 1999, Penn State.

Aris Winger: How are we feeling? Do we feel prepared and ready to go? How did it feel 1st year at Penn State, undergrad in general?

Seth Fortuna: Well, there are a lot of things going on with me in my personal life. There is a lot of flux just getting to Penn State. There's a little bit of luck there, because I only ended up applying to one school and if I hadn't gotten into Penn State I honestly don't know what I would have been doing. Actually, I remember working at a grocery store, and this Marine Corps recruiter kept coming through my line and was really trying to recruit me strongly. And so I had thought about maybe even joining the military instead of going to school.

But I got accepted to Penn State's main campus and ended up going. I was ready to get out for sure. I think that a lot of people don't manage that 1st year very well, for various reasons. Too much partying and all that, but I was able to manage my time fairly well. I think I did. I didn't excel academically there, but I think I did well enough, I guess. Set a good base to have success and graduate, and do all those things.

Aris Winger: With challenges in undergrad. Were there any roadblocks, or was it smooth sailing?

Seth Fortuna: I think my biggest challenge was that I didn't think I had a great mentor. I didn't appreciate how important that was. So, I think a lot of undergraduates or engineering undergraduates tend to do it because their parents are engineers, or maybe they're technical. Mine weren't; I just didn't understand what I was doing. My mom didn't go to college, my dad did, but as a business major, and I didn't really have any good people to kind of guide me and lead me. For example, like going to graduate school never even really crossed my mind once. I just figured if I was meant to go to graduate school, someone was going to tap me on the shoulder and tell me, Hey, you should go to graduate school, and that never happened. And so I just never bothered to apply, never even, I don't even think I thought about it.

In hindsight. I wish that someone had intervened and maybe just pushed me. And just at least told me that to think about it. But that never happened. And you know, part of that was probably my problem, because I didn't really seek out a mentor and didn't really appreciate the need for that. So that's 1 thing that I think looking back, I wish I had done a little bit differently.

Aris Winger: Yeah, that's powerful. That gets me because we were going to ask that later. And I'm glad you said it now. So, if we put you back. Do you know how that would look? Is this going to office hours? How would you envision young Seth doing this?

Seth Fortuna: Probably engaging the professors more. I always had this thing where I felt like professors were up on this pedestal that you're just a completely different cast system or something. Just not approachable people. When by and large they are. And you know now that I have a PhD. And I've interacted with plenty of professors, and I have friends who have gone off to be professors. They're just people like you and me, right? They have their own faults, just like you and I do. So I had to kind of tear that down in my head, or I should have been able to do that, or should have done that as an undergrad, and I didn't. I always avoided office hours for the most part and just didn't get to know the professor. So there really wasn't even anybody that would have been good as a mentor, because very few professors really knew me, kind of on a personal basis. I would say I didn't really seek out undergraduate research, either. And I think that's one thing that I wish I had done was actually try to do some more undergraduate research. And I think that that would have helped.

Aris Winger: Were you lost in undergrad?

Seth Fortuna: Lost?

Aris Winger: Yeah.

Seth Fortuna: Like in what way?

Aris Winger: Like you didn't have direction, or like you were just going through the motions, or working without purpose.

Seth Fortuna: I wouldn't say that I was lost. I think I was checking all the boxes doing the classes.

And seeing what I needed to do to graduate. But I definitely was in a state where any nudge in one direction was gonna change my momentum pretty strongly. And so that's what ended up happening when I ended up getting an internship. I guess it was in my junior year. I knew that I had a general sense that I needed to figure out what I wanted to do with my career and what industry I wanted to go into. But I was having trouble making that decision. And then I just kind of stumbled upon an internship in the semiconductor industry, and that, just like I said, was enough to just push me completely into that track, even though I maybe didn't do that deep down, thinking about whether or not this is actually the thing that I wanted to do with my life.

Aris Winger: So, the internship, how was that experience?

Seth Fortuna: It was very formative, for sure. It set kind of the basis for everything that followed. So I had the internship. It was really a co-op, so I think it was a total of one year, although not continuous. But I ended up working at that company after I graduated.

Aris Winger: So what skills are we getting there that you weren't getting in school that were helpful?

Seth Fortuna: At that time, I think schools do a better job of this now, but maybe 20 years ago, they weren't doing such a great job of making that connection between your class work in the real world. So that's something that's hard to just pick up, taking classes, because the focus is on the fundamentals and the math. So it's very easy not to see the bigger picture. Then, in the semiconductor industry, seeing how some of the concepts were applied in the real world, I think it helped make some connections in my brain to better put in context the schoolwork, the classwork that I was doing at that point.

Aris Winger: So now you go back to school after the internship. And are you more motivated, or does the class work make more sense? Going back to school after an internship like this, how does it impact you?

Seth Fortuna: I guess when I went back, I was pretty close to graduation, anyway. So there wasn't a whole lot of time to change direction. But I do remember taking one specific course, semiconductor physics, that I maybe wouldn't have taken or been inclined to take before the internship. So it may have focused me a little bit there. But honestly, I was so eager to graduate because I more or less put myself through school, loans, Pell grants, working over the summer and over Christmas breaks, and all these things. So I never really had much money. And during my college time, I wasn't getting a ton of support, and I was just so eager to find a job. That was, I think, my primary focus when I came back was like, Okay, I just want to wrap this up and then start making some money.

Aris Winger: Yeah, helpful. So then you finish and then.

Seth Fortuna: Yeah, I finished and then, I ended up getting a job with the same company [as the internship], although it was a different division, a different site. So this was Intel. I did an internship in Santa Clara. And then I got a job in Folsom, California. But now I'm trying to think how [I got the job], I don't even quite remember how. I feel like my resume was forwarded from my internship mentor to a hiring manager. And I think that's how that kicked off that whole interview process. And I ended up getting an interview there and got a job. And so I moved out there to the Sacramento Area and worked there for a couple of years. In that first job, I made a couple of realizations. First of all, I had actually had success in that job. And so I think generally I was doing very well. But I did come to the realization for the 1st time. The limitations of just having a bachelor's degree are on me.

Aris Winger: We definitely want to dig deep there. What were the limitations in your mind?

Seth Fortuna: I can just speak about the semiconductor industry. I don't really know how it is in other industries. Still, generally speaking, if you enter the semiconductor industry with a bachelor's degree, I had this notion that I was going to be going off and really doing engineering, like doing design work, making things. And all this stuff, right? But I think to a large extent, someone with their bachelor's degree is kind of just really expected to be a technician for the most part, like you're just doing stuff with your hands. You're basically being told what to do. You don't really have as much freedom and flexibility to kind of decide upon your own work, and do design work and things of that nature, and not to say that you can't end up doing that. But you're not necessarily going to be doing that kind of right out of the box, right? I had maybe these expectations that that was going to happen, or maybe even a sense of like. I don't know if entitlement might be too strong of a word. But I thought, Hey, you know, I came from a top 20 university. I had like a 3.7 GPA. Let me loose.

Let me work on some stuff, and that's not really what happened. I could recognize that some of that was just having a bachelor's degree, not having a graduate degree, which may have penalized me. It was gonna take me longer to do the work that I wanted to do just with the bachelor's degree. So I had already started, I think, 2 years into it. I'd already considered applying to graduate school and started collecting people to provide references. But I didn't pull the trigger. I even took the GRE. I got that far, but I didn't apply, and I ended up taking another job with Intel up in Oregon, which turned out to be a huge mistake.

Aris Winger: Because?

Seth Fortuna: Well, okay, because I was working more of a product-centric role. And, to be blunt. It was probably an easier job. And then I got moved up into more of an R&D role, where I was really surrounded by PhD folks. And then my lack of schooling really contrasted with them strongly, and I was doing some things that I thought really were technician-level work. And I got very frustrated there. There ended up being some layoffs, too, and my hiring manager, the person who really vouched for me, was really my mentor at that point, who brought me up to Oregon, got laid off, and I was just in like never, never land. I think I had 5 managers in one year. And so I was like, I gotta get out of here. So I finally pulled the trigger and applied to grad school, and I got in.

Aris Winger: This desire and or need to get more knowledge, go deeper into the content to understand, deeper. That seems to be motivating you here also.

Seth Fortuna: Yeah, for sure. I wanted to understand better how stuff works. And at that point, I was really getting more interested in light, like lasers and things like that, because we would use lasers in my job at Intel, and it's like man, these are kind of cool, like, how does even an LED work? I mean, that was something as simple as that. At that time I I had started getting this fascination with how light works and things of that nature, so that nudged me again, kind of in the direction of studying that more. That was kind of my focus when I was applying to grad school to do more classwork and research in that area.

Aris Winger: Yeah, so, Illinois. You're headed there.

Seth Fortuna: Yeah, Illinois. I ended up applying to probably 5 schools at that point. I think I got accepted to Illinois and Michigan. I probably would have gone to either place. Both schools are fairly decent for my field. But Illinois had a visit day, and I was never invited to a visit day at Michigan, so that was enough for me to choose Illinois. I generally enjoyed Illinois. It was a little bit more of a sleepy town than where I was living. I was living in downtown Portland at the time, and having the vibrancy of a city and all that, and then moving to Champaign. That was a little bit of a letdown initially, Illinois not having mountains and all that. But Illinois did grow on me, and I got to really like living in Champaign. And I actually had quite a bit of success doing research. I got a journal paper out quickly while I was there, and that's still my most highly cited journal paper; all that data was captured, basically, in the first 6 months that I was there. And so it was having really good success.

A couple of things happened that threw changes into my plans a little bit, upsetting the equilibrium there. I guess the 1st one was. I ended up having some medical issues. So I had to take a leave for a semester. And then I kind of decided that I didn't actually really like the research that I was doing. I said before, I was really interested in light and devices that emit light, and my advisor at that time was also interested in that. Still, a lot of the work we were doing was just growing semiconductor crystals and not necessarily making devices. And I wasn't too interested in growing semiconductors. I really wanted to make devices, and so there wasn't as much of that work going on. So that was the second thing. And then the 3rd thing was I ended up getting in this serious relationship with somebody. And they were graduating at the time. And they're basically ready to move. And I think the combination of having this health scare, meeting someone, and then also not really doing the work that I wanted to be doing, ended up making me leave just with my Master's degree and then going back into the industry, which was my next step.

Aris Winger: Okay, and so you go back to the industry where?

Seth Fortuna: This was in San Jose, kind of back in the same area where my 1st internship was. But now I was actually working for a light-emitting diode company. A little bit closer to where I wanted to be. Mostly doing reliability, engineering, and failure analysis. And so that was actually a bit of a frustrating thing for me, because when I got my master's and was applying, I really was applying to a lot more design-oriented jobs. The skills I had built up at Intel were mostly in failure analysis, fault isolation... figuring out why something broke in a semiconductor chip; those were the kind of skills that I picked up at Intel. But I really wanted to shed those skills. I wanted to do something else. But the only responses I was getting to my resumes that I sent out to various companies were the companies that were looking for people with those skills. And they wanted people who are doing that. After getting my Master's degree, and trying to really do something different, I found out that I couldn't find a job that would hire me to actually design devices. So I was kind of back to square one, almost.

Aris Winger: You felt boxed in.

Seth Fortuna: Yeah, for sure. I felt boxed in again. And the Master's degree just barely moved the needle for me. So, I still had the strong initiative to leave with the master's and try out the Bay Area again, because that's where my girlfriend at the time was. She was going to school at Berkeley, and so I ended up finding a job in that area. I did that for 2 years, and I just caught the bug, and I was like, I gotta continue my schooling because I'm not doing exactly what I want to do. I want to be the decider of my destiny. I want to be a decision maker for designers and not necessarily be told what to do or be handed what to work on. So then I went and got accepted to Berkeley for the PhD.

Aris Winger: I want to just make sure that I get this out. Many of us want to have the type of autonomy you speak about. It sounds like you are definitely trying to get more expertise in it. The more expertise you can get in terms of degrees, the gives avenues you have to this type of autonomy.

Seth Fortuna: Yeah, I'm not saying that's the only path, though. The other path could have been just to suck it up and just stay there for it. Because at the end of the day, I didn't graduate with my PhD until I was like 34-35. And if I had stayed at Intel for 15 years, I'm sure I would probably be making more money than I am right now, but I didn't want that path. I wanted to have more control over it. And so I preferred to go the academic route.

Now, in terms of financial success and all that stuff. If I wanted to make more money, I probably made the wrong decisions. I should have just sucked it up at Intel or stayed in the industry. So I think it was because I just enjoyed being in school and that environment. It's just more vibrant. Instead of being in the corporate world, working in a cubicle. It's just a lot more fun to be working and doing research in a university environment. So that's part of it, too. It's just an enjoyable experience being at a university.

Aris Winger: So while we're here, you definitely have experience in both worlds. Let's explore that. You've given your preferences. Could talk about just the differences between being in industry and academia that come out to you pretty immediately.

Seth Fortuna: So, I've mentored a number of undergraduates along the way, as a PhD student, and what I've noticed is that you get all these people who try to get these internships in research, and very few of them actually have any corporate experience. They'll come in with these undergraduate research experiences. Many people who want to go to grad school are dead set on going to grad school, so they don't spend time trying to get an internship with a company, and I always advise people to do that if they can, because I realize that while the corporate environment isn't necessarily my cup of tea. I think that the nature of that work actually appeals to a lot of people.

I think the goals and the nature of the work are such that your work is a little bit less nebulous. It's very clear what goals you're working towards, whereas academic work is often a little bit more open-ended. I think that can frustrate people sometimes like some people just want to be, if not told what to do, they want to have very, very clear priorities set for them. And that's just not always the case with research and development. So I think a lot of people really excel in the corporate environment, just because it fits better with their personality and things of that nature.

I'm not saying that, Oh, it's just better to be in to work in R&D or academia. I think it really depends on who you are as a person. So I always advise undergraduates to go off and spend a summer with a company if they can do that.

So, working for a company… there's always this push that you have to do it for the company. So they always have these quarterly meetings where they're just trying to motivate you to go out and work harder so we can improve this blah blah blah. But you know, at the end of the day, you work your butt off for a company, and they would very easily lay you off without really thinking twice about it, and so I was never willing to give my headspace to a company. I just didn't really like being a company person. I'm happy to do the work and job. But, to just become a citizen of a company, and just live and die, live and breathe whatever company I was working for. I just never really got into that, because the company gave me less than I was giving to the company. And so that's just how I feel about it, not to say that that's the right way. It's just how I feel about it.

So if I were to go back and work for a company, I'd much rather be at a startup. But my 1st desire is not to go back just as a technical person, just doing work at a company, not to say that I'm not going to do that in the future because of the way that things are with my job. I mean, the current funding situation is not so hot right now. So who knows where I'll be in like 2 years from now.

Aris Winger: Okay. So on your journey. At some point, you decide that you want to head to grad school. Where do you apply?

Seth Fortuna: I applied to Berkeley, obviously Stanford, UC San Diego, and I think UC Santa Barbara. I got into all the schools except Stanford. I ended up going to Berkeley, again, because I was still in that long-term relationship, and she was a student at Berkeley, so my decision was kind of chosen for me. In hindsight, that relationship dissolved, and I probably should have chosen based on the work that I was doing. I probably would have been better off going to a different school, just because the work that I was doing is not as strong at Berkeley as maybe some of those other schools that I had mentioned.

Aris Winger: But were you able to do stuff with lasers there or not?

Seth Fortuna: Yeah, I was making and designing light-emitting devices there. So yeah, I was doing the thing that I wanted to do. It was just that Berkeley had a smaller number of professors in that area. So there was less coursework available to me and things like that. But I was still happy at Berkeley. I was doing the stuff that I wanted to do. I didn't mean to give that impression, just that now looking back at it in hindsight, the stuff that I'm doing currently would have been a much better overlap with work that was being done at UC Santa Barbara. For example, I was recruited by a professor at UC Santa Barbara. I declined to go down there. But now he is working on one of my projects, a project that I'm the principal investigator on, and he's on my project. So it's just funny how that worked out right.

Aris Winger: Any lessons for being a professional from being in grad school that you had to pick up, learn?

Seth Fortuna: A couple of things come to mind. First of all, I think it's important for folks who are engineering graduate students to utilize all of the other amazing opportunities that they have in a university environment. Because once you leave it, it's gone. And once you go work for a company, or even work for a national lab like I am, it's different. You don't have access to all of these amazing diversity of resources.

Aris Winger: What do you mean? Access to things like what?

Seth Fortuna: Outside of engineering. There are things inside of engineering; there are always seminars and experts that come in and give talks. So I think it's important to go to those and see talks outside of your niche area. Don't get so focused on your own work, because, more likely than not, you're not going to be doing that work outside of school.

Aris Winger: Let me give you a scenario. Someone is in mechanical engineering. Are you saying that they're walking in the department's hallways, and they see a flyer for someone who's going to talk about civil or whatever? Are you saying they should still go to that, also?

Seth Fortuna: There's obviously only so much time that you have. So you have to pick and choose, but I should have been attending more of the computer science talks instead of just the electrical engineering talks. At that time, computer science was really ramping up. And now today, that whole field seems like it's eating the entire world. So I should have been more engaged in computer science back in school.

I don't know if you have to go the whole way over to the civil engineering department. But within your department, I think it's important to understand what other folks are doing because I often encounter problems that have been solved or people thought about 50 years ago.

And so there are very few new ideas that really emerge from science and engineering. And often, you can take something from a slightly different discipline and apply it to your field. And that's often a very fruitful way to go about finding unique solutions to problems. Just picking from adjacent fields. That just happens all the time. But that's the technical thing. I also think it's important for people to be a little bit more well-rounded. So go see talks well outside of engineering. You know, we got a lot of opportunities at Berkeley. We're kind of unique because we got quite a few luminaries that would come in, such as Supreme Court justices and things like that. You really need to set aside time to expose yourself to things like that.

Aris Winger: Why?

Seth Fortuna: First of all, you're not gonna really have that opportunity once you graduate. And I think it's just important to round out your experience to give you a broader sense of your place in the world and to understand different viewpoints. You know, just to make yourself a more well-informed citizen.

That's probably something to also connect back to the undergraduate. Penn State would kind of insist that you take a certain number of courses in fields outside of engineering. I'm sure schools are still doing that today, maybe even more so. And that was always kind of a frustration, I think, for engineering students, because it's like, 'I just want to take my classes, my normal engineering classes, and not take nutrition 101', or whatever the other class may be. I shared that frustration to some extent. But I also took a couple of classes outside of engineering that I still like to think about. I took a class on landscape architecture. I had not put any thought behind at all. But a lot of it was talking about the designs of cities, and how you should design a city to run efficiently, or how parks are designed, like how Central Park was designed, and things of that nature, something I never thought about at all. But I think about those topics all the time now that I'm out of school, and they've really kind of informed me on things like where I've decided to live.

Aris Winger: Yeah, powerful. Okay, so those are some lessons from the PhD experience. That is great. So then, after that?

Seth Fortuna: So after that, I graduated, and then a few months later, I got married. This is to someone completely different from the previous relationship. But I ended up getting married to somebody else, then I stuck around for 2 years with a postdoc, basically in my same position as during grad school. I just more or less extended what I was doing for another couple of years, because my wife at that time was a resident at a hospital, and she was kind of figuring out what she wanted to do with her life.

So we had all these upcoming big decisions. You know where to have kids, when to have kids, what job I was going to take after Berkeley, what job she was going to take after residency, and all these things. And so I think at that time most of the jobs that I would have been good for were mostly down in San Jose, Silicon Valley, the South Bay, and we decided that we didn't really want to move down there. We really liked where we were living in the Oakland, Berkeley area, but I didn't want to commute down there. That's quite a lot of commuting. And also it's quite expensive to live there. So we kind of came to the conclusion that it was going to be really hard to find the jobs that we wanted, and just to have enough money to really buy a home in a place that was desirable, and to raise a family and all that stuff, and so that pushed us towards looking outside of the Bay Area. That was mostly instigated by me. As a medical professional, my wife can more or less find work anywhere. Doctors are usually in high demand. So I was looking outside the Bay Area, looking strongly at Boston. And then and then I had a colleague who was in graduate school with me who was working at Sandia National Labs, and he told me about an opening they had for a postdoc there. I ended up applying and then getting that position. So that's how I ended up down here in Albuquerque.

Aris Winger: You've been there ever since.

Seth Fortuna: Yeah, 5 years now since 2019.

Aris Winger: Excellent. So, looking back now to undergrad, if you could add curriculum, add stuff to what you could have learned in undergrad, stuff that you might at some point during your journey that you would say, 'Well, wait! Why didn't someone teach me this?' 'Why didn't someone tell me that this was gonna happen?' What would be some of those things you wish you had been taught in undergrad?

Seth Fortuna: Yeah. First of all, there were a couple of decision points in undergrad where your department had a requirement where it was like, of these 3 classes, you have to take at least one. And so I can remember, there was a decision point where I had to choose between quantum mechanics, statics, and I don't remember what the 3rd class was, but it was something, like mechanics. And I was like, Oh, man, quantum sounds like too hard, too much math. But statistics, that doesn't sound too bad. I'll just sign up for that.

I really wish I had taken that quantum mechanics class, because that topic has just been like a bugaboo for me my entire career, and I just have not excelled at it.

I did take a class in matrix algebra. And oh my gosh, matrix algebra is so important these days that there should be a higher emphasis and more coursework in matrix algebra for engineers, because I encounter it all the time, and my skills are so poor. I really wish that I had had more schoolwork in that area.

So those are more concrete examples, but more generally. One of the things that I maybe didn't appreciate was how important the fundamentals are. Now I tell people that if you understood your undergraduate books from the front to cover to the back, you would be perfectly fine as a professional engineer, as a PhD-level engineer. What is most important is understanding the fundamentals because everything leads from the fundamentals, and with engineering, often, if you can get within a factor of 2, that's good enough. And if you need to get better than a factor of 2. Then you can do the more advanced science, the more advanced math. But for my work to get within a factor of 2 is often good enough. I can just jot something out in a notebook or on a whiteboard. Those simple equations that you learn in undergraduate studies. They serve you very well, and I think people often try to get hung up on the details as an undergraduate. Often, you don't need to understand something within 1% error as an engineer. So as an undergrad, if you're so focused on figuring out the problem, the solution to within 1%, then you start leaning on things like modeling and software packages. You get focused on those, and you completely lose the ability to utilize the more fundamental equations, which are so important.

Back-of-the-envelope calculations are very important to do. Division in your head, to work in different orders of magnitude in your head so that you could quickly answer a question in a meeting and not have to say, 'Oh, I'll get back to you on that'. To be able to quickly do math in your head so you can do stuff on the fly and quickly answer questions from a manager or a colleague. That's all very important.

Also memory. One thing I didn't appreciate, and I don't really have any empirical evidence to back this up. Still, I do really feel that the people who have the most success in a technical field, like professors and professionals, are people who have the greatest memories. They can remember people. I have a hard time remembering people, but to remember people and the work. To be able to remember a paper that you read like 3 years ago, to remember equations that you used 3 or 4 years ago, or whatever. It's so valuable because you can make decisions on the fly and not always have to crack open a textbook. I'm not sure how well you can really work on your memory; to some extent, that's probably innate. Maybe there are things that you can do to improve your memory capacity. I'm not sure. But anyway, those are a couple of things that come to mind that I've kind of seen, and I have learned over the years.

Aris Winger: Talk to us a little bit about teamwork and working on the team. How has that been easy? How is being on a team?

Seth Fortuna: Definitely, teamwork is important. I did get frustrated in undergrad. There was an emphasis in undergraduate school for team projects, and I always thought those poorly emulated the nature of team projects in the real world.

The emphasis was there. You have to work in a team, so you'd have all these team projects and your classes. But the way that you work in a team at an undergraduate school does not look like the way you work in a team in the real world. It's like I said, it's a poor emulation.

Maybe you know, over the 20 years I've been out of undergraduate school, they've improved upon that. I would say a couple of things, and maybe the things that I say are kind of at odds with each other, but to some extent, working in a team is often hard. Even though you have people on a team, it's often hard to get people to actually do the work because they have other stuff to do. They have other projects. So it's important for you to motivate people to do the work, especially if you're like the PI. Suppose you're the principal investigator. You're the person who owns the project or leads the team at the end of the day. If you fail, it's often on you. The people on your team don't always feel that. And so they're quite okay if they don't end up doing the work because maybe they don't need it. They have other stuff that they're working on. So you really need to motivate people to do the work.

And in school projects, certain people often do all the work, and then you have other people who will get the same grade, even though they didn't do as much. But motivating people to do the work is quite important because often people are busy and they have other things to do. It's very rare that you'll have a team where everybody does equal work. Again, it's always going to be one person who's really pushing the work along, and the other people are really just helping out. They're there to support that one main person. So, teamwork, usually it's like one person who has a main vision, or has a main task, and there are other people supporting that person.

Aris Winger: No, this was just happening to me, in which I was on a team of 5, and I was literally looking for the person you were talking about, the project leader, and then I realized that everybody thought that that was me.

Seth Fortuna: Oh, yeah.

Kyle Clark: That's been a common thing for me, too. Where suddenly you're sitting there, and you have this moment of "oh, everybody thinks I'm gonna be the one doing this work."

Aris Winger: So then, how does anything ever get done?

Seth Fortuna: Yeah, but now with my working mostly in R&D, it's a little bit different. Many of my projects are not structured, so I need to deliver something physical or tangible at the end of the day. In R&D, how this comes together often is quite interesting. You'll have people off doing their own thing. If I'm a team leader, I kind of have to make sure that there is some coherent message or some coherent story. But people don't always respond very well if you tell them exactly what to do, and so you need to give some people room to breathe and go and explore their own thing.

But you still need to somehow weave a coherent story so that you can. Prove to the people who gave you the money to do what you're doing that you went off and did something valuable, and they'll continue to give you money for some other project down the road. That's more focusing on an R&D team.

Now, if you're working on a project development team, that's a whole different thing. Because either the project was shipped or it wasn't. That's more black and white. With R&D, it's a little bit different because it's a little bit more of a gray area, more of a nebulous thing.

Aris Winger: I think you've done well telling us about just the R&D space in general, and why it's different. Is there anything else you want to say, just in general, about the R&D space? Why, it's different. What is its main purpose?

Seth Fortuna: I think the biggest thing, or one of the bigger things, is that in R&D, often our priorities shift very, very quickly. Our milestones that we have set are often fairly open-ended and might not have specific dates associated with them. So I think people struggle with that sometimes. I guess you get this in graduate school, too. You kinda have this sense of something that you're trying to do. But those, like intermediate stepping stone points, are not always very well defined or very clear. So I think people can struggle with that sometimes, because they do want those very clear stepping stones to reach toward their goal. And so it can be hard to motivate yourself sometimes because it's like, 'Well, I have like 20 things to do. I'm not even sure what priority number one is, and I can't really work on these 20 things at the same time. So what should I work on?'

I struggle with that all the time. Kind of setting, even just setting daily priorities. 'What is the thing that I should be focusing my efforts on now?' Especially when it comes to funding, because you need to make sure that next fiscal year you have enough money to continue working. And so you have to allot time, not only to do the work that you need to do now, but to get the money to do work next year. And how do you manage your time for that? What's more important, working on those projects that you have right now, or working on those projects that you're gonna get in the future? So time management, I think, is more challenging in an R&D environment than it is in a corporate environment. I think it's just clearer when you're working in a company what you need to be working on at any given time.

Aris Winger: Yeah, that's possible. Alright, we've got a couple more questions for you. So in your journey to get to where you are, what have you had to sacrifice?

Seth Fortuna: Oh boy, I think this is probably more specific to my journey. It's not gonna be, maybe not like a great general example, but I think we touched upon this a little bit. When I think about my career path, I probably would have maybe done it a little bit differently. I probably would have just preferred to have gone straight through graduate school, gotten the PhD. And just had that instead of going back and forth. So I think that's been a point of insecurity for me.

I used to go on LinkedIn all the time. But I have actually taken it off my phone. I still have an account just in case there's some random headhunter who is looking for someone for a job. But I choose not to go on LinkedIn, because you see things like 'so and so got a promotion', and 'so and so is now the VP of whatever.' And my career path has not put me on a career path to get promotions and go up the management chain, or put me on the path to making a serious amount of money. So I may have some insecurities about that.

I wish I had made some decisions differently with respect to my career trajectory so that I would maybe be a CTO of some company at this point in my career or something. But I think you just need to get comfortable with who you are and where you are in your career, and that takes some work. I don't know exactly what I'm sacrificing there.

Certainly, the more obvious thing is the work-life balance. Being an engineer does take a lot of time, right? And one thing that I found is when you're a student, an undergrad, or even a graduate student, you really feel like you have all the time in the world. If you don't do something well, I'll just do it tomorrow, because you don't have any other commitments. You might not be married. You may not have kids. But the second you get married, you start having kids, even just getting older. So many things start carving away at your time. You only have 24 hours in a day. Obviously, you have to sleep. But you think you have all this other time when you're young, but things quickly start carving away at that, and you have to make a decision. How much of that time am I going to be allowed to get carved up by your work? And that's a real decision.

For example, you can't go off and be a professor in a major research institution and expect that you're going to have as much time for your family as if you were to go work for a company where you can maybe leave things behind at the end of the day. Those are real decisions that you have to make.

And so I've maybe sacrificed some things, like when I didn't have a family and didn't have kids. I didn't do world travel or something like that, because I wanted to respect my company's 2-week vacation policy and things like that. But now I've chosen not to sacrifice my weekend time for my work. I used to work on the weekends pretty much all the time, certainly in grad school, and even starting out at Sandia. But now that I have 2 kids, I'm basically okay with the fact that I don't generally work on the weeknights. I generally don't work on the weekends, even though my peers are working evenings and weekends. So that if they're working more. Well, they're gonna have more output. They're gonna get more proposals. And they're gonna have more papers written. And so that's been a tough thing for me, I think, especially having a family later in life, is just being okay with that and understanding that being available for my family and not sacrificing that time is just more more important for me right now, and being okay with maybe not having as many paper papers published, and things of that nature.

Aris Winger: Great answer. Final question, as you know, the audience reading this might be an undergrad. This is your time to talk directly to them. What would you tell them about the journey, about going from undergrad to professional, what to look out for? Any advice at all, talk directly to them.

Seth Fortuna: Yeah, yeah, I would say that there are a few things that I would encourage. I would just emphasize that undergraduate schooling is the most important part of your knowledge base for engineering. Yeah, graduate school is important. But even if you didn't take any graduate schoolwork, and all you had was your undergraduate school work. Suppose you knew that foundational material from front to back, you're set. That's the most important thing.

When I open up a textbook because I have a problem that I'm encountering, even as someone with a PhD, I'm always cracking open an undergraduate textbook. I'm not cracking open some obscure graduate textbook because the fundamentals are the most important part. Understanding the fundamentals.

I think one thing that undergraduates fall in love with is modeling and simulations. It's really fun and cool to use simulation programs. But it's so much more important to be able to solve problems by hand. And again, just to get within a factor of 2. Because, as a professional, that's usually good enough. Fundamentals are so important.

Also, doing things outside of your classwork, outside of the engineering meeting, people having friends outside of engineering, having experiences outside of engineering, doing more socialization. Taking those classes outside of engineering and taking them seriously, putting some thought into utilizing that coursework for something that you find interesting. I think it is important to seek some opportunities for doing either undergraduate research or taking an internship. Not getting so hung up on having a 4.0 GPA. It's not that important. When I hire, when I look at resumes. I do not look at the GPA. Generally, if they're above a 3, I'm generally happy because what's more important to me is someone who's gone out and had experiences. And has clearly shown motivation and just joy for doing engineering. So I'm not hung up on GPA, but I think undergraduates can get too hung up on that.

12 - Krys Williams

ROLL WITH THE BUMPS IN THE PATH

Bumpy roads might compel us to get off the path. They might signal to us that we were never supposed to be on that trajectory to start. Time and time again, Materials Scientist, Physicist, and Mechanical Engineer Krystaufeux "Krys" Williams faced challenge after challenge, including impostor syndrome, at various levels and institutions. He was undeterred. His unyielding fascination with physics and to "learn more about materials interactions on the atomic scale" kept him going. Krys' engineering path spans the course of five institutions and many years of hard work and countless hours of dedication. It will remind you that if your passion is strong and you learn to tap into your resources and support, then you have a chance to achieve your goals and dreams, even when those around you say you can't.

Krys Williams, PhD

PhD and MS in Materials Science and Engineering, Penn State University

MS in Physics, Delaware State University

BS in Mechanical Engineering, Drexel University

BA in Physics, Lincoln University

Hometown: Washington, DC

Research Analyst, Institute for Defense Analyses

Aris Winger: Krys, welcome. I really appreciate you taking the time. Are you an engineer? Would you call yourself an engineer?

Krys Williams: I would call myself… I'm an engineer by training, but… if you ask me, I would consider myself more of a scientist. The degree that I received from my graduate institution was in materials science and engineering. With that being said, I would consider myself more of a scientist than an engineer.

Aris Winger: What does it mean to you to be an engineer?

Krys Williams: I still engage as an engineer in my work. What that means is that…things that an engineer does come down to almost the root of the word - engine. And originally, the engineer was solely focused on making adjustments to the engine to make it better, more efficient. And in the day-to-day job, an engineer is working to make a process that's already established more efficient, more effective. There's innovation there as well. But the system is usually already in place, in my mind. The engineer is trying to perfect that process, usually working in a team with many others, depending on how big the system or the engine is. A large team may take different components of that engine and improve the process, ensuring it doesn't lack efficiency. It's coming up with the next level or improvement to that engine. Even if you think about the automobile. In the next year, it's going to have some improvement or a new safety feature.

Aris Winger: And then the scientist?

Krys Williams: Now, to me, the scientist is the one who has a little more capacity for innovation. The scientist may have a system that's already established. If you think about pharmaceutical scientists, they may be working on a medicine that's already in place. But at the same time, they may be developing the next medicine that will help cure or delay the symptoms, get rid of the symptoms of COVID, or something like that. Scientists have a lot more capacity for innovation. That's what I really enjoy doing. That would be my ideal situation, coming up with something new.

Aris Winger: Great. Tell us about your undergraduate experience.

Krys Williams: My undergraduate degrees were in physics and mechanical engineering. I started at Lincoln University, and then…

Aris Winger: With the Amish.

Krys Williams: Yes, yes, with the Amish out in the country, and with no other resources, almost.

Aris Winger: HBCU amongst the Amish.

Krys Williams: And the way that came about was that I was somewhat undecided about what I wanted to do for college, and I wasn't diligent about filling out all my applications. But I knew my counselor really well, and when a recruiter came for this new science and engineering program that had been going on at Lincoln, I jumped at the opportunity, because at that point, I only had one acceptance letter. I was performing academically, but wasn't very strong with following through on college applications. I saw this as a chance to start my career. I hadn't been diligent up to that point.

Aris Winger: Was it a double major?

Krys Williams: The major was part of a dual degree program. Lincoln is a Liberal Arts Institution originally, and while they did have a science department, they didn't have strong engineering schools. They partnered with other institutions to get students who wanted to pursue engineering into a program elsewhere.

Aris Winger: You left after a certain number of years?

Krys Williams: Yes, and the way it's designed is as a 3, 2 program. You would originally spend three years at Lincoln and two years at the other university, which was Drexel University. And with the Co-Op, it became a little bit longer. It became a three-three for me, as the program offers the opportunity to spend six months working at a company during your undergraduate time. I had the opportunity to work at an actual company for six months in my educational process. And then I came back to finish the degree.

Aris Winger: What degree do you end up finishing with after 6 years? Is it a bachelor's

Krys Williams: I ended up with a bachelor's in physics, what they would call a BA in Physics, because of the liberal arts exposure as well as the scientific exposure. At Drexel, I received an undergraduate BS in Mechanical Engineering.

Aris Winger: Was there any imposter syndrome? Any concerns about preparation?

Krys Williams: Oh, very much, yes, very much, very much. The concerns about preparation were not from my perspective. I didn't have the vision going into undergraduate schooling at an HBCU, Lincoln University, to really understand the implications of pursuing two degrees, with the second one being at a predominantly white institution - Drexel University. I didn't consider the difference between the two places. One institution can be very nourishing and supportive. A larger institution can be very mechanical in its approach to helping students; you're just another number. You have to get through this weed-out process.

Aris Winger: Your class size tripled or quadrupled?

Krys Williams: Very much, very much. Compared to universities across the United States, Drexel is still somewhat small, but it has a very large number of students in engineering, and it's very competitive. I definitely faced imposter syndrome and…

Aris Winger: How did you deal with it? What's the secret formula?

Krys Williams: Wow! That's a good question.

Aris Winger: Somebody's reading this now, and they have imposter syndrome right now.

Krys Williams: I'm still dealing with it in a way. But the way I got through the Drexel part is one, say a lot of prayer, two, using the support programs that were in place at Drexel. One thing I didn't know was that there was a pre-summer program that helped some of the undergraduates at Drexel get acquainted with their process, their exposure to engineering. While I had that at Lincoln, I was able to take advantage of or embed myself in that support structure at Drexel, even though I didn't participate in that as a freshman undergraduate.

Aris Winger: What does that look like? Does that look like you deciding that you're going to go knock on somebody's door?

Krys Williams: Pretty much. Pretty much. It was me spending time in the Success Program office. That was in the main building on the 3rd floor. I spent time there, and even though I was still an outsider in that office in some ways, I knew that their goals aligned with mine regarding people needing support in understanding what this transition will be for someone like myself. In some ways, I knocked on the door and forced their hand to take me in. I asked for all the tricks of the trade to speak.

Aris Winger: This is interesting, because now this is not the same person who was coming out of high school to get the support that you need.

Krys Williams: Very true, very true, and it could have been that I've always been a somewhat social, more social person. However, it didn't come naturally to knock on the door and get the things I felt I needed. Somewhere along the way, I needed to become more persistent in looking for resources, even if I didn't know what they were.

Aris Winger: We're at Drexel. Any fundamental lessons before you graduate that need to be mentioned before you finish?

Krys Williams: Sure. Before I finished, there were quite a few things that I discovered about myself. I barely got through the engineering school process.

Aris Winger: What were the challenges?

Krys Williams: The challenges were my academic skills. I did really well in high school. I had an aptitude for math and science.

At this point, I had been through the L.A.S.E.R. (Lincoln's Advanced Science and Engineering Reinforcement) program at Lincoln University, which was designed to take students in the pre-summer and give them the training that they needed, including all of the basic engineering disciplines: physics, calculus, and those things. I pulled myself up and finally, towards the end, got my GPA up to earn scholarships and things like that. But transitioning to the engineering school at Drexel was much tougher than I had anticipated.

Aris Winger: Was it content, speed, environment, all of it?

Krys Williams: All of it. Inner city from a rural setting. Speed, content. The competition level.

Accessing different study groups, that's dynamic. Then the office hours: interacting more with the professors, having to pursue that relationship as opposed to having the professors pursue you when things aren't going as well as they should. You go from professors calling your dorm room to now going to an office hour and getting what you can from that, and then having to contribute to the study group, if you're deemed worthy enough to contribute to that study group. All of those things were skills that I had to pick up. And that's what caused me to struggle much in the transition.

Aris Winger: That's a learning curve.

Krys Williams: That was very challenging. I got through on the very low end of that learning curve.

One preacher used to say at Lincoln: "Some people graduate summa cum laude, some people graduate cum laude. And the rest of us graduate, 'Thank you, Lordy!'"

Aris Winger: Why didn't you switch majors? At the low point, why didn't you say, "This isn't the thing?" What kept you going?

Krys Williams: What kept me going…There was a bit of an intuition I felt that I had for some of the engineering concepts. It can take me a long time to read the writing on the wall, but I felt I had an intuition, and I believe my professors saw some of that intuition in the engineering classes. For that reason, I did not switch majors, and I'm not quite sure what I would have switched to. I felt I put my best foot forward at Lincoln and moved up the ranks. I felt at some point I would do the same at Drexel.

Aris Winger: You finish Drexel, and then you head off to what?

Krys Williams: After Drexel, I was looking to work. In that process, I put in a few applications. I had one acceptance letter. I didn't feel it was strong enough of a salary that I was looking for at the time.

Aris Winger: Are you still in Philadelphia at this time?

Krys Williams: I'm still in Philadelphia. I really wanted to stay there and start my career in that area. That was one of the factors, too. I didn't take the offer that I had because it wasn't close enough to where I wanted to live. After denying that offer because of pay and location, nothing else came. I think part of that was because it was around September 11th or before, and no opportunities were coming. I had to ask myself some tough questions. If I didn't have a job, could I really stay in Philly? I came back to my hometown and lived there for about 2 or 3 years, working as a teacher. During all that time, my desire was to go back to graduate school to pursue a program in physics.

Aris Winger: What did you teach?

Krys Williams: My very first job was at the University of the District of Columbia in their community outreach extension services, teaching adult learners who were trying to pursue their GED. I taught multiple subjects, mostly math and science. That was good for a while. It was grant-funded, and that funding ran out, and I taught high school for another half year or so at a Public Charter School in DC. By that time, I figure I am going to see what I can do with more jobs becoming available. But I was really thinking deeply about the graduate school thing.

Aris Winger: How does that come about? Is it because you had a deeper sense of wanting to know more? Why graduate school? What was coming up for you?

Krys Williams: Sure. I would say it was a combination of things. I wanted to learn deeper about the interactions of the atom and how that relates to material processes. One of probably my favorite courses in undergrad engineering was materials, or mechanics of materials, where part of the course was devoted to understanding materials at a deeper level. I was very curious about that. I wanted to look for opportunities to do it.

Once again, in a similar fashion to the high school version of myself, I didn't pursue it in terms of filling out applications and understanding what I needed to do. But I did speak with a friend who was starting a family around that time, my friend Andre. He told me that he had an opportunity to pursue graduate school, but because of his young family, he needed to focus on that. It turns out the people who were sponsoring this program, the Bridges to Doctorate Program, were looking for people to fill that role. I had worked with this office. They were embedded in the same office at Drexel University that I had worked in as an undergraduate, and I forced myself into that office. Things aligned, and I was off to my first graduate experience at this place.

Aris Winger: Where was this?

Krys Williams: This was in Delaware, at the University of Delaware, and I was pursuing my graduate degree in physics.

Aris Winger: And how was that experience?

Krys Williams: That was another experience that was very challenging for me. Going up to the next level… And if you recall from our conversation earlier, I had some exposure to the physics curriculum. But that curriculum was designed to send me to engineering school, more of what they call classical physics. In this environment, I'm competing with other graduate students who, for them, this is all they want to do is physics. I had some things to pick up at the higher undergraduate level with physics and Quantum physics. That's one of the things that made it difficult for me, apart from the large size of the campus, and it being a different environment altogether.

Aris Winger: Let's go deeper. We've all felt this. You're sitting in a class you realize you may not have the prerequisites. There's something that's missing here. You've never had quantum. You look over to the person next to you. They've taken quantum 2, 3, and 4. They're finishing the professor's sentences. Two things. One is about demoralization. How do you deal with that? Two, what do you do in terms of fixing that?

Krys Williams: Very good question. The gaps in your education are now your responsibility. Now, not only are you dealing with being at a PWI (predominantly white institution), you're dealing with competing internationally. Sometimes international students have taken variations of this course, I don't know, one or 2 times already.

But to answer your question: You now are responsible for making up those gaps, and no one tells you, but you feel that now you have to do what's necessary to get up to the race's starting point. You have to make up some things. They helped in some ways, allowing me to take a few undergraduate courses. I was also very supported by the Bridges to Doctorate program. And at the same time, one has to take it upon themselves to go to the library, find those resources. It took me a while to understand that this is not something that your professor is trying to convey to you. This is something on a national, international level that is available in many variations. I couldn't really grasp the concept of a quantum physics book being available, taught by a world-renowned physicist somewhere. How does one even start to grasp that? That was a question that I was dealing with. That was very much a challenge in my early graduate experience.

Aris Winger: But you made the attempts, pushed through it, and got more comfortable with it?

Krys Williams: For me, though, it took having to change to a different program, to a different school altogether. I transferred eventually to Delaware State University after that first experience at the University of Delaware. That's what it took for me to finally reboot and start again, essentially. At the same time, you're trying to prove to yourself that I can do this. Is this what I'm supposed to be doing? Lots of self-doubt. You're wondering what's going to become of your life at this point. That was a very challenging experience for me.

Aris Winger: Delaware state, what are they providing? What are they giving you that you weren't getting at the University of Delaware?

Krys Williams: Let's see, they were giving me…First, another chance. That was primarily what it was. And in some ways, I had matured. I think I've matured quite a bit, and I shifted the focus to myself. What can I do differently? While Delaware State is an HBCU, its research infrastructure was as good as the University of Delaware or Penn State, where I would go later. It wasn't like I was going to a place that was inferior. Even the support, I would say, was still about the same, but you get some comfort in seeing more faces like yours. You get some comfort in having a few more professors who understand the process, but I don't know if there was a lack of rigor there. And this time, I was a little more prepared in understanding what was being asked of me, what the playing field required now.

Aris Winger: We've heard the M word a couple of times, far in the interviews we've been doing, and it's "maturity." And if I could dream, I would inject our readers who are in undergraduate school now with all the maturity necessary to be successful. I want to unpack maturity. What are these elements of maturity that we need to get as quickly as possible for someone?

Krys Williams: You're in a position where you are on your own. You have your family back home. They may or may not understand that you're committing to something, and you don't want to have to come back home. At an HBCU where people look like you and have your same interests, there's the pull, of course, to kind of relax and do all the things that an African American student would enjoy. But at the same time, in the back of my head, I'm saying. "Krys, you gotta get yourself together. What are your goals? If you 'failed' the first time, then what's going to stop you from failing the second time?"

Dealing with these questions helped me mature. Though I could have done better when I had my TA assignments, I wanted to make sure that I did well with those assignments. When I had my quantum physics courses, I wanted to make sure that I had the elements down. I'm spending time looking at different lecturers this time. I'm looking at different professors now, understanding that the book can be easier to understand from one professor versus another. Books are written for different reasons.

Understanding that landscape now, I think, gave me a bit more maturity. And of course, looking at myself, saying, "Hey, I need to go and get this if I want it." I knew there were still going to be challenges; there were still gonna be biases. But realizing what I can do with what I have already.

Aris Winger: You're helping me a lot. You're helping me a lot here in terms of thinking about maturity being tied to: What are the self-reflection questions that you're asking yourself? And particularly the ones about: What are my goals? What am I trying to do here? That resonates with me a lot because I went through the motions when I wasn't mature. I was not thinking about what I was doing. I'm not operating with purpose. Hopefully, that helps someone who's reading this now.

Krys Williams: There could be cards stacked against you. But what do you want from the process? At the end of the day, I still had curiosity. I was still fascinated by materials and interactions. I'm pursuing physics. But at the end of the day, I really was curious about materials at a deep level, at the atomic level. . .

Aris Winger: This feels like a strong thread through this whole thing, your curiosity and commitment to that. Ok, so we finished Delaware State and then?

Krys Williams: Yep. Delaware State, at the time I was there, they did not have a P.. in Optical Physics. And by the time I finished that program, the master's in physics, I began looking for other PhD programs across the country. And that essentially was my objective. Or in some ways, I'm still trying to prove to myself that I can do this. I had some maturity, but in some ways, I wanted to stick it to whoever stuck it to me. I wanted to prove them wrong.

Aris Winger: You had people in mind? People who were not on your side. Haters?

Krys Williams: Exactly. They're questioning your resolve and whether you belong here, and in some ways, I want to prove to them that I belong here. I'm a part of this conversation. That's what spurred me on to pursue my doctorate in physics. But, looking back, I've always wanted a PhD. since my undergraduate. I heard someone saying, "You can do this." It was a guest lecturer coming to our school and saying, "What's your name, young man? Dr. Williams, how does that sound?" (after I told them my name) I kind of got that bug early. I always wanted to pursue a PhD. But the reason why I was pursuing it more in physics, even though I enjoyed it, was because I wanted to prove something either to myself or the naysayers.

At that point, I began dating someone (who is now my wife) who was pursuing her PhD. in education and Higher Education. Still, I had spent some time working in the office, dealing with diversity in science at Penn State University. As we get to know each other–I think this is kind of another divine appointment in my life–she's listening to my story and background. And she asked me a question. "Do you want to try and apply to our material science program? Because we have a really great program. Is this what you want to do? It sounds like what you want to do."

But I'm reading the cards here, nothing serious. You could probably guess what my response is. I respond, "No, I really want to pursue my dream, to be a cool physicist that can relate to people, and convey some of these difficult topics to them."

Aris Winger: Oh, Neil DeGrasse Tyson.

Krys Williams: Neil DeGrasse Tyson, some of the great physicists of our time, black physicists. But I'm going to be cooler. I'm going to go to the best physics university.

We have a few more conversations. She asked, "Why don't you just apply?" In the back of my mind, I think, "No, I'm determined." But going through the applications, and I did apply to appease her, I ended up taking that opportunity. It was the best choice I could have made.

Aris Winger: So you were at Penn State.

Krys Williams: I'm at Penn State at this point. I've been through the cycle a couple of times, and though I do have difficulty starting, it was where I needed to be. It was really cool learning about all of the great techniques. I'm becoming more of an experimentalist, which is something I already wanted to do. During my undergraduate and graduate experiences, I only had limited opportunities to be a research scientist in experimentation. I didn't have a chance to get exposure to a lot of the great experimental material science things. Now I'm at Penn State. I almost have to learn a new…

Aris Winger: I was about to ask about this. Go ahead.

Krys Williams: I almost have to learn a new language in terms of material science versus physics. They're very closely related in some ways, but in other ways, when it comes down to the nuances and the nomenclature, there are very distinct differences. I had to learn those things, and that was…

Aris Winger: And is this all on the run on the fly? And you're catching it. We're back to a new learning curve. How's that going?

Krys Williams: Another learning curve. I'm learning those things. It was very difficult at first. The lady that I'm in a relationship with is also aware of some of the resources that are available on campus. And of course, now I had that success story from Delaware state, learning to pursue and find other resources that give you access to the things you need to catch up to the curve.

Because this is another international competition, you're working with graduate students who, in some cases, are your buddies. But in most cases, they're vying for those same positions, scholarships, and levels you are vying for. But now I have the experience to let me seek out the resources that I needed to be successful. Those offices were very instrumental. But then I also had to pursue the research skills in the laboratory that would get me through to the next level.

Kyle Clark: You mentioned that this partner you had was helping you find resources. Were professors also helping you get to those if you did not have this one person in your life at the time? Were there other people who were helping find where these sources of help were?

Krys Williams: Yes, the short answer to that is, yes, I would say my girlfriend at the time (who is now my wife) and the people who she worked for in the Office of Science Diversity Initiatives were also able to point me to those professors who could determine that I might need a resource or training on this piece of equipment. They could point me to the professors to whom I would not have to prove myself. They were able to point me to those professors to ask something like, "Hey, do you have an extra book on XYZ instruments? Do you have something that could help Krys out?" There were professors there who were very instrumental in helping me get to where I am now.

Aris Winger: Any other major lessons at Penn State?

Krys Williams: I did have to make some critical changes to who my advisor was. I was fortunate enough to find a very supportive advisor (Dr. Digby Macdonald), whom I didn't start with at the time. Not that my previous advisor wasn't supportive, but I became aware that it was helpful to have an advisor inside my own major, if you will, or within my school. That became a really important point at this level. You're learning that advisors and professors may be vying for and supporting you behind closed doors. You need someone who could do that. You need someone who trusts your skills. While you have to be responsible in bringing your highest level of work, there are some things that are happening that you aren't necessarily aware of at that time. You need someone, an advisor, who can fight those battles for you.

Aris Winger: After finishing Penn State, and then you're in the workforce now...

Krys Williams: Workforce, even before I finish. That's another level to this story. I, for some reason or another, once I get aligned with the advisor, I'm reading the economy, if you will. I'm reading the writing on the wall and what's going on. Around the time when the economy was faltering, I became aware of an opportunity to work at a national lab to do my thesis research. I'm faced with a dilemma: do I finish the traditional path of a graduate student and finish out my research portion, or work at a lab while finishing?

At this point, I'm finished with my coursework. I have to figure out what field of research I want to engage in. When an opportunity came up to work back in the area where I'm from, Washington, DC, I took the opportunity before finishing my degree.

It came in the package of a program that was designed to bring graduate or undergraduate students to a national lab, allow them to do research, and earn a salary. It probably was above what the typical graduate student would earn, but not as much as, say, a full professional that the lab would earn. I took that opportunity while I was still a graduate student, which helped me feel like what I was doing was worth it. All the sacrifice was worthwhile, given that I could take care of myself and now my newly formed family, and finish out what I started.

Aris Winger: And how was it working in the lab? Now, at this point, what are you calling yourself? Are you a scientist at this point? Are you an engineer?

Krys Williams: . At this point, I am officially a materials research engineer, although I consider myself a professional scientist. And while I hadn't quite completed the doctoral program, I felt my contributions were very important to the main mission of the group that I was in. That was kind of laid out by the foundation that my advisor started in his field of material science, this subarea of electrochemistry and corrosion research. I felt that was the foundation that was laid. And in my group, I was able to bring my mechanical aptitude to that field, and that was the area, the niche, that I was carving out for myself.

Aris Winger: What are you working on today?

Krys Williams: Well, I worked in my position at the National Lab for about 9 to 10 years.

Aris Winger: Oh, wow!

Krys Williams: And of course, some of that, or 4 of those years, was spent as a student employee. And part of the program was an agreement that you would convert noncompetitively. Essentially, I didn't have to do a Postdoc. I did the postdoc while I was a research engineer student. I transitioned out of that role and now to a research analyst role (at another company). I had to put aside my experimental research skill set to pick up another skill set, which is in analytics.

Now I am, even though I'm still working with systems and materials and mechanical engineering, I'm now doing it more in an analytical way, as you may have noticed, the trend in analytics. Everyone is trying to analyze data. That's essentially what I'm doing, but in the context of mechanical and materials expertise that's required.

Aris Winger: As you think back on your undergraduate experience, what would have been part of the curriculum that you wish they had told you?

Krys Williams: I think if I had it to do all over again, I would hope that those differences in the institutions and the levels of competition could have been relayed a little better to me.

Aris Winger: Here are some things that you need to expect in the change of institution.

Krys Williams: Yes. There could be warnings. Sometimes when you're in the environment, there's a different set of survival techniques that you need to adjust to make the adjustment. I found that connections are very important if you are going to make that transition in your career.

Aris Winger: Are you saying that you wish you had had better mentoring also?

Krys Williams: I believe that's the case. I believe that mentoring is very, very important. Sometimes their goal is in, say, your 1st institution is to get you finished. And that's a worthy goal to get you. I want to get you through Lincoln. It's going to be tough. There might be some challenges along the way, but there're going to be some bigger challenges, even bigger challenges in the next place that you go to. And let's see if we can get you a few resources to deal with those challenges. Sometimes you're dealing with people who are used to one tool set, and that tool set may not be the best tool set for all of the things that they have to face, and it'll be tricky, giving those things to the student.

Aris Winger: What are you still trying to learn day to day in your work as a professional?

Krys Williams: Believe it or not, as a professional, I'm still finding myself trying to prove myself, trying to improve myself. Trying to find my strengths and hone in on those things, and I find I am finding success. I still have challenges in my day-to-day work. Of course, the stakes are a lot higher. You're working with people making decisions for our country's best interests and things like that. And the stakes are higher. But at the end of the day, I believe one has to be confident in their ability, despite failures.

I'm learning to take my strengths and contribute to the teams that I participate with in a meaningful way. Overcoming and passing down as much as I can, even as I see the younger PhDs come into my group. We're a company that kind of brings in people with master's and PhDs. I can see a lot of times that they're coming fresh out of the lab. Sometimes they aren't ready for those interactions with these high-level people.

Aris Winger: What do you mean?

Krys Williams: In my role as an analyst, we're expected not only to analyze the system, but we're also expected to deliver the information to an audience via writing memos. We have to convey our very complex subject matter to an audience who may have a generic technical background. Then the information will trickle down to an audience who is your average everyday citizen, your average taxpayer.

We feel the pressure. That was my most recent struggle, I would say, in technical writing, taking those very complex ideas and making them make sense to the everyday person. There was another learning curve.

Aris Winger: I have 2 more questions for you. The first is: what have you sacrificed in order to be here?

Krys Williams: Wow! I think I have sacrificed the ability to enjoy things a lot earlier. Even starting a family earlier (I am now married to the woman from Penn State and have a teen son).

Even buying a house earlier. During these transitions, back and forth in graduate school, the money wasn't always guaranteed. I had to find various resources, either teaching assistantships, research assistantships, that weren't always coming in the most timely manner. I had to put aside stability, early stability, for this goal of professional success later. I think that was my biggest sacrifice. No regrets, certainly. I am able to enjoy a lot more now than I have in the past. My buddies might have teased me before. Now they can see the fruits of their labor.

I think that was the sacrifice. And of course, you, in some ways, miss some of the moments, some of those key moments with family members and things like that. You get there for the big ones. But sometimes you miss those moments. You have to figure out if you're going to spend this time in the lab, or am I going to get back for a birthday? You kind of sacrifice those sometimes.

Aris Winger: Final question. We got a reader here who is an undergrad in engineering, or otherwise thinking about going into engineering. Talk to them directly. What would you say to them about going through the struggle, about getting through, about whether it's worth it? The whole thing, whatever you want to say to them. They're reading now.

Krys Williams: To the reader who is getting ready to take on the challenge of the undergraduate engineering experience, I would say there is going to be a lot of hard work. The struggle is not guaranteed at the beginning, but know that if you do find an initial difficulty or initial struggle, there is a way to get through it, and based on my experience, sometimes you look for those resources that are there at some places. And if there are some supportive network structures at your institution, pursue them, look for them actively. It's going to be on you, but if some people reach out to you, let them know what you're dealing with. Don't feel you have to do it all on your own, because I'm sure you're going to be strong. I'm sure you've been great, and that's gotten you to this point. But at some point in your life, you're going to need a few extra resources and new tools in your toolkit. Don't be afraid to ask for help. Look for those resources and adapt. And we look forward to making these transitions easier for you. But there will be some challenges along the way. I wish you the best, and I'm rooting for you.

13 - Joseph Harman

VALUE THE PEOPLE AROUND YOU

Being a problem solver means that you are dealing with contexts so complex that you could not possibly imagine completing the required tasks alone. Engineering is inherently tied to good relationships and working with others to solve complex problems. Computational Protein Engineer Joseph Harman has valued relationships with others from early on, and it has paid robust dividends. One fateful conversation at lunch with a visiting seminar speaker changed everything for him, leading to working in a Nobel Prize-winning lab and pursuing a career in early drug discovery using protein engineering. Upon reading his story, it will become evident that the successful path of an engineer is not solitary, but intertwined with the relationships that are developed and cultivated along the way.

Joseph Harman, PhD

Senior Scientist, Computational Protein Engineering, A-Alpha Bio

PhD in Chemistry & Biochemistry, University of Oregon

BA in Biochemistry, Willamette University

Hometown: Philomath, Oregon

Aris Winger: Joseph, do you consider yourself an engineer?

Joseph Harman: That's a funny question. I started out in biochemistry, and then I kind of drifted into protein engineering. I'm mostly a biochemist, but my current job is all computational drug design.. I'm a form of engineer at the moment, although I'm just as much a biologist.

Aris Winger: What does being an engineer mean to you?

Joseph Harman: Oh, man, that's a good question. I think, practically speaking, engineers are people who build things. I'm not a formally trained engineer, but in my work, I try to build proteins that are useful. We try to make useful drugs and diagnostic tools, and I think that most engineers build something in some form, or try to make something that's useful for people.

Aris Winger: Let's go back in time. It's the summer before undergrad, and as you're going into that, how are you feeling? Do you feel prepared? And how was the 1st year of undergrad?

Joseph Harman: That is a deep step into the past. Let's see. At the time I was heading to undergrad, I wanted to be a medical doctor. Looking back at that point, I was a completely different person. As far as specifically the summer before college. Wow! I am really blanking on that one - I feel like I was just a kid. I played a sport in college, so I was pretty focused on training for that, too.

Aris Winger: What did you play?

Joseph Harman: I played football at a small Division 3 school. I was focused on getting ready for football camp, doing well in school, and moving out of my parents' house. I don't think I had much engineering in mind at all at that point.

Aris Winger: When did thoughts of engineering start? Undergrad was still all pre-med biology for the most part?

Joseph Harman: Engineering and research began to cross my radar when I started doing internships in the summers. I was trying to figure out what I wanted to do, and I was still on this medicine track for 2 to 3 years of undergrad. It was around then that I met Kyle. Kyle and I worked together the summer before my senior year of undergrad, and Kyle, I don't know if you remember this, but me and one other student worked in the lab with you. Emily was training to be an engineer, and I was studying biochemistry and biophysics. I think somewhere we decided to basically swap projects to learn more about each other's areas of research. I took on a project that was a bit more engineering-heavy than I was familiar with. And we worked together to figure things out on both ends, because I had never worked with several of the more material characterization-focused instruments that we were using for the project. Between my experience with Kyle at LBNL (Lawrence Berkeley National Laboratory) and a couple of other summer internships, that's where I found that medicine wasn't quite the thing I wanted to do. Some of these other areas, particularly in research, were more to my interest.

Aris Winger: Excellent, and that was Junior/Senior year?

Joseph Harman: Yes, that's correct. I did start doing summer internships right away in college, starting after my freshman year. I bounced around quite a bit in different research areas, and that's kind of a theme in my career. I worked in a research lab at a winery after my freshman year in college. I also worked at a biotech company over the summer, and briefly worked at a children's clinic in Peru. I was still focused on medicine at that point. Then the last summer was with Kyle at LBNL, working on fuel cell membranes. So I had 3 very different summer research experiences as an undergrad, trying to figure out what I wanted to do.

Aris Winger: Do you feel it was beneficial for these internships, summer experiences to be different from each other?

Joseph Harman: Everybody's got a different experience. Some people come in and they know that this is the thing I was born to do, and they do it. I really had to bounce around and figure it out. I didn't have a ton of people in my family who had done that type of work or anything. My mom was a teacher. My dad was an accountant, and I really had some things to figure out when I was heading to college.

Aris Winger: Such as?

Joseph Harman: Mostly transitioning and learning what professional scientific research and engineering look like. Going to graduate school for chemistry rather than medical school was challenging to figure out. My undergraduate school had no graduate science program, so I had no idea what graduate school in the sciences was like. I think bouncing around through those different experiences, and especially meeting a lot of different people, such as Kyle and other people who've done PhDs and worked in research settings, I learned a ton about what going to graduate school looked like. It was pretty foreign to me at that point.

Aris Winger: Great. Before we leave undergrad, any monumental moments, challenges, mentors, or support people you met?

Joseph Harman: I definitely had some really great mentors. I had an advisor in undergrad named Sarah Kirk. I was in the middle of applying to medical school and panicked about whether this was the right decision for me, as 21-year-olds do, and I decided that it wasn't going to be for me. I started looking at graduate programs, and she really helped me navigate that process when I didn't quite know what I was looking for. When you're looking at grad schools, what Professor do you work for? What school do you go to? What research do you want to work on? Each program and lab is different.. There's no common application for Phd programs. I think that this particular professor really helped me navigate that and figure it out.

Aris Winger: And how did you meet Sarah Kirk?

Joseph Harman: She was my advisor and also one of my professors. Organic chemistry, a couple of other classes.

Aris Winger: Excellent. As we leave undergrad, how did you decide where to go for graduate school?

Joseph Harman: I mentioned that there was some last-minute panic figuring out what I wanted to do. I did know that I wanted to do biochemistry. I enjoyed the research that I'd done in that area. I was looking at programs, applied to a few schools, went through the process of getting in some, not getting in others, and going through interviews, and then I ended up going to the University of Oregon, which was great for me, because that's where I'm from. I ended up being close to family, and the department I ended up in was quite diverse in the type of research they did. It was a smaller department that does quite a bit of basic research, with people doing zebrafish genetics and neuroscience and working in various other areas. I found a place where I could rotate through a few labs and continue this process of figuring out what I wanted to do. I came in with a bit more of an inorganic chemistry background from my undergraduate research for my thesis and from a couple of the internships I'd done.. During my 1st year of grad school, which included 3 different lab rotations, I really started gravitating toward a bit more classic biochemistry, purifying proteins, figuring out what they're doing, that kind of thing.

Aris Winger: How was the transition?

Joseph Harman: It was mostly good. The 1st year of grad school is kind of funny because it's really busy and feels similar to undergrad. You're taking classes, typically teaching a class or two, and doing research in your rotation labs. Taking classes made it feel a bit like undergrad. But there were also definitely some changes in intensity in certain areas. And the onus was on you.. This is your Phd, your dissertation someday.. You have to take responsibility for what you're doing. And that part's definitely different from undergrad.

Aris Winger: Did you have to go through a qualifying exam?

Joseph Harman: We did do a qualifying exam. It was halfway through our second year, and it was definitely a big hurdle. The main times that people choose to leave graduate school are often after rotations if they don't feel they can find a good fit for a lab, or after the qualifying exam. Those are kind of the two big hurdles. After that, I think most people typically stick it out.

Aris Winger: Did you end up with an advisor to help with writing your thesis? And what area?

Joseph Harman: I continued in the biochemistry track and found a great professor named Mike Harms to work with as my advisor.. He did his Phd in biophysics, where he studied how proteins fold, doing experiments like protein NMR, and really getting into the atomic details of proteins. And then he did a postdoc in evolutionary biology. He really started thinking about how proteins evolve to perform certain functions in humans. Then he combined the two research together in his lab at Oregon. We were thinking about how proteins evolve new functions and properties, and then going in and taking those proteins and doing fairly detailed physical studies of them, mechanistically, looking at things like - how does this protein wiggle around? How does it do its job? What parts of the protein are running the engine? I really enjoyed this because there was a high-level aspect of how proteins perform their functions. How is protein history written in humans? How do they do what they do? And we attempted to answer those questions. And then gaining a mechanistic understanding of how we think something works was very cool.

Aris Winger: Okay, now tell us about your 1st job out of graduate school.

Joseph Harman: Let's see. I went and did a postdoc. I think this is probably a huge turning point, I would say the biggest turning point in my career now that I'm kind of reflecting.

Aris Winger: Alright!

Joseph Harman: I had a professor come give a talk when I was close to the end of graduate school. I don't think I was writing my thesis or my dissertation, but I was pretty close. He gave a seminar and I took him out to lunch, kind of like the standard 'graduate student trying to get some free food' situation, and we really hit it off. This professor was from the University of Washington. His name is Jesse Zalatan, and he's a synthetic biologist. He worked on CRISPR activation, where people are trying to recruit activator proteins to certain parts of the genome using CRISPR machinery and turn genes on. We got to talking. He had some really interesting ideas about trying to use protein design to engineer these gene activation systems he was studying.. At that time, I wasn't well-versed in protein engineering.

I was more trying to understand how proteins evolved to where they are now, not trying to engineer them to do something that I want them to do. Jesse brought up David Baker's lab at UW. And he started pitching a couple of collaborative projects where we could design some proteins for CRISPR activation and test them out in his lab, and he got me connected with David. I went up there and interviewed, and showed what I've been working on in molecular protein evolution. I ended up doing a postdoc with David. Definitely bounced around a bit on different types of projects there. And I think part of this was a product of, once again, being in a new field. We worked on the CRISPR activation stuff and a couple of other protein engineering for synthetic biology projects. I really dove off and got interested in some of the other areas that David's lab was working on because it's a very, very unique place. There were something like 50 grad students and 50 postdocs when I was there. It's a giant lab, a ton of really smart people to learn from. And I really gravitated toward a lot of the cell signaling research that was going on.

My Phd work was in toll receptors and the evolution of proteins that activate them, and I was already interested in mammalian cell signaling. A lot of the people working in protein engineering in that space work on cytokines and Cytokine receptors. And that was great for at least 2 reasons. It was an area I knew a bit about, brought some expertise in, and was excited about. In my current work, people are interested in cytokines as therapies and therapeutics. It's definitely been a big turning point for me working in those areas, as the main stuff that I worked on in David's lab was trying to engineer our own cytokines that can activate certain Cytokine receptors that might not natively interact with each other, might not have a native ligand that pulls them together. And David's lab continues to do these incredible projects where we are kind of hacking biology to make it do what we want - especially since protein engineering tools have really matured in the last 3 or 4 years.

In fact, it's been a crazy few weeks for me and everybody in protein design recently, because David won the Nobel Prize 3 months ago. He went to Stockholm and brought along a bunch of former and current members of the lab. It was incredible. It was a huge recognition for all of the work that David and generations of protein engineers have worked on for decades, and I was grateful to play a small part in that during my time there.

Aris Winger: Thank you for sharing that. When you say you meet this person who comes for the talk. What does that mean? That means that you did what?

Joseph Harman: A professor visited and spoke at a weekly student seminar. I think one thing that you hear from people like me, and you'll hear this from people like David Baker, is that taking advantage of interactions with people whenever you can is critical. These off-the-cuff generic moments can really change your life in a lot of ways. That was exactly what this was for me. I literally signed up to take a speaker to lunch and didn't know them. I don't think they were even hosted by my lab. I didn't have any connection to them, but we really hit it off. It turned out we had a lot in common.

Aris Winger: This was one-on-one?

Joseph Harman: It was 4 or 5 grad students, but it was great. And we nerded out. I think I kind of cornered him on the walk back. We got to talking about ideas, and I think I emailed him that same day and sent a couple more ideas his way, and he really kind of started the process for me.

I think as I'm telling you this story, I realize that you pick up these mentors over time, and find people that will go to bat for you, and kind of capitalizing on those moments, but also really valuing the people around you can go a long way.

Aris Winger: So, now you're at David's lab. I'm wondering about the wandering eye. You're looking over at other's research or topics and say, Whoa, that's interesting. How do you feel comfortable with looking at other things and not feeling like, oh, I've got to stay in my lane and do my thing?

Joseph Harman: That's absolutely tough, and uniquely tough in a giant lab. There aren't that many examples of those really huge labs like David Baker's research group. It was something we thought about a lot. I think we did our best to be really intentional and communicate, make sure that. People working on the same things talk to each other.

If you let random activity happen with a bunch of smart people working in a lab, people are going to end up working on the same thing and gravitate toward the same interesting ideas. It definitely was a unique challenge with so many people and an abundance of resources. You kind of had to be cordial and try to work together where you could, at times, kind of split stuff as needed into people's buckets. Definitely, a hard problem, though.

Aris Winger: Tell us about leaving graduate school. You're doing the postdoc. You're in the professional world in lots of ways. What is it that you wish that you had been taught, or that was part of the curriculum in undergrad? Something that later on you were like, "Why didn't anyone teach me this?" Or "why didn't they tell me that this is going to be important?"

Joseph Harman: That's really tough... It's a hindsight 2020 kind of thing. There was one thing I noticed that was a huge benefit of these internships. I went to a primarily undergraduate institution that had no graduate sciences programs at the time.. I talked to my friends who went to bigger schools that had graduate programs. And they would, in some cases, work in a lab for 4 years, publish papers, and really get deep into something before going to graduate school.

Either version can definitely work. It worked out for me but was a bit more on-the-fly learning. I think if you want to go to graduate school, it can be really helpful to know, obviously, what graduate school is. This is where doing summer internships taught me a lot, including working with Kyle. I got that example over the 3 to 4 months we worked together, and that was literally one of the only examples I got of what graduate school looks like before going to graduate school.

I think it's important to put some thought into what you think your long-term plan is and try to carve out opportunities for yourself, even if you bounce around a bit to get there. I do feel I've had friends over the years who worked in a fairly obscure area of research that was kind of a dead end. And they ended up career switching or regretting where they were headed. I'm not saying everybody should go get a data science degree and chase AI and whatnot. But try to find that magic mix of things that other people care about, things that you care about, and things that you are good at.

And I think mentors really help with that, too, because sometimes it's hard to even ask the questions you don't know how to ask. I think seeking out people who can help you parse through everything and the various opportunities in front of you is critical.

Aris Winger: Do you feel like you had a long-term plan?

Joseph Harman: I think I had long-term goals, but I wasn't quite sure how to achieve them. I also had some non-negotiables.

My interests changed a lot over time. I had things that I was looking for and an idea of what I wanted to do. But I went from inorganic chemist to medicine, organic chemistry, biochemistry, and protein engineering. And even now, my past job was about 50% working in the lab, and 50% doing computational protein design work. Now I'm fully on the computer doing protein design on a machine learning team.

So now, saying all that, I guess I don't think I had a plan, but I did try to keep my eye out for good situations and good people, which were some of my non-negotiables. I think that's really important, for example, when you're picking a graduate lab.

And I think you could translate that to any career step, identify the things that are really important to you, and try to find places and people that match that.

Aris Winger: Great. Ok, we finished the postdoc. Where do we head after that?

Joseph Harman: My postdoc. I was there for a little over 2 years. It was a pretty tough time. It was during COVID. I started in the middle of COVID Summer 2020. My daughter was born about a year later. It was a bit crazy for me.

I left my postdoc after 2 years. Close to a dozen startups in Seattle came from the Baker lab, and former graduate students and postdocs primarily started them. They're in various research areas, mostly therapeutic, some diagnostics, and some enzyme engineering work. So I went and worked at one of those startups, called Monod Bio. Named after the biochemist Jacques Monod, and it was a really cool opportunity. A postdoc and a graduate student from the Baker Lab had started the company around 2020. They were doing de novo protein design for diagnostic applications, meaning we're literally trying to make proteins on the computer, never before seen in nature, that will bind to a target and, in our case, function as a biosensor or diagnostic tool. . De novo proteins can be a tough sell in therapeutics because they're largely untested in trials. It's unclear how immunogenic they will be. You still have to go through FDA approval in diagnostics, but the proteins we engineer for diagnostic purposes don't end up in people as drugs. The goal is to detect something from a patient sample, so there's a lot more freedom to kind of go crazy with the tools and the proteins that we test as diagnostics. That's what Monod Bio works on.

I had worked previously with the grad student who had started that company, and we'd worked on a couple of projects together, and got along really well. And as I realized, hey, I'm ready to leave my postdoc, looking for a job. I got in touch with him and interviewed, and we took off. I think I was their 10th employee. I think they got up to 25 employees while I was there. And it was great. It was definitely a classic startup, a little bit crazy.

Aris Winger: Meaning what? What does it mean to work for a startup for you?

Joseph Harman: To be fair. I don't have a larger company comparison. My current work experience has been at two biotech startups. But a startup typically means that everybody's got several hats on, and everybody is trying to get this thing going, so it's a lot of excitement and groundbreaking research, but sometimes a little crazy.

I have these hilarious memories of when we moved into a new building one month after starting at Monod. We moved into a new biotech space in Seattle, and it wasn't even plumbed properly to do chemistry. We had to call all of these contractors to get a gas line in there, and there seemed to be some new challenge every day just to do the basic things we needed to do. I learned a lot from being part of the crazy experience of trying to get a company off the ground and learning what it takes to do that.

Aris Winger: And what happens after that? At some point, you decide to leave your first job for your current one.

Joseph Harman: I had a really great opportunity fall into my lap that led to my current job. I had been at Monod for a year and a half. Things were going pretty well. We put out a patent on one of our projects that was pretty exciting to be a part of.

I had been doing quite a bit of lab work at that point, working as a manager, and also doing computational protein design on the computer. I really found myself gravitating toward the computational protein design side of my work. Around that same time, various protein design research areas really began to mature. We can now use AI methods to generate proteins, to do things we want, and then go test them in the lab and see if they work. It's incredible. And it's really fast and fun to work on and iterate on. I was familiar with another company in town, called A-Alpha Bio, that measures protein interactions en masse using library-on-library yeast display technology.. They routinely measured millions of interaction networks in a single experiment. They collected these massive data sets measuring the strength of proteins binding to each other, a key property of protein-based therapeutics. A-Alpha Bio had a computational protein design role open up. I realized that they needed somebody with my background who could come in and start applying these kinds of fresh tools that we have toward protein engineering and design efforts.. It was a longer interview process. I had to do homework. It was a bit more of a tech interview to some degree.

Aris Winger: Why do you say it fell into your lap?

Joseph Harman: I say it fell into my lap in the sense that I wasn't actively looking and wasn't on the job hunt. One day, I saw the job posting and was like, Wow, that might be the perfect fit for me.

Now I work at A-Alpha on a machine learning team within a data science department. This was definitely an opportunity to jump into more formal programming and software development. The team I'm on is a mixture of ML scientists, data scientists, bioinformaticians, and software engineers. I often talk about protein structures and biology to my colleagues. And they spend a lot of time teaching me about how to write good code..

Aris Winger: That's good. Let's stay there for a second. Now you're on the team. What are the qualities, skills, and characteristics of being a good team member for you?

Joseph Harman: I think this is the kind of thing I enjoy most about working at a start-up. You're all on the same team. We all have mostly the same goals. We want to push our stuff forward, and we have to lean on each other's strengths. We'll come up with a research project and get the freedom to run with it, and really figure out from start to finish what the project looks like as a team.

We often start with the biology underlying a project that we want to take on. But then, we need to start thinking practically about how to do what we want to do?? Do we need a pretty quick test? Am I gonna go, throw a project together on my computer, and is it kind of isolated to me? Or do I need to take the time to make more of a reusable pipeline that we're gonna use over and over again? Do we have to start thinking about scaling what we've made??

That's where I really start planning. Then I need to go and communicate with my colleagues. How do we do this? How can we build this thing out together?

The other piece is fairly standard team dynamics. My team meets once a week. We catch up on the projects we're working on and check in on whether anybody needs anything. Is anybody stuck on something?

I do have the luxury now of working hybrid, often working remotely from home but occasionally going into the office. I have a nice balance of sometimes operating fully on Slack and other times going into the office and whiteboarding things out. I think communicating a lot and thinking about how to communicate effectively has been really important.

Aris Winger: I take it that they help you transition into the new position?

Joseph Harman: Definitely. I think it depends on the position. But in my case, I came in and they had a few specific projects they wanted to do. There was a bit of a jump in on some stuff, and then there were some longer-term projects that I definitely had to learn a lot from my colleagues about, such as I'd never used AWS before this job, and things like that.

Aris Winger: How is the learning curve? How do you figure this new role and toolset out?

Joseph Harman: Definitely leaning on colleagues a lot, and those weekly meetings, asking people questions, lots of Slack messages. I kind of pull from all of the standard sources. YouTube as needed. ChatGPT has been a lifesaver as a new to production programmer. It gets my code about 80% of the way there, and then it's my job to review it and make the code work. Deciphering what is most useful for a given task, getting rid of parts that are not the most satisfying answer.

Aris Winger: That's great. You're doing lots of communication about things you don't know, and talk to me a little bit about pride and ego, and not knowing something. Did you have to face feelings of, Oh, I don't know. Am I supposed to know? Or have you always felt comfortable with, if I don't know, I'm gonna ask?

Joseph Harman: That's a good one. I feel imposter syndrome stuff pops up for everybody, no matter who you are. I am lucky enough to be somewhat extroverted, and I don't mind appearing dumb at times. I'm often the person in the room asking what's probably a dumb question. But I encourage people to do that.

The other thing. I think that's important. It is giving people, whatever approach they have, opportunities to ask those questions. I think, for example, I've had a couple of managers over the years who do a really good job of giving people different types of space to learn and ask the things they need to ask.

Aris Winger: How? How does that happen? How do they do that?

Joseph Harman: Try to provide different spaces for expression. You can have big group things where the experts are probably gonna take over, small group things, or one-on-one meetings. Make sure that people have these different venues. We try to do different topical things. We'll have a machine learning lunch and learn. We try to do journal clubs, etc, to find or provide different ways to make things stick. I think hands-on projects are also great for people's learning purposes - getting a project where part of the goal is to learn and develop in a new area can be super helpful.

Aris Winger: Alright, a couple more questions. To be where you are now, what have you had to sacrifice?

Joseph Harman: Let's see... living in Seattle is very expensive. No, that's not, that's a sacrifice, but not a very serious one. I had mentioned the postdoc thing, leaving a little bit earlier than intended. I think the thing I faced was that I've got a young family in an expensive place, and I'm doing a postdoc and not making much money, and I did, at that point, make the decision to leave my postdoc. I need to get a job that can meet my family's needs, and I don't think I would call that a sacrifice necessarily, but it was a big change that took me some time to come to grips with.

I didn't necessarily want to leave. I left a couple of postdoc projects, kind of unfinished, and it can be hard to leave those types of situations, especially now, looking back. David won the Nobel Prize. I could have been in the lab when that happened. How cool would that have been!

I think that was one sacrifice, and I think generally, figuring out family life in the midst of a career is tough for everybody. My wife definitely, too, has had to work through that. She's gone through a couple of job transitions, and we had to navigate all the craziness of childcare and two people working. Other sacrifices, I wouldn't say, are anything too crazy. Our families are pretty far away, and we're here in Seattle kind of constrained geographically a bit by our jobs but I think that's I think that pretty much covers it.

Aris Winger: Thank you. Last question. As we're going to have lots of people reading the book. Some of the people are going to be undergrads, thinking about being in engineering or engineering majors. This is your time to talk directly to them. What would you say to them as they're going through the process of being in STEM in general? They may be struggling and not know what they should be doing. Whatever you want to say to them, this is your chance.

Joseph Harman: I think finding good mentors is one of the best things you can do. And find them in different forms. If you can find people who you can learn from about how they got to where they got, start trying to align what you want based on what they're doing, and talk about how they got there. I think I've been really, really lucky to have those people in multiple steps.

You heard how I wandered all over different research areas and interests. And I think that's totally fine because I ended up here. There's nothing wrong with that, and I think, especially as an undergrad when you don't know what you want to do, you don't have to beat yourself up and be hard on yourself for not knowing what you want to do. It's perfectly fine to keep testing things out and seeing what sticks. I certainly did a lot of that.

But then, as you're kind of evolving your process, and really figuring out who you are and who you want to be as a professional, finding those people that click with you is important. That's what happened with my graduate mentor. The things we worked on in his lab, the protein evolution stuff, were really cool, but honestly, that was kind of a bonus. It was more the person I was working with and the way we worked together, the way he supported me as a young scientist.

Even now, in my current career, as I was interviewing for my current role, I was trying to figure out who these people are, what they are about, and how they conduct themselves. Do they take care of their people? Do they support people to grow and learn? And I definitely needed that kind of support. I think that finding good people that you can support too is important.

It's a little bit different for undergrads. It's a little bit more one-sided. You're kind of looking for people who can mentor you. But as you grow in your career, you wanna return the favor. And I feel I'm now starting to get to that point.

As you get older, you're gonna be somebody that other people are going to look to and ask you questions. How'd you get here? What did you do? What did you think? And you'll want to try to do for others what other people did for you.

14 – KiYett Brown

YOU'RE NOT SUPPOSED TO KNOW EVERYTHING

Destiny calls. For Traffic Engineer KiYett Brown, she knew she was going to be an engineer for some time. Life intervened, and she found herself serving communities as a teacher. After a few too many years of commitment, she had her moment, sitting at a desk during her free period: "This is not what I'm supposed to be doing." Soon thereafter, she embarked on the path lit by what was residing within her, a deep commitment to solving the problems of the road. This path was not easy, but when destiny calls, the bumps feel a lot smaller. Enjoy her story here.

KiYett Brown, PhD

Traffic Engineer, Jacobs

PhD & MS in Civil Engineering, Florida Agricultural & Mechanical University

BS in Mathematics, Emory & Henry University

BA in Physics, Emory & Henry University

Hometown: Mount Airy, North Carolina

Aris Winger: Welcome, KiYett. Are you an engineer?

KiYett Brown: I am.

Aris Winger: And what does that mean to you?

KiYett Brown: Oh, making the world better. My discipline is civil engineering. My concentration is transportation. So I basically design anything that can move on a surface level, whether it's vehicles, pedestrians, or bicyclists.

Aris Winger: So when you're in traffic, you're just like, Oh, my God! This could be done so much better.

KiYett Brown: Sometimes. I wonder why it is like this? But then other times, I know why this is happening, and it makes sense to me. It may not make sense to other people, and I think a lot of the frustration I get from most people is why there is always so much construction.

KiYett Brown: And then my answer is, Well, do you want the roads to be safer and better or not?

Aris Winger: Fantastic. Thank you. So let's go through the journey. So right before undergrad, your Summer before you go into Emory and Henry, how are we feeling about going into college? Are we feeling excited? Do you feel well prepared?

KiYett Brown: I'm excited. Do I feel like I'm well prepared? Yes and no. You can only be prepared for what you know, and so there are a lot of things that you don't know. So there's a lot of nervousness, excitement, and anxiety around it.

But overall, I felt just excited to start something new, and to begin the process of what it is that I know. I know what I wanted to do, and wanted to become.

Aris Winger: And in the undergraduate space, any lessons learned or challenges? Anything you had to endure or encounter?

KiYett Brown: For the most part, no. I don't think that there were any lessons learned…I mean, of course, there were some lessons learned, but professionally, I don't think there were any lessons learned.

I think that the work that I did in undergrad prepared me for what I saw in grad school. So I don't think that there was anything that's like I would do over or do differently.

Aris Winger: Double major in math and physics?

KiYett Brown: Yes.

Aris Winger: After undergrad, what are we thinking?

KiYett Brown: So after undergrad, I did not go straight into grad school. I taught high school math for five years. I gave my brain a break for a little bit, and then I went to grad school.

Aris Winger: How was the teaching? How was that experience?

KiYett Brown: It was. It was good. It was nice. I got to meet a lot of great students, so I taught math, but I also taught physics for 2 years.

I got a lot of connections through that process, whether it be with students that I taught or basketball players that I coached. Some of their parents were engineers or worked at FAMU in the administrative offices. It really set me up for connections to make grad school easier.

Aris Winger: Why are you deciding to go to grad school? What compels you to go?

KiYett Brown: Well, I never wanted to teach. That was not something that I wanted to do. I've always wanted to do engineering. I just felt like I wasn't prepared mentally to go straight into grad school after undergrad.

Aris Winger: What does that mean?

KiYett Brown: Like…I wasn't. I didn't want to go back to studying and reading and the assignments and homework. I wanted… I needed a break.

And so teaching kept my mind sharp as far as the mathematics aspects and physics aspects of engineering. But it wasn't like a day-to-day grind all the time.

Aris Winger: So, at some point, how do you know when it's the right time? Like, at some point, you're just like…

KiYett Brown: Honestly, it was like an epiphany .. I realized this is not what I'm supposed to be doing. It was a conversation that I had with myself, like "Kiyett. What are you doing? This is where… we're not…

Aris Winger: Do you remember where this was? Were you at home? Were you…

KiYett Brown: I was probably at school, work, or high school. I told myself, "This is not what I wanted to do in life, and you've been here too long, like you were supposed to be here for like a year or 2 years."

And then the 2 years became 5 years. And it's like this is too long. So do what you know you need to do and what you said you're going to do.

I was cool with making the money… I mean, even though it's not like a lot of money, right? But if I went back to school, then I would have to be full-time. So I kind of got comfortable with getting a paycheck and doing whatever I wanted to do with that.

Aris Winger: And the people who are around you, the family and the support system. What are they saying? Are they pushing you to get back earlier?

KiYett Brown: No, they're just letting me fly by the seat of my pants, "whatever you want to do."

Aris Winger: So then, at some point, you decide to apply. Where did you apply?

KiYett Brown: I applied to FAMU because I was in Tallahassee. So I was teaching in Tallahassee, Florida. So I applied to FAMU, and FAMU has a great engineering program, and they're an HBCU.

Aris Winger: Is that important to you?

KiYett Brown: It is. It was important to me. Because growing up, I never saw engineers who look like me, and so to be in a space with people who not only look like me, but are pursuing greatness, and whatever aspect that is for them…It was important to me to be a part of that culture and a part of that community.

Aris Winger: What is it that you get from that?

KiYett Brown: You get a sense of belonging and a sense of "They did it, so I can do it." They look like me. They've gone through the same struggles, whether it be because they're Black or because they're Black and a woman. They've gone through. They know what it takes to get there, and they're gonna push me to make sure that I achieve greatness in whatever aspect that looks like for me.

Aris Winger: Is that the only place you applied?

KiYett Brown: That is the only place I applied.

Aris Winger: And if you hadn't gotten in there, then what?

KiYett Brown: Oh, I was getting in!

Aris Winger: How was that transition?

KiYett Brown: It was great. It was an easy transition because I had made up my mind that this is what I want to do. So I was in the headspace to give it my all and pursue my dream of becoming an engineer.

Aris Winger: And a support system with mentors?

KiYett Brown: Yeah, it was awesome. They were there. I didn't have to try too hard to gain support and mentors at FAMU. All of the professors were very willing to help and guide me along my path.

Aris Winger: Tell me about some.

KiYett Brown: So one of the students that I taught in the High School, her dad was the Dean of graduate admissions and before kind of before and after the application process, he and I had conversations about what it is I want to do what it is I'm trying to achieve, and he kind of connected me to the right people

He helped me talk to the right person who set me up for success, and he made sure I took this class and took it with this professor, because the class is going to be hard, but he knew I was going to get out of it what I needed to get out of it. And so having that was, I don't know if I would get that anywhere else.

Aris Winger: And study groups?

KiYett Brown: Study groups. Yeah, they were kind of formed like, right off the bat.

Aris Winger: How? How is that right off the bat?

KiYett Brown: They just... I mean... So you're in class and sitting next to the person. And you're like, "You know what he's talking about?" And they're like, "No."

And I'm like, "Okay, so what are you doing after class? You have class after this?" They say, "No, I don't have class after this." Okay? Oh, well, let's go to office hours. So they just kind of form, naturally. Yeah.

Aris Winger: So this is one of the things that I think we're trying to uncover, is that that's not natural... like you had to do something.

KiYett Brown: Yeah.

Aris Winger: We're gonna have some people reading this who aren't finding study groups who are trying to figure out how to do that. So by reaching out, we're discovering it's tied to your personality. The likelihood for someone to say what you said requires some way of being that isn't worried about rejection, to have to admit that you don't know what you're talking about.

KiYett Brown: Yeah, you gotta admit that like... because you're not gonna know everything, even when you make a 4.0 in school and go to grad school. Make a 4.0, and when you get into an industry, you're still not gonna know everything because the industry is so different, like the concepts of understanding. What happens and why is great.

But what you do day to day in the industry is nothing like what you do in the classroom. So you're never gonna know everything. And you're always gonna have to ask questions.

Aris Winger: So saying to yourself, "I'm not supposed to know everything," kind of gives you permission.

Aris Winger: So then study groups form. And are they qualifying exams?

KiYett Brown: For my master's, no.

Aris Winger: For the Phd. Yes, okay. How was the master's experience?

KiYett Brown: That's honestly… that's where I was supposed to stop. I wasn't supposed to go on.

Aris Winger: Oh, really?

KiYett Brown: Yeah, my thought was, "Oh, I'm gonna get in, get this master's. And I'm gonna work." And that was the end of it.

Then one of my lovely professors explained that I could do a Phd. And I said, "Oh, you're right, I could, but I'm not going to." He responded with "But why not? And I didn't have a reason why not.

He explained that he just applied for this grant and that I could apply for it, and he was sure that I would get it because he thought I fit all of the qualifications for it.

He then explained that obtaining a Ph.D would be free and comes with a stipend. I just didn't have a reason to say no…I am not married or have any kids. Why would I not do it now?

And so that was the transition from master's to Ph.D. It happened because I was only going to stop at my master's.

Aris Winger: And the transition to the Phd program? Were there any…

KiYett Brown: It was easy. It was seamless because I stayed in the same school, so I didn't have to take any more tests or anything. They just admitted me straight into the Phd. Program. The classes didn't become harder; they just involved more work. So it required better time management on my part.

Aris Winger: And the qualifying exam?

KiYett Brown: The qualifying exam doesn't happen until year three of the Phd program. So you take… I took classes. I had to take so many hours of classes. And then, while you're taking those classes, you're working on your prelim. But your prelim consists of your dissertation, like the first three-ish chapters. So you have to kind of tell them what it is you're planning on studying and how you're going to achieve it. And then you have a committee. So my committee was made up of five people: my advisor, and then three other professors in the engineering department, and a professor outside of the engineering department.

They pick a day. Each of them has one day, and they send you questions in the morning, you have all day to answer them, and then you send them back in the evening.

And then at the end of that week, you present what you're going to talk about in your dissertation. And then at the end of that presentation. They tell you whether you pass or not, and then you go on, stop taking classes, and just write your dissertation full-time.

Aris Winger: How is that process, the qualifying exam?

KiYett Brown: Oh, it was nerve-wracking because they can ask you questions about any class that you took at any time. So they have your class schedule. They know what you've taken. They know what you should know. And they can ask you whatever questions they want to ask you about any of those classes.

Aris Winger: Did you get surprised by any of the questions?

KiYett Brown: No. I had taken enough classes with the professors that I knew what they were going to ask or the types of questions they were going to ask.

Aris Winger: How do you know that?

KiYett Brown: I knew that one professor was only gonna ask me questions about coding and Matlab, and how to do linear regression. I knew that that was going to happen. And it happened because those were the type of classes that I took with him, and also those are the type of questions he would always ask me when I'm talking about my dissertation topic and things like that. You spend so much time with your committee over the years, and each of them has certain specialities. So you get an idea of what they are going to ask you based on conversations, meetings, and classes that you have with them. Nothing is concrete, but you have an idea of what to expect.

Aris Winger: And then the dissertation writing, how was that?

KiYett Brown: It was a little stressful because it was 2020, happening right in the middle of it. And I had some family things happen in the middle of it. It was helter-skelter. But yeah. We did it. We got through it.

Aris Winger: And then afterwards, where do you end up going after that?

KiYett Brown: I got a job at Crawford, Murphy, and Tilly in Indianapolis, Indiana.

Aris Winger: So you moved?

KiYett Brown: I moved. Yeah, I left Florida. I moved to Indianapolis, and they threw me into projects as soon as I arrived. They were like, "Oh, you have a Ph.D. You know what you're doing."

Aris Winger: And so how was that transition?

KiYett Brown: I didn't know what I was doing. No, I did. I did know what I was doing, as far as writing reports, doing safety analysis, and doing any type of statistical analysis they wanted me to do. Like I got that. But as far as the design…So colleges don't have…they use Autodesk or Civil 3D. But they don't use that in industry. They use micro stations, open roads, and so it's a bit of a learning curve.

But overall, the transition was nice. I had a great company that supported me, which gave me training and sent me to conferences if I wanted to go. So it was a really nice transition from school, academic to industry. It really was.

Aris Winger: I'm thinking about this learning curve. How does the company help you out with the learning curve?

KiYett Brown: I think I was fortunate to have a company that understood. I know a lot about…

I've done more, I guess, in-depth studying, and concentration, as far as transportation and traffic is concerned, because you don't get that far in depth with just an undergrad in civil engineering degree, you don't. You may take one transportation class, and that's it. At the same time, I studied this for my master's and my Phd. So I have more knowledge of the transportation world. But not when it comes to design. And they understood that.

They told me they were going to use my strengths. They knew that I didn't know design that well and decided to provide help in that area.

Aris Winger: How does that conversation come about?

KiYett Brown: So I had a mentor. So they set me up in the mentorship program, and my mentor,

She was also in the company, but wasn't like a direct supervisor. So it was someone that I felt comfortable talking to about what I don't really know or what I didn't understand, not only about software, but also about company relations.

It works. So I think that companies should have something like that. And I understand that not all companies do.

Aris Winger: A mentorship program?

KiYett Brown: The mentorship program has an "open door, ask me anything, I'm not gonna judge" policy. You like it. Sometimes I think people are afraid to ask questions because they don't want to seem like a burden, or don't know what they're doing, or it takes them twice as long to do it as a more experienced engineer.

Kyle Clark: So when you're at this company, people are saying they have an open-door policy and "ask me anything…" because I've been at a few companies that do this, and it comes down to trust…You say it was easier to talk to them because they weren't your direct supervisor.

KiYett Brown: True. But okay. So also, my direct supervisor…I think that I had a really good interview with him.

So I got to feel out the type of person that they were. Also, before moving to Indianapolis, I went up there for a weekend. I got to be around the employees that I was going to be working with. That made it easier to talk to them. I started to build a rapport with people, especially as soon as I knew that's where I was going to go. Once I knew I was going to accept the offer, I started reaching out to people in the company to say, "Hey, I'm coming!" And they reached out to me to say, "Let us help you find an apartment. Let us help you navigate the system," because, like, I'm new to the industry, but also new to the area. I think that also matters and makes a difference, and that also helped because they made it clear that they were here to help me. So it didn't make me feel bad about asking them questions.

Aris Winger: I wanted to make sure we get this point out pretty clearly. It sounds like we believe that companies should be judgment-free zones.

KiYett Brown: They should be. You should be "allowed" to show up as your whole self when you go to work. I think that is the best way to get the most production out of your employees when they feel their best selves within the work environment.

Aris Winger: I just wanted to make sure we were clear about that.

So, at this point, you're in this professional job. Is there anything that you wish you had gotten from undergrad in terms of skills? Is there anything you had to learn on your own where you said to yourself, "Why wasn't I taught something like this? Why didn't anybody teach me this?"

KiYett Brown: Networking skills. I feel like that's the only thing where I was a deer in the headlights. The other soft skills, I think I had those, you know. But if you put me in a room with people I don't know, and you want me to talk to five people. I'm not really comfortable doing that. But I think I'm uncomfortable because I didn't have a lot of exposure to it.

Aris Winger: Well, teach us right now. So how do you do it?

KiYett Brown: I don't know. I still don't. I still struggle with it. But I'm getting better at it because they want me to be more involved with client relations. And so I'm getting better at talking to people that I don't know, but it is still… I still have to give myself a pep talk in the car like "girl. You gotta talk to people you don't know. So just put your face on and talk to people you don't know." And I give myself a goal, like to talk to three people you don't know.

Because if you talk to 3 people you don't know, one of those people is going to introduce you to someone else. Right? So if you make the first step to say, "Okay, I'm gonna talk to this person, even though I don't know them." They're gonna open up your networking pool. And that's what I've realized. But my networking skills are still… That's something that I wish I had gotten more acclimated to.

Aris Winger: So, how long did you stay in Indianapolis?

KiYett Brown: I stayed in Indianapolis for two years. It was too cold. It snowed all the time, and it was just not… and I didn't have family that was close by, so I realized I needed something else.

The company was great. If I could pick the company up and put it into a community where…Also, Indianapolis doesn't have an identity as a city. So it's hard to find your place, like where you fit in. It's hard to find a community. And I was a part of NSBE, the National Society of Black Engineers. I was a part of Women in Transportation. I was a part of the Institute of Transportation Engineers. I was a part of all of these professional organizations that introduced me to people in my community. Even though they are engineers, they're still, they're broader. They have broader interests and hobbies. And so that worked, but didn't. It got me some community, but so far away from family.

Aris Winger: So what were you missing?

KiYett Brown: There was no one who looked like me. I'm still in the Midwest, right? Even though it's Indianapolis, it's a huge metropolitan area. I'm still in the Midwest, and it feels very midwest-ish. It's not Chicago, you know. And so diversity for me was missing the piece. I was really missing the community and family.

So yeah, I had to move. So I'm back in North Carolina now, where my family is.

Aris Winger: So you applied for a job?

KiYett Brown: Applied to a job. I am with Jacobs now. And also, I probably should have paid more attention to it, but the company that I was working for in Indianapolis didn't have any people of color in leadership positions. And so when I went to leadership meetings, I was the only person of color in the room… like in the whole room.

Aris Winger: Looking back, you would have…

KiYett Brown: Paid more attention to that when applying at first, and something that I like about Jacobs is that the CEO is a person of color. They have industry leaders all the way down, who are people of color. For me, I know that there's no glass ceiling. Right? So that's what that means for me. That may not mean the same thing for everybody else. But that's what it means for me: that there's no glass ceiling.

KiYett Brown: So I'm with Jacobs now, and I love it. It's a great company.

Aris Winger: What do you do?

KiYett Brown: Oh, man, right now I'm working on a project that is taking all of my time. We are putting in intelligent transportation systems in Georgia along its interstate system, to one day have… so that they have the technological equipment to communicate with autonomous and connected vehicles.

There are certain things that they can do and implement now, like Cctvs and putting in fiber optic cable and all that stuff. The project that we're working on is like 200 and something miles of highway. So it's taking all of my time.

Aris Winger: Why is it taking up your time?

KiYett Brown: Because they want to start this year.

Aris Winger: Got it. So this is something about the time crunch.

KiYett Brown: Yes.

Aris Winger: So I am wondering about how you communicate that something can't be done. How do you communicate that?

KiYett Brown: Well, I did.

Aris Winger: Oh, you did.

KiYett Brown: But I did so… I was supposed to only be working on a section of this project. And my section is done, and the next section is not done, and the people who were supposed to be working on it have not started it. And since my section is done and I know what I'm doing, they're like, "Oh, you can do it."

Aris Winger: Well, you're being too nice.

KiYett Brown: Am I being too nice?

Aris Winger: So, is there punishment for doing your job well? You complete something, and they just give you more?

KiYett Brown: Yes and no, so I will say that I did have a week off… where I did not have any work that needed to be done immediately. Right? And I was supposed to just be a support system for the next group.

I let the week pass. I said, "Oh, they're working. They got it. They haven't asked me any questions. Yeah, I don't know why they haven't asked me any questions, because there are questions to be asked. But I wasn't. You know…I wasn't pressing the issue, and then I talked to my supervisor, and I said, "Hey, they haven't asked me any questions," and he replied, "Well, have you looked in the drawings yet to see what they have done and what they haven't done?"

I hadn't because I told them to ask me questions, right? If they have questions, ask me. And then I opened the drawing, and there was nothing in it. So at that point, my supervisor concluded that someone had dropped the ball somewhere. It wasn't me. But for the next week, 2 weeks or so, 3 weeks, they asked me to work on getting it up to speed to where we can actually submit something. And so.

Aris Winger: And so what are the feelings at that point?

KiYett Brown: I don't know what feelings I had. My feelings were…I know that I can do it right. It's not a question about capability. But my feelings were, "Why didn't they?" The person who was supposed to do it. What are they working on?

I don't know their work schedule or their workload. But I just feel like something somewhere was miscommunicated. And maybe they feel like they had time to work on it, but then they didn't. But then they didn't tell anyone about it either.

Aris Winger: So, talk to me a little bit about teams. How is teamwork? The skills you need for teamwork…Did you feel like you got prepared to be on the team?

KiYett Brown: Yes, in grad school. Yes. So at FAMU, one of the nice things they do with their engineering courses…Each one has a group project. All engineering courses have a group project in class that's outside of your homework and individual stuff you have to do, and you are assigned this group project at random.

The professors have a tendency to single out people whom they know didn't do the work. So everyone does work because no one wants to… because of that, I was well prepared for teamwork. I would say, "Okay, this is how we're gonna split this up. And this is how often we're gonna meet and...

Aris Winger: But wait, it sounds like, are you leading this? Oftentimes?

KiYett Brown: I am one of the leads. Yeah.

Aris Winger: So, tell me about some of these teamwork skills that show up.

KiYett Brown: Accountability. So whether it's a teammate or yourself. Right?

So if you're in a meeting and there are actionable items. You get assigned that actionable item, or if you take on the job, then just make sure that it gets done right, because when we have the next meeting, we anticipate that that's done, so we can move forward. We have multiple deadlines to meet on every single project. And these deadlines are set by the client. So in this case, the client would be the Georgia Department of Transportation, right? So they tell us when we have to be certain.

Aris Winger: Benchmarks.

KiYett Brown:

So it's all about communication and accountability. So if I say that I'm going to do something, then I hold myself accountable to do it, and if I can't do it, something has come up, or I've been pulled into another project, then I make sure whoever I'm working with knows. And I give them a rundown of what I did accomplish and what I did not accomplish.

I think that the only way to really make sure that you get that from your team is you do it yourself. You show how it's done, because not everyone works the same way in a team. But if they see that I'm organized, have notes, and know who is doing what, then they will have expectations that they should have their work done. And that's true because I don't want to do it.

Aris Winger: And so now what's the goal? Now, what are you trying to do? What are your future goals for you?

KiYett Brown: This year, I am going to take my PE. So that's the professional exam. To become an engineer, because then I get to stamp plans.

Aris Winger: Tell me more. I don't know what you mean.

KiYett Brown: So right now, I do the design work. I send it to a professional engineer like my supervisor, and he looks over it. He makes sure that it's okay and puts his stamp on it to say that these plans are good to go. This is ready to be built.

But then he's also able to be a project manager or to be over projects. I want to be over a project and say, "This is my project." I can't do that if I don't have a PE.

Aris Winger: Okay, so what's required? What do you have to do?

KiYett Brown: Oh, with a 9-hour test.

Aris Winger: How are we preparing?

KiYett Brown: We're going to study. There are classes that you can sign up for and take, so we'll do one of those classes.

Aris Winger: Are you studying today differently than when you used to study in school?

KiYett Brown: It's more strategic studying, I would say.

There are certain aspects of this exam, or even the previous exam that I had to take before this, to get your engineering and training license. So you have the FE, which is engineering in training. And then you work underneath the PE for so many years, and then you're eligible to take the PE yourself.

KiYett Brown: So with studying for both the 1st test, I skipped all of the math stuff. Right?

This is because I know it. I don't need to study Algebra 2.

But the bridges stuff! Oh, I suck at that. So it's more geared towards knowing that most of the questions are going to be bridge questions. So I'm going to study bridge questions and not necessarily the other stuff I do daily that I actually understand and know how to do. So it's a little different.

Aris Winger: When did we plan on taking that?

KiYett Brown: Oh, we're going to shoot for September. They say you need 6 months to study.

Aris Winger: September 2025.

KiYett Brown: So I'm gonna take my full 6 months to study and then some.

Aris Winger: Tell me about balance.

KiYett Brown: But I haven't started studying yet. So that's the thing. I haven't started studying yet, because I don't know which study class I'm gonna sign up for yet. So once I figure that out, then we'll make that happen.

Aris Winger: Talk to me about confidence. You seem very confident.

KiYett Brown: In what?

Aris Winger: In everything.

KiYett Brown: Because I know what I'm doing, and I love what I'm doing.

Aris Winger: I'm talking about from the beginning, from undergrad.

KiYett Brown: Because I knew what I wanted to do. There was never a question about… Do I want to be an engineer? Yes. And do I want to do civil engineering? Yes.

I teetered between… but initially wanted to do bridges, but then I got into a transportation class and realized this was so much better for me.

And so that's kind of where I'm stuck. So I did start out with bridge work and bridge design, but then I eventually moved on to transportation. But I've always wanted to be a civil engineer.

KC: Being somebody who… knowing a little bit of background of the Emory and Henry connection here…you wanted to go into engineering. I didn't know I wanted to go into engineering. Emory and Henry is not an engineering school.

KiYett Brown: No, it is not.

KC: You've also talked about the importance of being around people that look like you, which Emory and Henry is also not one of those places.

KiYett Brown: It is not. But those things… Okay… Emory. Yes, it was not an engineering school, but I went to play basketball, and I knew that I could get my foundation with math and physics from Emory. So I wasn't concerned about the engineering part.

Aris Winger: Why weren't you concerned about that?

KiYett Brown: Because I know I'm smart.

Aris Winger: So this is what I wanted to unpack. Where does that come from? So, where's the imposter syndrome like?

KiYett Brown: I feel like that's innate. It just is. It's just there. It's always there.

Aris Winger: What's there? The imposter syndrome.

KiYett Brown: The imposter syndrome. Yes. There's always a sense of "do I really belong here?"

Aris Winger: Oh, so when it shows up, you are treating it as if it's right on schedule.

KiYett Brown: Yeah, right.

Aris Winger: Yeah, yeah, got it. Okay.

KiYett Brown: Being around my people who look like me did not happen until later in life.

So that was something that I grew into after I moved to Florida, and I got to experience more, and then that became more important to me.

Needing to have a sense of community of people who look like me, that was not out of the gate.

Aris Winger: A couple of more questions for you. What if you had to sacrifice?

KiYett Brown: hmm! That's a tough question. Comfortability.

Aris Winger: Meaning what?

KiYett Brown: Meaning allowing yourself to get stuck in a rut. Like I could have just.

I had these dreams of being an engineer, but I could have just stuck to teaching and then gone into administration. Or you know, I could have been stuck in that sense because that was comfortable. Right? That didn't push me beyond what I knew I was capable of doing, right?

The process of going from a master's to Phd. Was. I had to give up comfort, right? Because I… getting my master's was easy, right? The classes were

KiYett Brown: I mean, they were classes, but they weren't hard, right?

Jumping from that level from master's to Phd. Like, there was a level of comfort that I had to give up in order to do that.

Aris Winger: What does giving up comfort from a master's to a PhD look like? What's an example?

KiYett Brown: Not reading outside of class. I couldn't do that in my Phd. Not doing extra research or going the extra mile. They say you have to have 5 resources. But for a Phd, that's the minimum of what they want to see. But if you don't do more, they will ask you why you didn't do more.

So knowing that more is required of me, let me know I have to be uncomfortable with actually giving them more.

I would also say in some aspects, relationships. For me personally, I feel like people come and go for a reason.

Aris Winger: There are some people you have to…

KiYett Brown: Yeah, we can't be friends.

Aris Winger: Yeah, we're not gonna see each other as much...

KiYett Brown: Yeah, yeah.. But even so, even within my friend group, even the friends who were very supportive, they understood. I can't hang out. I can't go. I can't go out. I can't go out this weekend, or it's a Wednesday, and I can't see y'all like. I gotta study. I got a paper to write. I have XY and Z to do.

Aris Winger: Was it always easy for you to say no? Or did you have to learn how to say no?

KiYett Brown: Oh, no, it was easy. It was easy for me to say no because I knew that this was something that I knew I wanted to do, something that I was passionate about doing. And so it was very easy to say, "I can't do this today."

Y'all can hit me up next month or next week, or actually, when this is over, we can party. We can hang out, and we can do all the things. Whatever you want to do when I'm done.

Aris Winger: Last question. You know that the reader might be someone who is an undergrad who might be at an institution that doesn't have an engineering degree. So they're doing math, physics, or someone who is struggling. This is your time to just talk directly to them. What advice do you have for them about the journey?

KiYett Brown: Figure out your why and remind yourself of your "why." Daily. If you figure out your why... Why are you doing this? Why do you want to do this? Why is this important to you? Then you're not gonna stop achieving your why.

And it's going to be hard. And there are going to be times when you want to quit, but you have to bring yourself back to your why. That's what I would say.

15 - Robert Hodge

Fail Forward

The walls of a classroom can be confining. Symbolically, homework assignments with closed-form solutions, and presentations and projects with rubrics can do a poor job at simulating what you really encounter in problem-solving in the real world. How do we get this experience? Industrial and Systems Engineer (and Entrepreneur) Robert Hodge was approached by two friends who were working on a side project: building a new and innovative golf shoe. Failure was ever present. He realized this could be a gift, a necessary part of the process. His story informs us to "Stay the course, and it'll pay off ... don't get discouraged" because setbacks aren't necessarily holes in our path but potential springboards towards our goal.

Robert Hodge

President at ForeLife Golf | Energy Providers Consultant

BS in Industrial & Systems Engineering, Virginia Tech

Hometown: Blacksburg, Virginia

Aris Winger: Robert Hodge, are you an engineer?

Robert Hodge: I am.

Aris Winger: What does that mean to you?

Robert Hodge: As an engineer, I really want to solve problems and then create solutions. That's kind of what it means to me. Sometimes it's challenging problems that don't necessarily have a clear-cut answer forward. It's a mix of defining problems, breaking them into workable solutions, and working towards that end result.

Aris Winger: I'll stay here for a moment about things not being clear-cut. Talk to me about coming from a space educationally, where lots of problems we solve in school are clear-cut. And then, all of a sudden, these engineering problems are no longer clear-cut. How do we make this adjustment, or do you get used to it, this ambiguity about where to go next? How do you train yourself to be with that?

Robert Hodge: That's a good question. The first thing that comes to mind is you're looking at a textbook. You're an undergraduate, and someone goes to the grocery store and buys 50 watermelons. It doesn't seem like a practical problem and solution. That's part of the disconnect. I think the way that I've practiced is by learning by doing rather than doing a clear-cut problem. That's the way I learn best.

Aris Winger: You are one of our younger interviewees. Your story will certainly resonate with people who are undergraduates who are reading this at this very moment. Take us a little bit before you go to undergrad. How are you feeling? Do you feel you're prepared? What was that summer? Then how was the first semester?

Robert Hodge: The summer leading up to college, I knew I wanted to be an engineer. I wasn't sure which discipline yet, but I liked solving problems and had always been a numbers guy, so that's the path I was leaning toward. At the time, I was working my summer lifeguarding job and getting ready for the next chapter in college. That summer, I summited Mount Kilimanjaro with my uncle to celebrate the hard work of high school and reset before starting college. I felt prepared from my high school experience and honestly wasn't really thinking about it too much.

Aris Winger: What was your introduction to engineering?

Robert Hodge: My first introduction to engineering was through family. I'd help my dad fix things around the house, pick my uncle's brain about what he was working on in his career, and hear stories about my grandfather's work in engineering higher education. In high school, my first real step into it was a 9th-grade drafting course where we were hand-drawing mechanical designs. The class sparked my interest and eventually led me into chemistry, calculus, and more mechanical design courses.

Aris Winger: First Semester of College?

Robert Hodge: My first semester was a mix of general engineering courses, including multivariable calculus and intro to engineering, where they walk you through the different disciplines, learn foundational topics, and complete a team design project. I also took a couple of electives outside of the College of Engineering. I had a pretty rigorous high school experience, so in a way it felt like a continuation of that, which was good. It was definitely challenging. Physics, for one, was tough.

Aris Winger: What was challenging about it?

Robert Hodge: The course content was pretty abstract, making it tough to wrap my head around it initially. I feel at times you gotta hit your head against the wall, do all the practice problems, and fail in order to learn the path forward.

Aris Winger: Talk to me about failing forward. Unpack that for me.

Robert Hodge: For me, failing forward means starting by trying to solve problems on my own. If I get stuck, then I go back to my notes and back to the textbook. It might mean calling a friend, going to the professor, or visiting the TA's office hours. It's finding the way to learn the material and adapting to be able to solve those problems. It's finding the ways that I can remember it and have it as a tool in my tool bag going forward, the next four or five years.

Aris Winger: Did you always know how to fail forward?

Robert Hodge: As a first-year, I don't think I knew that at the time. That's a great question. I think I was caught in the details, and it was almost learning for regurgitation.

Aris Winger: When did that change?

Robert Hodge: I would say that changed kind of later on in college: junior or senior year, where you're actively applying theories in class. You're working with other students. You've got three years of coursework under your belt, and it's time to leap into applying it to help a real company solve one of its pressing business needs. This would happen in our senior design course.

Aris Winger: If you could go back, would you have done things differently? Would the regurgitation be less? Would you have done it exactly the same?

Robert Hodge: I feel it would be very similar. I would challenge my freshman-year self to think about the bigger picture. Go beyond the super-scoped out homework assignment or test. Why are we talking about this now? Take a step back. Appreciating rather than being in the weeds to answer the very specific technical questions at the time. Take that extra step to think about how this would be useful. Am I interested in it? Could it be a possible career path? I was not keen on any of that in my first two years of college. That came later on.

Aris Winger: Where are our readers supposed to look for the big picture?

Robert Hodge: For me, the big picture came from getting involved outside the classroom, research, talking with professors, and having those broader conversations. It's an extra step or effort beyond the coursework. The coursework built the foundation, but those experiences helped me connect the dots and see how everything fit together.

Aris Winger: Did you go to office hours often? Were you connected to professors?

Robert Hodge: It depended on the course. For the ones I found difficult, I made a point to go to office hours. The TA and I would work through problems together, I'd show them my thought process and what I had done so far. I never walked in with a blank sheet of paper. We would talk about it step-by-step. For classes, I felt more comfortable with the course content. I usually just ask a buddy if a smaller question comes up.

Aris Winger: How is this buddy made? Is this someone you knew ahead of time? How are we getting to know other people in the major?

Robert Hodge: The first engineering course put us into teams, so right from the start, I was working on group projects with other students, and a great way to meet peers. My roommate was also an engineer, and we were in many of the same courses. Between dorms, classes, and getting involved on campus, I kept meeting more students in engineering.

You're slowly expanding that network. By the end of your freshman year, you are determining your discipline. Your cohort goes from several thousand people to a couple of hundred people.

Aris Winger: How did you decide on your discipline?

Robert Hodge: That first year engineering course was learning about the different disciplines. I ultimately chose industrial and systems engineering because I have always been interested in business strategy. I saw a clear connection between the coursework and business management, while still staying close to the technical work. That combination really drew me in.

Aris Winger: This is at the end of your freshman year?

Robert Hodge: Yup!

Aris Winger: Now you're taking classes in that.

Robert Hodge: Yes. Correct.

Aris Winger: Are there internships that you're doing?

Robert Hodge: I did two internships. The first internship was after my sophomore year. I went to school during COVID. Things were all over the place. It was a little bit hard to find an internship. Still, ultimately, I reached out and worked at a small program management and business solutions consulting firm in my college town called Transformative Management Solutions. It was a business analyst role. Effectively, they were building a financial solution for Federal contractors using earned value management. They were teaching me kind of how to use Power Apps and Power BI platforms to help them more on the technical side. But then, in addition to learning those technical skills, I was also able to learn the financial side of tracking cost and schedule variance, identifying key performance indicators, and helping support the design of dashboards to house all this information.

That was my first technical role, which was good.

Aris Winger: Sounds like that experience was impactful.

Robert Hodge: It was. I worked directly with the owner, meeting a couple of times a week to talk through the features we were building. He coached me on the fundamentals, knew the platforms and tools we were using, and could explain how everything worked together. As the owner, he also understood the overall vision, which was a super helpful context. The one-on-one mentorship in a smaller environment helped me see an idea through from start to finish.

Aris Winger: Then the other internship was?

Robert Hodge: My second internship was the summer after my junior year down in Fort Worth, Texas, working at Lockheed Martin in the program management office for F-35 mods and upgrades. It was a really cool experience and also my first time being away from home, since I went to college in my hometown. I learned a lot about myself that summer.

Aris Winger: What'd you learn?

Robert Hodge: I learned a ton at Lockheed, both in the job and outside of it. It was my first time really living away from home, so I had to figure out a routine and get used to a totally new environment. Most of the summer was just learning the processes, how decisions get made on the F-35, all the different groups that have a say, which was super cool. I worked really closely with my manager, who was an awesome mentor. He made a point to make me feel part of the team, invited me to meetings just to listen in, and gave me chances to learn.

The two big projects I worked on were pretty different. One was user interface and experience testing for a new dashboard tool, really digging into each feature, checking the visuals and drill downs, and seeing if it was intuitive and easy to use. The other was helping close out contract line items and chip away at the backlog, which honestly felt like a scavenger hunt, piecing together the story and evidence for each one and coordinating to get it wrapped up.

Being at a big company, I also learned that the work moves more slowly, with more data handoffs and sign-offs before things happen. For the process I was working on, a modification, retrofit, or new equipment installed on an aircraft could take years. So I did not get that same start-to-finish feeling I had at the smaller company, but I came away with a whole new appreciation for how huge, complex projects get done. And on the fun side, there was a big group of interns that summer, which was a blast. I made a ton of new friends, and having that social piece alongside the work made the whole experience even better.

Aris Winger: You have this interesting perspective, two very different internships. Looking back, would you have chosen two very different internships like this?

Robert Hodge: Absolutely. Having that really small and that really big company experience really helped me figure out parts that I really liked about the small company. I really liked the transparency. I really like hands-on work. I thought I learned a little more from doing that smaller internship.

But it was incredible working for a large company and seeing the end product of an F-35 jet. I thought that was super cool. Even though it was super zoomed up, having both of those experiences helped me kind of figure out what size company I wanted to work for after graduation.

I concluded that I liked the smaller environment a little more, which kind of led me to my current company, where I work.

Aris Winger: Talk to me about routine. You say you learned about routine. Did first or second year Robert have a routine?

Robert Hodge: I did not.

Aris Winger: Why is routine important? What's routine about?

Robert Hodge: Routine to me is just about keeping myself in a good spot so I can show up and do well. Eating decent food, getting enough sleep, and having some structure every day.

Freshman and sophomore years, there's so much going on. You wake up and you go to the gym. You go to your classes. Friends want to hang out, clubs are going on, and college sports are going on. You're trying to apply for that internship for the coming summer, and you don't want to miss out on anything, and quite honestly, I think it wore me out.

I really started to notice in my sophomore year, after having moved to Texas. There was a lot less going on Monday through Friday. Monday through Thursday, I was focused on work. We worked 10-hour shifts. I'd wake up at 5 or 6 am. Recharge, eat a good breakfast, go to work, hang out with friends in the evening, and then kind of turn in. Having that schedule, that routine dialed in, I performed better, and I was a lot more satisfied, and felt I was achieving more while doing less.

Aris Winger: Do you come back after that to school, and you're keeping the routine, or you're getting more structure?

Robert Hodge: I feel that was the intention. When I came back from Texas, I tried to keep those habits going, but honestly, they kind of fell to the wayside. In my senior year, I realized I had all these big aspirations from that internship experience, and I wanted to actually work them into my daily life. That is when I tried to become a lot more intentional and aware about keeping those routines. **Aris Winger:** Tell me about the professors you're meeting. Do we have any mentors?

Robert Hodge: Yep. Two mentors come to mind. The first was a professor I had for my intro-level engineering course. I had him in both the first and second semesters. In the first semester, we were doing a lot of coding in MATLAB, including programming a LEGO robot to follow a line on a piece of paper. In the second semester, our team was building a fixed-wing drone, so we went from coding to creating something physical, which was totally different but a really good experience. I really enjoyed having him as a professor for going the extra mile to make the course content relatable, fun, and practical.

This same professor ran an undergraduate research group. At the end of my freshman year, I applied to join and ended up working on a team with a friend of mine. That is when we started working more one-on-one and got to know each other better. What was interesting about that research was that it was studying how virtual collaboration environments that engineering students were using were impacting their teamwork and perceived levels of success. It was a social science experiment and very different from my usual technical work. This was my first crack at doing research and looking into something totally new, with a great mentor helping lead the charge.

What we were testing was in those 1st and second, or those 1st year engineering courses. How are people structuring their project management? Are they using GroupMe, or are they using Snapchat to talk about this? Are they setting up a virtual collaboration environment? Are they setting up a Google Drive? Are they setting up Microsoft Teams? Is it Slack? We really wanted to understand how people were working together. We wanted to see if having a virtual collaboration environment helped a student offload the cognitive load of keeping track of things.

There were 6 first-year engineering courses. Three of them were instructed to create a virtual collaboration environment. They had to report to us what they were using. The other three chose their own adventure. We created Likert-style surveys as a metric.

Then, the other researcher and I, along with the professor, had to work together to design an experiment, build out these surveys, define what we were really trying to learn, and figure out a way to quantify the results. And that was the first real experience I had with that.

Aris Winger: In some ways, you also see the professors struggle with these things.

Robert Hodge: Absolutely, this professor also had never done a project like this before. He was there on the front lines with us, learning while we were doing it, and we were kind of doing it as a team, which humanized it.

Aris Winger: That's good for the administrators who might be reading now. Those types of experiences are influential and important. Great. Tell us about mentor number two.

Robert Hodge: Mentor number two was one of the leaders at the Virginia Tech Apex Center for Entrepreneurs. During my sophomore year, a couple of buddies and I started our own golf shoe company, which is how we first got connected. We ended up joining their start-up incubator program, and he really showed us the ropes, everything from marketing our products to general best practices for starting a company. He was one of our go-to resources whenever we ran into a roadblock, and he also pushed us to new heights by helping us prepare and enter pitch competitions.

Aris Winger: Talk to me about identity. You were an industrial engineering major. When you look over at the entrepreneur stuff, there's not a part of you that says, "I can't do that. I'm an engineer." Talk to the reader about someone who says, "I'm an engineer. I have to stick with engineering. I can't look outside." Why is that even beneficial for you as an engineer?

Robert Hodge: I got into entrepreneurship in my sophomore year. Two of my close friends started a golf shoe company over winter break my sophomore year, and when they told me about it, I thought it was the coolest thing ever. I had some overlapping experience from classes like manufacturing processes lab, industrial cost control, and even production planning/inventory control, so I told them to keep me in mind if they needed an extra set of hands. Eventually, I got involved, and it didn't even feel like work.

To answer your question, this was the first time that opened my eyes to being able to work outside of Matlab or Excel, and really build out these ideas, and still be an engineer. It has been a really satisfying experience, and I am still working on it to this day.

But I will say, struggling in physics, struggling in statics, and building the research experiment, I think, prepared me to jump into the entrepreneurial cross-functional venture. It was all very technically different, but it taught me not to be discouraged if it's not a linear path forward. It taught me how to think of ideas and really take a very big question and break it into manageable steps to go forward.

Aris Winger: What year is this happening in for you?

Robert Hodge: This was my sophomore year before that business analyst internship.

Aris Winger: You've had a couple of years of internships at this point, and we're in senior year.

Robert Hodge: I was starting to figure things out. I was always interested in technology strategy and consulting to satisfy the technical side of things. Also, I was thinking of being a consultant and a driver of ideas and solutions, helping solve problems. It almost felt like entrepreneurship, something that I had already been doing and really liked.

By senior year, I started to look at full-time consulting job opportunities. That's where I work during the day, while I work on the shoe company in the evenings and weekends. You jump into senior year, and offers are going out in October and November ahead of the next summer start date; the process starts pretty early.

Aris Winger: Are you going to job fairs?

Robert Hodge: Yep, every year I went to our large engineering expo, which is student-run. A ton of companies come to it. I'm walking around with my stack of resumes, my elevator pitch ready to go and meeting recruiters, and talking to them about my journey throughout college, and what I'm interested in, asking them about their experience and company.

Aris Winger: Are there consulting jobs there?

Robert Hodge: . That is how I found the current company I work at, Guidehouse. Many of the other large consulting firms were there as well. It's really hard to land a technical internship after your freshman year, and one of the course requirements in our freshman year was to go to the career fair. You had to send a picture that you're there and dress up, and go walk around, see the environment, and talk to a couple of companies. Just really trying to immerse yourself and build those relationships. This is your best and most personal avenue to get these jobs. Put yourself out there and give it a try in a very low-stress environment. Take a swing at it.

Aris Winger: You did that in your 1st year.

Robert Hodge: Yup. It felt very frustrating at the time. Wait a second? Why am I here? Everyone told me it was tough to land a job or intern after freshman year. But when the next year rolls around, I've already done this before, and it is a familiar experience.

Aris Winger: You get some offers. You decide on the place you are now. Why did you pick them?

Robert Hodge: I chose Guidehouse because it was aligned with my interest in technology and was a smaller and up-and-coming company. It felt really scrappy, fast-paced, collaborative, and it almost felt like a startup. The company is only about six years old, still building out infrastructure, still asking questions, and figuring out its identity. It felt very similar to building my own company, and the people I talked with during the interview process really resonated with me. The opportunities I was looking at were in technology and strategy implementation, and the role I have is focused on that in the energy sector. Which actually surprised me, and I didn't even know that was an opportunity available ahead of learning about it at our career fair.

Aris Winger: We've been interested in this balance between curiosity and fear. You were offered the energy opportunity. Where is imposter syndrome? Where is the "Oh, that's not my area." Where is that for you?

Robert Hodge: I sometimes felt very out of place during my internships. I would tell myself, "They picked me. Why would they pick me?" Through putting myself out there and being a leader in my college fraternity, undergraduate research, and entrepreneurial stuff. I had failed many times. I stood up and talked to the whole fraternity, and I was stuttering the whole time. That was embarrassing. What can I do next time to not have that happen? Oh, be more prepared. In our first shoe production run, we received 400 pairs of our first shoe line, which ended up being made out of the wrong material, and we had to figure out what to do next.

But putting myself out there and seeing it as an opportunity rather than a worry about failing. And worrying about what people are going to think. I felt that before, and it doesn't feel good. I was beating myself up. I'm very much a perfectionist.

Seeing those moments as opportunities rather than being scared.

Having done that a couple of times, it built up my confidence and my skills. Really talking to people, too. It's not something that's scary for me because I've had the practice, being very extroverted, and coming out of my shell in college and meeting a whole bunch of new people. It didn't really feel like a scary opportunity.

I decided to read up on the energy space and be ready to go. But it is a little nerve-racking. I had no full-time experience before this new company. I know nobody. What can I do before that to read up and figure out what we do? I asked my manager to send me some materials in advance. I read the website, and I was looking at projects and clients on LinkedIn.

I would say three to four months in advance, senior year. It takes a bit more capacity to take on something like that. What I would also do is very informal. I signed up for an energy blog. They would email me. I would read the emails every day. It doesn't have to be super structured or rigid. I was trying to build my foundation.

Aris Winger: You're immersing yourself.

Robert Hodge: Yep, absolutely.

Getting ready to hear what kind of lingo they're talking, and being willing to show up and try. And then that's kind of the mentality that I took.

Aris Winger: Now you're in the workforce. If you could go back to Virginia Tech and add to their curriculum any of the skills, any of the things that when you got into the workforce, you wish you were taught, what would you add? What would you wish you had been taught in undergrad that you had to figure out in terms of how to be an engineer in the workforce?

Robert Hodge: A couple of immediate things come to mind. The first is the tools we use in the workforce. Not everyone has an internship or is working the same kinds of jobs. If you can level the playing field and teach people those tools that they're going to be using going forward, that takes some of that unknown element out of it. Then they could spend time thinking about the ideas, learning about the company, or the work itself, and not having to deal with some of those distractions. That's number one.

Number two: Whether maybe an entrepreneurial class or a class on building and scoping ideas. That's what I learned through my shoe company. We were a small team of friends. What meeting cadence works for us? What's the structure of each meeting look like? Having no experience in manufacturing other than classes. We had no experience in shoe design, either. How are we going to build a shoe that's going to compete with your big players on the market? I got a lot out of that experience. It doesn't necessarily have to be a consumer product.

Getting that experience, taking an idea from start to finish, getting the whole building process, and scaling an idea process. I think that opened up my eyes to paying attention to the bigger picture.

I mentioned what I would tell my freshman-year self. What are the ideas of interest? What do I want to keep going forward?

I think the third thing is something that I have, but not everyone has. We had a course in my major that was called Careers in ISE, and essentially, there wasn't really too much structure to it. They would invite alumni working in the field. They would come, talk to us, give a presentation, and that was really helpful to connect the dots.

Aris Winger: Connecting the dots between what?

Robert Hodge: Tangible career paths outside of college. A lot of people came in from consulting. Lots of CFOs came from our college. They spoke to specific experiences in Blacksburg, our college town, and how it helped propel them in their careers from start to wherever they were, and they talked about key lessons they learned. It was helpful getting a fresh perspective.

Aris Winger: You are our last interview. That's special in lots of ways. We may not put you last in the book. After hearing 16 interviews, some themes have come up. I want to take this moment because you said something that others have said. It was this project that you were talking about that was completely outside of the coursework. Something that you are trying to build from scratch, and all of the education you get from that. That transforms you in ways that you may not get in the classroom. It sounds like it was super important and influential for you.

Robert Hodge: Absolutely

Aris Winger: What did you learn from the project that you didn't get in the classroom?

Robert Hodge: I think, from a technical point of view, learning about sourcing materials from several different areas or vendors, how all those timelines come together, and they interact to form a product. I didn't.... I didn't get that in the classroom.

I'm battling with lead times to get all these products and materials. It all comes together. That's a process. There's shipping to get the product to the warehouse.

Aris Winger: I'm looking at an expert over here. Dr. Clark has been doing this stuff for over a decade. Kyle, can you imagine having this experience as a sophomore?

Kyle Clark: It would have been very helpful. In our classes, we get presented with these problems that might be trying to simulate it, but they rarely give you a lead time change in the middle of a project.

It's been one of the biggest problems in my career. The biggest delay is that your supplier or a part didn't show up on time, or it showed up, and it broke. Or it was the wrong one. And I've had a number of projects get pushed by months because of stuff like that. I'm sure this happens with the shoe business.

Robert Hodge: Absolutely. Our very first production order, we've been working on design and several versions of the shoes, and the order is here. We've got pre-orders. We've already collected payment of some sort months in advance. We're getting ready to deliver all these units. We came to find out that one of the materials was made incorrectly. It was a critical component of where the laces lace through it. After a couple of uses, it ultimately ripped off the shoe, and we couldn't sell the shoes. They were unusable.

Twenty-four hours of "Oh, we're down bad. What are we gonna do?"

Then it's the next day. You wake up. Now let's go solve the problem, and we can work it out with the vendor. But that was the "Oh shit" moment. It's "Let me recollect myself, and figure it out."

We were supposed to launch, and we received these units. It was January of my senior year. January of 2023. That set us back 7 months, and then we officially relaunched 7 months later. Summer of 2023.

Aris Winger: Let me put a pin here. If we had to choose, we would definitely ask every reader to get that side project together, do something from scratch. You're gonna get so much stuff that you can't even put a finger on. That's gonna help you later. That feels like something we have to say.

Robert Hodge: For sure. And the other idea that I would say was really transformational for me was understanding how organizations work. Do you hear a company's mission statement, or what they're all about? Then you think of the various technical departments. Thinking about it from a strategy perspective and how that contributes to that big, bold vision. How do all these things tie into that?

That's another thing. From the experience that I've learned when I'm working as a consultant, I see the big picture. I can then understand a little bit more easily why people are doing certain things. That was also beneficial.

Aris Winger: We're jumbled and out of order a little bit because this is happening simultaneously with traditional schooling.

Robert Hodge: Yes.

Aris Winger: Take us back as much as you want to fill in, that you haven't already said about this venture.

Robert Hodge: Yep, the venture started. My sophomore year. Two of my older friends were seniors at the time. They started the business, and I offered my help. They threw me a bone, per se, and they were trying to help me get experience on my resume to land an internship.

It turns out this is the experience, even for 6 months, that helped me land the internship at Lockheed Martin; One of the bosses had an interest in golf, and that's kind of how it kind of shook out. But I think it helped me land that opportunity. All of this was happening at the same time, and we were working with a contract shoe designer who took on our project on the side. They worked for big box stores. He was our technical expert. We had this vision. We had guiding principles of how we wanted our shoe to look, and he helped us transform it into a reality. We started sketching. We started to get prototypes.

That prototyping period started in the summer of my sophomore year and lasted up until the summer of my junior year. We were getting prototypes and saying, This material works great. This sole was great. Let's use this kind of rubber compound with it. This is the kind of mudguard we want to use.

Aris Winger: Were the other two engineers?

Robert Hodge: One was focused on computer science, and the other was economics.

The vision around this was that we all got super into golf over COVID. Being college kids, golf's really expensive. We all were getting hand-me-down golf clubs at Goodwill, and we were out there in our tennis shoes. We thought to ourselves, Why are there no golf shoes that are affordable, stylish, and comfortable? Those were our 3 pillars that we wanted to design a shoe around. All of our current buddies who had golf shoes… Midway through a round of golf, their feet would start to hurt. We wanted a shoe that you can lace up at home. You can go play some golf, go to the grocery store, go to the bar, or go to class. We wanted to make it a versatile, everyday shoe.

We took that idea and learned the shoe landscape. The biggest surprise that I had was how tough marketing is. From a technical point of view, getting the website up was easy for us. Merging it with the business processes was something we had some experience with in classes. And YouTube and AI were great resources for us. We looked up how to do something and watched a quick video on it, and became mini pros at it afterwards.

But the messaging and the storytelling, I would say, were kind of the big nugget that was able to combine with my technical work, and I think it helped me become a better communicator. It really helped propel me to be able to step up and be a leader. It's been transformational.

Aris Winger: A couple more questions. What are the goals of the company? Where do you want to be in the future? What do the next 2, 3, 5 years look like for you?

Robert Hodge: Our company's goal is to reimagine the traditional golf shoe and experience on and off the course in our shoes. We've had our first shoe launch of four hundred units. We've got them around the United States in around twenty-five states. We've garnered feedback. Hey? This was great, this is something we could have some work on. And we're back in the redesign process for our second launch, which was really helpful. And we built this community. The short-term goal for the year is, Hey, let's get a shoe design or a recipe that we want to scale with. And then, now, we're really trying to leverage the community to create opportunities with pro golfers. To really go from ordering 400 to ordering thousands of pairs. We've put in the work to build the foundation, resources, and design, and how we design the shoe is, hey? You kind of have a silhouette or some model. And then it's you're playing with incremental design updates, colors, instead of materials, and different sole patterns and designs. It kind of goes more into a plug-and-play mode.

Aris Winger: What I've learned from you in the last 15 minutes, that every time you talk about something, at least for the business, some element of the business that you're doing or figuring out. You mentioned a person you mentioned somebody. It was the designer earlier. And then. And I'm thinking, in the next 5 years, there's somebody also that's gonna come along and add some element that sparks it and makes it explode. I'm excited for you.

Robert Hodge: Oh, thank you. You learn the ins and outs of business, and you learn about seeing things as opportunities. It stunk that the 1st ones were made incorrectly, but it taught us something about our supply chain. It's Whoa! I didn't even see that it was a curveball. We're better equipped to do it next time, and you said it was the 2 friends who helped get me involved in this and work my way up. It's the people who make it happen and build the ideas. I was at a fraternity leadership retreat my sophomore year, and they had a guest speaker come in. One of the things that he said stuck with me, and is one of my guiding acronyms that I live by, is RBO: relationship before opportunity. And it's with the shoe company, whether it's the designer, whether it's the customer, whether it's my boss at work, whether it's the barista at Starbucks. It all comes back to the relationship before opportunity. That's what we're thinking about when we're connecting with golf pros, store owners, or even players. That's what we think about, and we don't want to make a quick buck. Our team wants to build something that's sustainable and lasting.

Aris Winger: Two more questions in order to be where you are now. And in your position. What have you had to sacrifice?

Robert Hodge: I would say a lot of time with friends. And in college, doing undergraduate research, or being a leader in a fraternity and working on a business, it came at the expense of everyone's out doing this really fun thing now, we're headed to this party, or we're going to the football game. And it's I'm sitting there in front of my TV for white noise. And I'm going on my computer, and we would have a lot of late-night design calls that would take 3, 4, 5 hours. I remember the 1st summer that I got involved with this. We're on our family beach trip, and it's 10:30 at night, and everyone's about to go to bed. And I'm now cracking open my computer. And my parents are like, "What are you doing?" And I'm about to discuss t-shirt and shoe designs now, I gotta go out on the balcony, good night. I'll see you guys tomorrow? I'd say a lot of time. That's the big one.

Aris Winger: Excellent. Last question. Somebody's reading these words, and they're an undergraduate. They're in engineering. They're feeling good. They might not be feeling good. They may be on track, they may be lost. This is your chance to talk directly to them. Get whatever advice, whatever helped you, whatever you want to say to them.

Robert Hodge: I would say, stay the course. There's light at the end of the tunnel, there are really hard courses, there may be something that you're scared to tackle, or you don't necessarily want to wake up early every morning, but I would say it's worth it. And I would say, I talked to you both about the importance of a routine, and from all my experiences I've learned, and the kind of approach that I take is that habits compound. If I can do a little bit each and every day, it'll really stack up, and don't be discouraged that you have a bad day or something doesn't go your way. I think, specifically for the Shoe Company, or whether you start it as a job. There's a delayed gratification. I think we're now starting to see some success with the shoes we started 5 years ago. In the job, I didn't feel comfortable with the material or my clients, or the work, until 15 months later. Stay the course, and it'll pay off. And don't get discouraged, for sure.

16 - Danny Murphy

ENGINEER RESPONSIBLY

There might come a time when you need someone to look you in the eye and let you know they care about you. This was the beginning of a redemptive arc for Professor Danny Murphy that might shock you. Finding himself deep within a "survivalist form of despair," the spark his first mentor gave him provided a pathway to starting school, undoubtedly saving his life. What you are about to read is the telling of a journey of a humble man who found purpose in both his calling as an engineer and in being a mentor for others, like the man who turned his life around did for him.

Danny Murphy (Papa Murph)

Assistant Professor of Mechatronics at Central Virginia Community College

A3 Educator of the Year, 2024

BS in Electronics Engineering Technology at DeVry University

Hometown: Oakland, Maryland

Aris Winger: Danny, thank you very much for doing this. Are you an engineer?

Danny Murphy: I am.

Aris Winger: And what does being an engineer mean to you?

Danny Murphy: Gosh! That's a big question, isn't it? Let me start by saying what being an engineer means to me, specifically within the context of my engineering career, as opposed to the bigger question of what it means to everybody else.

I've spent about 25 to 26 years now as an automation engineer, specifically a controls engineer. Typically, automation and controls engineers will design the electrical equipment and program the software responsible for making automated machinery run. Now, obviously, engineering has a much broader scope than that. But that's what it means in the context of my career.

Danny Murphy: Engineering in a nutshell would be the art and science of responsibly creating a robust product.

Aris Winger: Go ahead, break that down. You say responsibly. Why is responsibility a part of this?

Danny Murphy: Otherwise, you're kind of a proliferator of chaos, aren't you? If you're not responsibly designing something from logical methods in a parameterized scope of function, then you're not really creating. You're an agent of dynamic change, which doesn't really mean anything in terms of creating an engineered product. Engineering requires the engineer to be responsible enough to properly learn what they're doing and disciplined enough to apply the principles that they've learned, or else they're not really a creator. They're a fiddler.

Aris Winger: Appreciate that. Now take us back. We're going to go through the journey. Take us back to shortly before you went to university, the summer before the year before you went to university. How are you feeling about going into college? How was the 1st year of undergraduate? What is the time like as you're transitioning to undergraduate school?

Danny Murphy: The journey for me… It's a long and rather complicated one, but to summarize it, moving to college to me was synonymous with moving out of functional homelessness.

It began a life that otherwise very likely would have ended early.

I was a teenager in the nineties, which means that it was my responsibility to confuse rebelliousness with independence. My parents and I at the time didn't get along very well, and I was either 16 or 17 when they kind of had enough with my attitude, and they kicked me out of the house. For a while, I did what any teenage, homeless person would do, which is mooch off of friends and girlfriends and stuff like that until enough people had said, "You can't do that anymore." And that began the steep decline into existential terror, and I spent a lot of time in my car and a lot of time in abandoned buildings. A lens factory had shut down near McDonald's, which had some dry places to sleep, even if they were rather cold. It was cold where I grew up. I spent quite a long period of time bouncing back and forth between quasi-survivable places before I had the opportunity to go up to college and get an apartment with a few people who were barely willing to tolerate me.

Aris Winger: I want to unpack this opportunity. Fill in the blanks for us about how college even shows up for you as an opportunity, a possibility.

Danny Murphy: I'm glad you asked that. That's a really important part of my life and directed how I became me.

I had a number of very good teachers, but one that sticks out in my mind as a transformative influence, and that would be Steve Cosner. He was my electronics teacher in high school. Steve was your classic boomer in the nineties. Kind of gruff, not particularly compassionate. But I remember him telling me one day, Look, I can tell something's up, and I really don't want to get involved, but you smell bad, and you're not going down a good path. Let's get you straightened up and at least get you some good grades. There's a chance that you can get a scholarship and move on to college instead of whatever it is you're doing now.

And he did. He spent some extra time with me. He was constantly encouraging at a time when there were a lot of people who were anything but encouraging. And he, among a few other things, kind of navigated me into the electronics type of field. Largely because that's what he was teaching, and we always try to assimilate our idols, don't we?

He told me about DeVry University. It was called DeVry Institute of Technology back then, and they were a good school, but they were kind of known for their cheesy commercials. They had a merit-based scholarship program for 2 people a year based on SAT scores, essays, and other factors that could get a full scholarship. I was like, it's not going to be me, obviously, but what have I got to lose?

I worked with Mr. Cosner and got my grades up. I took the SAT tests and did reasonably well. And he came to me very excited one day, saying, You've gotten the half scholarship. And I thought, that's neat, but that's getting exactly halfway to the moon. You're still stuck. I played happy to let him know how appreciative I was for the work that he'd done, but secretly kind of resigned myself to a life of nothingness, however long that would be.

Something or another happened, but one of the two selected full scholars decided to move on to another college, and by default, I was bumped up into that full scholarship bracket.

Now keep in mind. There are a lot of financial programs nowadays for a lot of people to get school paid for, but at least as far as what I knew about back then, it wasn't the same. What getting a full scholarship meant to me was, I thought of Willy Wonka. It's a golden ticket! And, for contrast, at the time I was squatting in a walled-off section of a woman's house, sleeping on a discarded mattress with a hole in it where the emergency crew had used a Sawzall to cut out the brain matter from where the last guy lay down and shot himself.

I refer to those times as "the suicide mattress." And that, that's the context. You're asking me what it was to go from that and on to college. For me, it was escaping a very survivalist form of despair and adjusting from Appalachia to Columbus, Ohio. That city had a million people. It was terrifying in and of itself for a boy who grew up in the woods. But you could make $7.50 an hour up there. Oh, my God! What are you gonna do with that much money?

I was escaping a life where I once ate nothing but a raw potato a day for 30 days straight, and going up to a place where I could go to a grocery store and buy a loaf of bread and some beans or something, and live in a place that had heat with people who talk to you. It was an incredible, incredible change for me.

Now, as college went on, I didn't focus very well. I never have. I tend to live in a very scattered form of thought. Sitting in a classroom and listening to people talk to me for hours and hours a day was extremely challenging for me, and later on, that particular form of hell is what made me decide to teach in the way that I currently do.

Aris Winger: Ok, so you get to college, find a dorm, get a roommate, all of that stuff, and then what?

Danny Murphy: The way that Devry worked is rather than having on-campus dorms, they secured apartment complexes for multiple students at a rate of roughly 200% what the apartment would cost without the school's help. A bunch of us were pre-selected based on some type of survey. There were 4 guys in a 2-bedroom apartment in a not particularly bad part of town, a lower-middle-class residential area with a golf course nearby and within driving distance of plenty of work opportunities, which I didn't have back home.

Aris Winger: So you're working also?

Danny Murphy: I think I worked 4 and a half hours a day while I went to school. I had a little part-time job. I was a computer tech at a place that did estimating solution software for auto body shops, which was a lucky development in itself..

I had a friend in high school named Bobby who was a self-taught computer expert. We hung out a lot, and he taught me a ton about hardware, but his understanding was orders of magnitude beyond mine. Anyway, we were nerding out in a computer store one evening. I think Bobby was considering upgrading his desktop to 16 megabytes of RAM, and a realtor was getting frustrated that customer service couldn't help fix a laptop he desperately needed.

So Bobby's talking about motherboards and BIOS settings. I'm just standing there looking competent by association, and the realtor walks over to me and asks, "Do you know anything about this? Could you fix this for me?" And I knew that I didn't know how to fix the laptop, but I also knew I was destitute and squatting in the corner of an abandoned lens factory, so I said, "Yes, absolutely!"

He gave it to me, and I took it back to one of the places that I was crashing that happened to have an electrical outlet. And I thought, What am I gonna do? How am I gonna fix this thing? I don't know the 1st thing about what I'm doing. So I looked around in the DOS file system and found some temporary files. They didn't look like they should be there. I deleted them, and oh, my gosh! On restart, everything came up and was working again! So I brought it back to this realtor. He told me that's great. What do I owe you? And I told him, Don't pay me anything. You must know about apartments or houses in the area that are having trouble being rented. Give me permission to squat in one of those places until I get up to college. And he was sure, of course, it didn't cost him anything, and it gave me access to water, a gas stove, and all the things that I needed to wash and get a job. The job, by the way, was Computer Tech at the store where I'd met him.

So, back when I went up to Columbus, Ohio, I was able to list that on my resume to get another computer tech job, one that paid real money. For context where I grew up, the minimum wage, I think, was $4.25 an hour, and my 1st job moving up to Columbus was $7.50 an hour, and I thought I was the luckiest human being in the world to have a stable income at a place that was stupid enough to trust me to do something.

And then to leave there and go to a campus where I could go and get educated for free, in the hopes that someday I would have the hope of doing something real with my life. And then, of course, to have the group of fairly rational and normal guys that I room with, to have some type of fraternal community.

Aris Winger: Oh, wow! Now you're in your 1st year. How is the 1st year of college going for you?

Danny Murphy: My 1st year in college was fine. Apparently, a lot of the other students came from high schools that didn't have an electronics program. I breezed through the DC and AC circuits, all the labs. The math wasn't particularly challenging. At that point, I think sitting still in the classrooms was the most difficult thing for me.

Now that particular school did have labs. I don't want to criticize any due to my particular learning style, because that would be ridiculous, but these labs! You follow the list, you did the tasks, and it led you somewhere, but you had no idea what you were doing. In fact, most people would race through the labs as quickly as humanly possible. And I think this is true for most students, unless they are unusually interested. You blow through the lab as soon as possible so you can have an extra 10 minutes a night of beer drinking time at the end, and you learn nothing. You put some weird-shaped components in a breadboard, and you hook them up with something, and you apply some voltage. Whatever the hell voltage that the lab tells you to put on it, you measure something. You have no idea what you measure, and then you pack up and get out of there, and you get a 95 on the lab, and you don't know what the 5 points you missed were from, and that happens for a while. Then, you sit in the classroom. You listen to somebody who, if at least they're animated and have an interesting voice, can get you to pay attention every once in a while. But by and large, you don't know what the hell's going on. Then you go to work, and you're constantly tired.

But there's heat and electricity, and you can eat some beans; it's heaven. That's what my 1st year was.

Aris Winger: And if you could go back and tell Danny now to do labs differently, what would you tell him?

Danny Murphy: Just spend the extra few minutes that it would take to comfortably do the lab at a reasonable pace. Take notes, step back, and read through it before you do it. Ask What are you doing? What does that mean? If you weren't paying attention when the professor told you what it meant, go look it up.

The Internet existed in the late 1990s. We had tools to do research. Don't just follow a list of instructions to finish them. That's how people die sad. Find out what you're doing, why you're doing it, and then do it. I don't know why that doesn't occur to us before we get too old for it to matter for a large portion of our lives. But it matters in labs, too. Get your own damn context about what the thing is supposed to mean, and then pursue it as though it could teach you something, because it does. That's what I would tell Danny, my past self.

Aris Winger: Undergraduate time in general? Are you doing internships, meeting mentors? Who are the people in your life during that time?

Danny Murphy: For anyone who works while they go to college full-time, it's just a nonstop grind. You wake up in the morning, hope your car will start so you can get to work, go to class, try to absorb the material, and sit there giving commiserative glances to the other tired people trying to crush information into their overflowing skulls. The bonds you form with your classmates are born of empathy, and can be pretty strong.

I was fortunate in that our professors were typically selected from industry. I can't express how critical that is for the real development of an engineering mindset. There are a few things, and this isn't just true of academia; this is true of any discipline that needs to interface with any other discipline… There are a few things worse than somebody who lives their life within that isolated discipline and never contextualizes what they're doing within the realm of how it fits into society, and academia is often criticized for that. Academia is unfairly criticized about that, given that other disciplines aren't equally criticized for the same flaw.

But I was fortunate to have professors who came from industry because that meant that they knew how the knowledge was being applied and how to create what would be a self-sustaining academic course that resonated with the needs of industry.

There were several of my professors that I wouldn't say I worshipped, but who brought context from what it was to work in the field and gave some form of meaning behind the mathematical equations. I was always very grateful for that mentorship. I would say they would have been available had I sought more guidance, but it was a matter of limitations on time. There's work, there's food, there's sleep, there's class, and there's homework. Apart from that, you do very little. I did very little other than that.

Aris Winger: Before we leave the undergraduate experience. Is there anything else from that time that you want to bring up?

Danny Murphy: It was wonderful to make a journey with like-minded people and develop friendships that we often fairly casually cast aside once we move to a different locality. The treasure that you have, not only during college, but during high school or any type of schooling. To be around people of the same age who are in the same type of learning category and range of mental development is such a beautiful, beautiful thing.

You graduate, and you think Cool, good luck everyone, whoever the hell you were, now onto my real life. But in reflection, those friendships… I would encourage anyone going through the same journey to cherish them with the intent of sustaining them for the rest of their lives. There are a few people I've kept in touch with, primarily Greg VanMeter. He became a Green Beret, and we still talk, once every 2 months, which is a lot. I graduated in '99. That's 26 years. That's 150-something conversations. I'll take that.

Aris Winger: After undergrad, where do you head?

Danny Murphy: After I graduated, I started looking around. Our engineering degree offered 3 main focuses. One was telecoms, one was computer networking, and one was controls. I knew I hated networking because that was horrible. Telecoms, I didn't fully understand intuitively. That left whatever "Controls" were.

I think it's rare that someone who has gone through such an abbreviated amount of study can really grasp what it is (the subject matter). You think you know when you graduate, but you have no idea until you get in the workforce.

I thought controls would have something to do with closed-loop feedback; that's pretty much all I knew. So I looked at a couple of places. One of them was in Massachusetts, and one of them happened to be in Hagerstown, Maryland. They did types of machinery for mining and vehicle assembly, and stuff like that. And I thought, I'll give that a shot.

I moved to the Maryland, West Virginia, and Pennsylvania areas, and I remember they hired me as a staff engineer. I had "Engineer" in my title, which was a large portion of why I selected that role, because, wow! You get engineering in your title, and you can brag to your parents about it and the people who criticized you in high school. That was pretty much the depth of my decision-making back then. And to anyone who knows what controls engineers do at this particular point in human history, back then, they largely wrote code that controlled big machines that make stuff, if I had to dumb it down into something I could have understood at the time. And there are generally 2 or 3 platforms of software that are widely used throughout the industry, even if there are thousands that are used in some manner. Ours was Allen-Bradley/Rockwell Software Studio 5000, at least that's what they call it now. It was RSLogix 5000 back then.

Anyone going into that position should have been not only aware of, but proficient in this software. I wasn't. In school, we'd studied some archaic and irrelevant substitute, in a single lab I blew through too quickly and didn't understand. So I walked in on my 1st day of my engineering career, and I looked at the software that was up on my workstation. And I was like, "Oh, that's pretty. What's that?" And they gave me this horrified look and said It's software that makes up 90% of your job! What do you mean, "What's that?"

That was an embarrassing 1st day. It was instantly obvious I couldn't do what they'd hired me to do. They spent some time putting me out in the panel shop so I could see what an electrical panel looked like because, of course, I didn't know. I'd done everything on a breadboard, and nobody uses those in controls. I spent some time doing AutoCAD drafting stuff for several years. I spent some time in factories trying to troubleshoot nightmarish problems under nightmarish pressure, until I got to learn enough to kind of fumble through what it was I was supposed to do.

Aris Winger: How did you learn the software?

Danny Murphy: You sit down and you do it. Somebody says there's a bug in the code, so you open it up and look through it as though you were looking through the Dead Sea Scrolls to try to absorb something that doesn't make sense by osmosis. I think you learn it the same way that a baby learns the native language of its parents by sitting in front of them for so long that eventually patterns start to string themselves together. The better way to learn it would be to take a training course on it. But that's not a luxury I had, and you'd be horrified at how many engineers learn by fumbling through. You make a lot of dumb mistakes and stumble until you can walk and run, metaphorically.

Aris Winger: You have now this 1st job out of school.

Aris Winger: We can jump all over the place here. But what would you have wished they had taught you in school that you needed out in the professional world? Whether that's content or any type of skill. Anything that when you were out in the professional world, you're thinking I wish someone had taught me this or this should be part of engineering 101, or whatever, in addition to the content stuff you mentioned that we need to be talking about in undergrad?

Danny Murphy: I'm really glad you asked that question, because that defined my own curriculum once I started teaching. What would I wish I had had in school in order to be better prepared for industry? Exercises developed using industry-standard equipment that simulated real-world projects I was likely to see in a professional environment.

I don't know if you've looked at a modern electronics curriculum. But it's been about the same since the eighties. Here's a resistor. Here's a capacitor, here's 16 PIN chips. There's a theory that has to go into learning anything, and often the theory starts out being very abstract. But once you learn the abstract stuff, if you don't eventually use it to solve a real-world problem in an industry-approved way, you'll have no context and no idea how to meaningfully contribute. You'll be limited to janky, useless science projects, which is a very disappointing reality for many new engineers.

I could jump ahead to when I began teaching. The 1st mistake I made was, I assumed that my sphere of knowledge was the only one that mattered, and I could do it alone.

Within about a semester, I realized I have to be humble as a professor, and I have to reach out to people in industry, and I have to ask them, "Hey, I'm trying to teach this thing, and guess what? As much as I want to believe I know everything, I bet you understand it better than me."

Guess what, that sentence there will endear you to a lot of engineers and industry that are already convinced they know better.. And you can't approach the industry with your hand out because they're in it for the profit and don't want to give anybody anything for free. Why the hell would they? If they were, they'd be in a charity. But if you work with them to supply them with some students that they need, and to be a meaningful part of their goals, then you can start to ask them. Hey, is there a way that I could bring you in to be a guest speaker in the class? Can I get your insight on this exercise I created?

This works especially with the younger industry professionals looking to stack badges in their resume. You say, Come in and talk to people about what you do. And you get a couple of people doing that. And that allows students a little bit of an idea of what's really going on in industry. Then you can hook someone in and say, Hey, you make panels? Can you bring a panel in and show us? And they'll say, Yes, of course. And try to wire it up, or something. You ask, can you bring in your laptop with some code that's not protected by intellectual property rights and show them what the code looks like on an industry-standard software platform?

But really, it's the responsibility of the schools, and it's a difficult responsibility to fulfill to provide the students with what's standard in industry. Think of it this way: industry-standard equipment is often prohibitively expensive. Try to get it in the classroom, and you have a program that prices itself out of competitiveness with other schools. So you find a less expensive alternative, but then students learn using a product that they'll never see in their professional careers. It's a delicate balance, and if whoever is in charge of decision-making isn't intimately familiar with the industry they claim to serve, the graduating class won't be prepared, and they'll learn that very soon.

Aris Winger: And skill-wise, are there any lessons in terms of day-to-day of being an engineer that we can get across to our young people early?

Danny Murphy: Oh, my experience with engineering is very different from what I see upcoming generations seeming to expect on various social media platforms. The expectation is that you graduate with 90% of the relevant knowledge and a hundred percent of the status. And you're instantaneously able to demand and negotiate great things for yourself, because you've achieved a certain level of education. And to some, to some degree, that can happen.

But the thing that people should be prepared for when entering engineering is that engineering is a heavy cross to bear. You're constantly making decisions throughout the day, and if your focus wanders, somebody might die. Or they might die 2 or 3 years down the road. Or a 1st of its kind piece of prototype equipment might balloon into a whole product line that's unsafe and damages things. If you're a chemical engineer, you might design something that stays in the environment forever. We've heard a little bit about that recently

There have been times when I've worked on projects where I was designing hydrogen furnaces for military night vision, and you wake up in the middle of the night thinking, "Did I control the vacuum process on that in such a way that it's not going to explode?" It's an almost torturous self-sacrifice to dedicate the amount of mental focus to what you're doing to ensure the safety of all the people that your product could potentially negatively impact if you fail. That's what engineering is. Engineering is suffering so that others don't have to.

Aris Winger: Now, you are in the workforce. What is the journey there? You get your 1st job afterwards, and then where do you go from there?

Danny Murphy: The 1st job, I spent about 4 years there. I was able to help develop the Harley-Davidson Softail Assembly line, which was a lot of fun. From there, I came from Maryland down to Lynchburg, Virginia. I found that the amount of engineering work in Lynchburg, Virginia, at least at that time, was incredible. A hub of OEMs. I thought of it back then as the engineering Mecca.

I came down to Lynchburg and worked briefly at a second job that had to do with troubleshooting and installing various beverage processing equipment. Machines that put bottles on pallets, things like that. It was a fine job, but it was at a small company, and I found that I thought I would probably want to have something with a little bit more of a future for me personally in it. I won't say anything bad about the job. It was a fine job.

From there, I went to a different company that did different types of beverage processing equipment, things like case-packers and bottle fillers. They advertised about 25% travel, which ended up being about 70% travel, and that's fairly typical throughout certain types of engineering. The amount of travel is misrepresented in the interview. People buy a house, move in, and then become dependent on the company.. I stayed there a year or so and then went to the next company that focused on prototype machinery. I stayed there for about 13 years, and the prototype machinery was incredible. Because you have to make something new, people would come to us and say, We can't find anyone that makes this type of machine. Can you do it? And the owner would say, Sure, we can do anything, and they'd come to the engineers and say, Can you do this? And we'd say, of course not. That's impossible, and then we'd eventually get it done. That was a lot of hard work and long hours, but some of my best projects that I'm most proud of came out of that particular duration of work. We did systems for the ALMA Observatory, Earth's most powerful radio telescope. There are 66 parabolic dishes located up at the top of the Chilean Andes. I got to travel to the mountain peaks to install my equipment.. That was pretty life-changing.

Danny Murphy: From there, I moved on to another company that worked on non-destructive testing and stayed there for a little while. I mentioned suffering in engineering, and this place was a good example. So, commissioning a project is incredibly stressful. Sales staff or administrators will arbitrarily set a timeline for project completion. These are people who don't actually do the work for a living, so it's almost tempting to forgive them for being wrong, but as an engineer, you're expected to meet schedules, whether they're realistic or not. I remember these guys allotted 2 days for an equipment startup I insisted would take a week. I ended up getting it working in 4 days, but the time crunch was so great that we didn't eat the entire time. I would sleep 2 hours a night under the lunch table in the break room in the factory. It was terrible and ridiculously unsafe. They'll never tell you that you can't sleep or eat; of course, they'll just leave you no other option. It's tough on the people doing the work.

At that particular job, I thought, What am I doing? What am I doing to myself? I'm gonna find a way to literally do anything else. And that's when, at the same time, the local community college was saying they were trying to develop a mechatronics program. I'd never heard that word before. What the hell's mechatronics? And I started working with them to adjunct teach a class on PLC programming. And it was interesting because the professor who had approached me about helping out with the class needed someone who could help her teach electronics. And I don't know if you understand what that would mean to me, given my history with my electronics teacher from high school.

Aris Winger: Please, tell me.

Danny Murphy: It was a cosmic imperative. It was this incredibly random opportunity. Hey? Remember that electronics teacher, who kind of made the difference between life and death for you. Would you do that? How do you say no to that?

And I know that teaching electronics doesn't necessarily involve being a mentor to people's lives, or you wouldn't think it does. But I thought,

I wonder if there would be any chance if I were to be in that role, if I could ever impact someone's life as much as that man impacted mine.

It turns out that life gives you that opportunity, in that role as a professor, about 3 times a year. Being a professor gives you an incredible chance to find people who need somebody to believe in them. And sometimes that matters more than any of the technical details that you teach them. Last Thursday, I had a young man tell me, after the robot lab. My dad died when I was 3, and you're the 1st person who has believed in me since then.

I went through the adjunct phase, and I'm now an assistant professor at the Community College. I don't believe there's a lot of opportunity, unless I were to go pursue a Master's degree, for me to get up past Assistant Professor. It looks like the associate professor and professor titles are reserved for people with certain levels of academic education and not necessarily industry experience, which I think is regrettable. But I understand where that comes from.

And that brings me up from my 1st job to now.

Aris Winger: That's powerful. Thank you for that. What are your goals today? What are you trying to do today and moving forward?

Danny Murphy: I need to find a way to help more people. I've been thinking a lot about how I can expand the number of students that I can reach. Because I have to admit that the real, satisfying life challenge that I found in teaching has a little less to do with the technical details and a lot more to do with the mentorship. In fact, sometimes I think of how satisfying it was to design machinery. When you design a machine, you make something productive out of something that's not productive, and that's great when you can do it with, say, metal and plastic. But it's deeply meaningful when you can do it with a human life. And moving forward, that's what I'm trying to do. And I'll be honest with you, I haven't figured out how to do that yet. That's what I'm working on.

Aris Winger: That's powerful. A couple more questions for you. To be where you are now, what have you had to sacrifice?

Danny Murphy: That's a really good question. It hasn't been much of a sacrifice. The things you sacrifice are the nights at the bar with friends or the hikes out on the weekends. Sometimes, when you have to work extra, there's that. But largely, the things that I've had to sacrifice fall under the realm of recreation. Which is a very fair payment to produce things of value that I can be happy about. There are a lot of my projects that are global in nature. I got to design the cryostat positioning systems for the world's most powerful deep space telescope! I designed the hydrogen furnaces that supply our US Army and special forces' night vision! There was a cost. But I think the sacrifice is worth the satisfaction.

Aris Winger: There's something about your journey. Looking back on your journey and what you've gone through. Are you proud of yourself?

Danny Murphy: I'm very aware there are a lot of smart people in the world, and I bet when they design something, they do it well. And I do my best. But I'm not the sharpest tool in the shed. I happened to be tenacious, and I think that tenacity comes from where I came from as a 16-year-old, where you died if you didn't figure it out. And that's the way I approach my engineering projects. If I don't figure this out, nobody else will, and something bad will happen.

Am I proud of that? If you're running away from a wolf and you get away. Are you proud of yourself? No, you got away from the wolf. I wouldn't say I'm proud of myself.

What I would say more than that is I'm unbelievably grateful to have gotten to walk a path through a forest that had fewer predators. There are people out there in the world who are trying to keep the bombs from falling on them. All I had to do was find a place to sleep. How many people would be happy about that? So no, I'm not proud of myself. I'm very grateful to how many people there were to help me along, and I feel responsible for proliferating that encouragement.

Aris Winger: Last question. As we're gonna have lots of different people reading this, particularly some undergrads who are thinking about engineering, people who are in different phases of it. Some people feel they're doing a great job. Some people who feel they're not. This is your time, your chance to talk to them directly. What do you have to say to them about the journey? Anything you want to tell them? Go ahead and tell them now directly.

Danny Murphy: It's not all about you, but some of it's about you. Oh, don't make the mistake that I made early on, and think that because you have a title, that means you have some inherent worth. Your worth, I feel, comes from what you can contribute to your society, the people around you, and your family. And balance those things, because those are very different things. Your society, the people around you, and your family. An imbalance could mean your employer makes a lot of money off of your life at the expense of you having time with your kids.

Then again, if you are one of the people who really like a work-life balance, then you could find that you allow yourself to remain very ordinary at the expense of pursuing something hard and doing something worthwhile.

Step out of your own ego and work with the people around you. Don't look down on people who have a lower education than you, because sometimes they have the answers you don't. And don't assume that people with more education than you are always trying to pull one over on you.

THEMES

We thought this project was important because there is a gap between what the school was saying was needed to be a successful engineer and what actually happens when we enter the real world as an engineer. As Cooper said, "...pencil whipping or documentation, or sitting in meetings and making sure people are all on the same page feels different than what you picture."

If we could dream, there would be an adjacent set of topics we would treat just as important as Mechanics and Inorganic Chemistry. This book is the first step in that dream.

What would those topics be? We compiled some themes that we thought stood out directly from the authors directly from the authors. In each of these areas, we name-name-drop a sampling of the authors tied to a particular theme. You'll also notice that some of the themes apply not just to succeeding in engineering but to life as well. As you read the themes, think about other authors' stories and how they relate to the theme as well.

Level Up

Krys, Cory and Sibel all make it clear that college is a completely different beast than high school. It takes more work. It's like a job. It's on you. It's about the big picture (see the next theme). Studying takes on a whole new meaning. Studying for a test? Forget that. You're studying to be an engineer. Leveling up means demanding of yourself what it takes to meet the moment. This means changing who you are and how you relate to others and how you communicate, collaborate, lead, serve and empathize with others.

The Big Picture

Ariel, KiYett and Anthony were all pretty explicit about it. Find your "why." It makes sense. You are about to dedicate at least the next 1,200 days in pursuit of a goal. You should, reasonably, start to be clear of exactly why you are doing that. When the rough parts come, knowing the big picture keeps you going. Being on a road you chose gives you momentum, a crucial key to happiness and fulfillment. Begin to understand your purpose and your mission because someone as talented and unique as you shouldn't be wandering around aimlessly. It's a disservice to the world and not even close to what you deserve for yourself and your life.

Reflect

Alex, Cory, and Jesse did a ton of reflection. Reflection saved Jesse's life. Cory reflected with us and called himself a "doofus" in undergrad before leveling up (see the first theme) the second time around. There is no improvement without deep reflection. What does this look like? It's unabashedly honest. It asks the hard questions. What role did I play in what happened? What are my strengths and weaknesses? How can I get in my own way? When you start to really dig into these questions and answer them with unfiltered clarity, amazing things will start to happen. You will start to develop a sense of ownership over your own life, providing you the primary avenue to the personal freedom and self-actualization that we all seek.

Prioritize What Matters (and Discard What Doesn't)

We explicitly and deliberately asked about sacrifice. It's because we each only have so much bandwidth. The stories of Seth, Joseph, and Katrien stand out in this area as their sacrifices go against the grain. Katrien sacrifices the traditional family structure for her business and Seth embraces his commitment to family instead of diving Full Speed Ahead into his career. There are no wrong answers. What you choose to prioritize (and sacrifice) reflects what you consider important. When you start to discard what ultimately doesn't matter, it will feel hard at first. But as you start to be around what you consider important more often, you start to be who you truly are, a worthy goal we should all be striving towards.

Mental Health

How are you doing? We as a society have turned this all important question into a formal nicety. Jesse, Danny, and Cooper each in their own way discuss the challenges that can show up for us in how we feel along the journey, whether it's burnout, feeling the pressure of success or the crippling state of your current environment. Each of these can lead you down the wrong path. Each of these authors dealt with their challenges in the same way, through tapping into their support networks and mentors, getting advice and new perspectives to help them make it from day to day. They realized that they were not alone and you should realize that you are also not alone. Whether you realize it or not, at this moment, there is someone that you could call who would listen to you say what you need to say out loud, when you need to be heard. Never forget that. As our authors can attest, knowing this piece of information can be the difference between life and death.

If you or someone you know needs support, contact the 988 Suicide & Crisis Lifeline. You can call or text 988 anytime, or chat online at https://988lifeline.org/. This service is free, confidential, and available 24/7.

Ask Questions

One of the biggest myths about success is its correlation to having the answers, when in so many ways it's about having the courage to ask the right questions. Ariel, Austin, and Kiyett are our champion question askers. Faced with moments in which they didn't know, they spoke up. They voiced their lack of knowledge in spite of being scared because they realized that getting the information they needed was far more important than continuing the facade of knowing. It required them to check their ego and embrace humility. You might be put in a situation where you are "supposed" to know. Ask the question. More often than not you and your career will be better for it.

Serve Others

Engineers are the ultimate problem solvers. The problems they solve are often not their own, but someone else's. Inherently, an engineer's problem solving serves a purpose and often people. Anthony, Danny, and Robert all see their work beyond the application of science to the larger picture. How do people benefit from this? When you work as a servant in engineering, not only do you change as a person, you find a whole new level of purpose in what you are doing.

Learn to Work with Others

Engineering is not a solitary exercise. Problems are so complex that in order to make progress, you'll need lots of different ideas and perspectives. Joseph, Cooper, and Alex rave about the benefits of being able to collaborate with others and to work on teams. While there are always challenges working with others, the benefits outweigh the costs. Learning to communicate and work with others effectively is just as important as any science you learn in your classes. After all, what's the alternative? An engineer on an island solves very few problems, diminishing their purpose from the start.

Network to Expand Your Reach and Foster Opportunity

Nikeem got a LinkedIn message that changed his life forever. Opportunity presented itself in part because he presented himself as available to his network. Your chances at opportunity are directly proportional to the size of your network. KiYett sat outside in her car before going into a networking event, pushing herself to "just meet three people." She knows. Anthony didn't even see the point of going to the Engineering Expo as a first year student. But that was the class assignment. What he didn't know at the time was that with every hand he shook, every conversation he had, even the small ones, and with every resume he shared, even though it was sparse, the more he increased his opportunity. He would eventually find the group in which he vibed with the best, gathering the boldness to say that he would work for them for free as labor to get connected. You can guess what happened next. Network and opportunity go hand and hand. The next time you say to yourself "I want opportunities," ask yourself "Who do I know and who knows me?"

Handle the Move to a New Arena

Krys found himself at five different institutions on his way to a doctorate in engineering. How many new situations must that have been for him? Both Danny and Austin at their new job right out of training both realized they didn't know the software that was required in order for them to do their job. They both flourished. How? When you are in a new environment after a transition, a major key to success is the support system you are transitioning to. Those new people should be ready and willing to help out. Most importantly, you must be mentally prepared to learn and be comfortable being on a learning curve. This could range from learning a new programming language to how team meetings are run at the new company. When you find yourself in transition to a new place, ask yourself one question and declare to yourself a statement: (1) Who can support me here? (2) It's not as much about what I know now as much as how willing I am to learn whatever it takes to be successful.

Explore More and Get Uncomfortable

Problems and engineering are so complicated that paradoxically you'll need more than engineering skills to solve them. Where do these skills come from? Cory, Alex and Katrien would offer that their success was deeply tied to spending significant time outside traditional engineering solving problems. Alex spent a significant amount of time during his engineering study in the law and business school. Katrien works with engineers *and* fashion designers everyday. Learning how other disciplines solve problems has at least two benefits. First, you never know when an out of the box method or idea might be the very thing you need for your problem. Second, you will become accustomed to working with other ways of thinking, which is crucial for solving problems involving stakeholders from a variety of backgrounds and areas. The discipline of engineering has solved world problems across cultures, country boundaries, and experience. If you are interested in solving those problems then you need to train in solving problems across different perspectives in response. This won't be comfortable. That's good. It's outstanding or comfortable. It's impossible to be both. Getting uncomfortable means you are choosing outstanding.

Expect and Prepare for the Unexpected

As much as we want to act as if we know what's to come or we try to plan our life deterministically like a jigsaw puzzle, life has a way of humbling us, reminding us that we have far less control. Seth, Sibel and Nikeem experienced job loss, serious health scares, and being thrown out of class, respectively and unexpectedly. They all rebounded. How? They were very much rooted in purpose (see above for the bigger picture) and we're open to adapting. When you have an idea of your bigger picture then you anticipate the bumps and the road. If you are open to adapting, when the road you are on starts to crumble, new ones become easier to envision. The next time life intervenes into your well-made plans, what a difference it might make for you to say to yourself "This was an unexpected obstacle. I knew they were going to come. I am prepared to adapt."

Build a Group of Supporters

You can't do it alone. Time and again Cooper, Jesse, and Austin relied on their supporters for a variety of assistance. Cooper as a first year student shared space with people who gave him invaluable advice on what to expect and what to avoid over the next four years of his education. Austin had unwavering support from his family on his path, especially when he switched paths in the midst of a global pandemic The first thing Jesse did in one of his darkest moments was visit his supporters, asking them for their feedback and advice. Who's your crew? Who are the people who will listen to you intently and give you honest feedback, not for any other reason than because they know and care about *you*. Your choice of your supporters is just as important as any content you may learn in any course.

Build Relationships with Mentors

Navigating a path is better with a trusted guide. This doesn't mean the guide tells you exactly where to go. They may have been on a similar path and might be able to give some thoughts on what to expect and (perhaps more importantly) what you might want to avoid. Good mentorship is so important that Joseph named it as the prominent topic that he wanted readers of his story to understand as the most crucial part of his success. Ariel had an open rotation of mentors, making sure she always had a personal avenue to learn more from people who knew more. As the saying goes, you are a product of the people around you. It would follow pretty easily that if you have goals you want to achieve that you would have as one of these people someone that already traversed a similar path and was willing to share openly and honestly with you about the journey. How do you find a mentor? Be direct. Joseph was direct. Ariel was downright bold. The key to finding mentors relies around a few thoughts. First, you'll be surprised how many will say yes because it is often a part of their mission to mentor and they enjoy being able to help others through sharing their own journey. Second, you don't need too much time for the life changing advice you could possibly get. So don't think that you are wasting their time because you won't be using that much of it. Third, the reward for getting a yes far outweighs them saying no when you ask. After all, if we put 10 people in front of you and told you that only one of them would be your mentor but that the two of you would have a one-hour conversation that will forever change your life, wouldn't you just go ahead and ask all of them in order to find the one?

Show Up Consistently

Would you hire someone who showed up once in a while, who wasn't around because of their mood that day, or because they didn't feel like it? Zero of the authors have these qualities. Show up and show up consistently. This theme stands out in a special way. It undoubtedly is exhibited by every single author. Each of them kept at it. Nikeem and Austin grinded through application after application for *months*. Do you think any of these authors went to class sporadically? Of course not. To be an engineer, to be at the top of your field, to be an expert, to be a professional, you can't have lapses. You not only have to show up, but you have to *keep* showing up. The crucial implication here is that if you keep showing up, then that means you show up on the bad days too. You show up on the days that you don't want to show up. You put in the effort on the days when you don't feel like it. It's a must to be a successful problem solver.

CONCLUSION

"Someone needs to tell those tales. When the battles are fought and won and lost...There's magic in that. It's in the listener, and for each and every ear it will be different, and it will affect them in ways they can never predict. From the mundane to the profound. You may tell a tale that takes up residence in someone's soul, becomes their blood and self and purpose. That tale will move them and drive them and who knows what they might do because of it, because of your words. That is your role, your gift. "
— Erin Morgenstern, The Night Circus

We hope you have enjoyed the time with the authors' stories. Our goal in this project was rooted in the hope that your soul was the residence for some moment of their tales and that you might indeed do something life-life-altering because of it.

We were overwhelmed with the plethora of advice and nuggets of information that they were willing to share. We'll be coming back again and again to the houses they have built, without question.

In the previous chapter, we discussed some overarching themes and closed the book with some moments that will stick with us. We hope you enjoyed the journey of reading their stories at any fraction of the amount we had in bringing them to you. It was an honor.

Never stop believing that you can turn it around.

What Was

Nikeem is on the subway in order to get on the bus to head to college after being told to leave his high school math class. Sibel is in tears, saying to herself that it's too hard. A baby-faced Anthony is terrified before entering the Engineering Expo. Austin is on his way to work the overnight shift at the hotel. Katrien is exhausted working on Nanoscience during the day and fashion design at night. Danny is staring at that mattress, knowing there is nowhere else to sleep. Cory is on the boat, realizing the clock is ticking and he's in a young man's game. Ki-Yett has watched two years of a two-year two-year pause turn into five. Alex is staring at a D in multivariable calculus after his first semester. Ariel is unsure and scared to go outside the box for this new job. Seth is taking orders to do the mundane when his soul aches to explore. Krys is told time and again that Dr. in front of his name is impossible. Cooper gets knocked down by impostor syndrome. Robert gets a large shipment of orders that are all wrong. Joseph is lost, jumping around from workplace to workplace, not really knowing where he should be. Jesse is thinking it's probably best if he were no longer around.

What Is

Nikeem takes full advantage of a reach out to crush an interview to be a Cyber Security Engineer. Sibel embraces the hard as a requirement for the next level. Anthony finds the vibe and commits to engineering as service. Austin grinds his way through the boot camp to Capital One. Katrien does both to get access to her personal freedom. Danny is the professor we all wish we had. Cory finds his priorities and the freedom in never sacrificing them. KiYett says enough and takes control of her life. Alex is staring at an A in multivariable calculus after his second semester as a launch to bigger and brighter things. Ariel is scared and does it anyway. Seth listens to himself and goes for more. Krys Williams, Ph.D. Cooper gets back up and scores a TKO on impostor syndrome. Robert turns a setback into a springboard. Joseph realizes that there is a difference between being lost and being who you are. Jesse fights for himself, wins, and the world is better for it.

THAT'S NOT THE END!

Join the FREE Problem Solvers Community!

Thank you so much for reading the book. As a token of our appreciation for buying and reading the book, come join the Problem Solvers Community!

If you are looking to become an engineering professional and want to learn the outside-the-classroom skills needed to succeed, all while connecting with fellow strivers with similar goals, join the (completely free!!) community!

Get Access and Connections to Information and Resources	Get Answers to Important Questions along your Journey
✓ Periodic "Ask an Engineer" Sessions ✓ Access to the Hidden Curriculum: The Sixteen Crucial Skills needed to be an Engineer ✓ Connect with others who are seeking to become an engineer ✓ Connect with Current Engineers and hear their stories ✓ Access to free development resources that will give you an edge in becoming an engineer	* What do I have to do in order to level up and be prepared to become an engineer? * How do I get an internship? * How do I get a mentor? * How do you deal with impostor syndrome? * How do you handle a job interview? * How do I know if graduate school is right for me? * What are the best ways to network and meet others?

CONCLUSION

We Hope to See You There!
Here's a Small Sample of Professionals that you'll connect with

Robert Hodge

Energy Providers Consultant

KiYett Brown

Traffic Engineer
Jacobs

Jesse Milliken-Callan

Water Resource Control Engineer

Cory Payne

Sales Engineer
Charlatte

Join the Community at
https://tinyurl.com/BeAProblemSolver

www.ingramcontent.com/pod-product-compliance
Lightning Source LLC
Chambersburg PA
CBHW071147070526
44584CB00019B/2685